David Fincher: Interviews

Conversations with Filmmakers Series
Gerald Peary, General Editor

David Fincher

INTERVIEWS

Edited by Laurence F. Knapp

University Press of Mississippi / Jackson

www.upress.state.ms.us

The University Press of Mississippi is a member
of the Association of American University Presses.

Copyright © 2014 by University Press of Mississippi
All rights reserved
Manufactured in the United States of America

First printing 2014
∞
Library of Congress Cataloging-in-Publication Data

Fincher, David.
  David Fincher: interviews / edited by Laurence F. Knapp.
    pages cm — (Conversations with filmmakers series)
  Includes bibliographical references and index.
  Includes filmography.
  ISBN 978-1-62846-036-0 (hardback) — ISBN 978-1-62846-037-7 (ebook) 1. Fincher,
David—Interviews. 2. Motion picture producers and directors—United States—In-
terviews. I. Knapp, Laurence F., 1965– editor of compilation. II. Title.
  PN1998.3.F54A3 2014
  791.4302'33092—dc23   2014008216

British Library Cataloging-in-Publication Data available

Contents

Introduction

"I don't enjoy doing interviews, because I don't like being part of the noise. I just don't want to be grist for the mill."[1]

David Fincher hates being defined as an auteur. While many directors such as Tyler Perry, Quentin Tarantino, or Joss Whedon accept their celebrity status as part of their identity, Fincher does not want to be associated with a particular image or theme: "I don't want to be a Winchell's Donut. Even if my last name is 'Winchell.' I want to be able to make something like *Zodiac*. I mean, shouldn't your movies, if they are truly personal, change the way you change?"[2] Fincher clings to the old-fashioned belief that his films should do all the communicating: "I don't in my heart believe that a director should do interviews just to sell the movie. I worry that it demystifies it too much. And, I mean, you can't fix the movie by explaining to people the context in which you made it. It's not like they're going to enjoy it more. If you've fucked up they're still going to ask for their eight bucks back."[3] As Fincher confesses to Stephan Littger, "A director is like a quarterback. You get way too much credit when it works and way too much blame when it doesn't."[4]

For directors like Spike Lee or Kevin Smith, film is an odyssey of self-discovery and self-promotion. Fincher prefers self-effacement, but his need for absolute control compels him, begrudgingly, to take ownership of his work: "I have many, many friends who are vice-presidents and presidents of production at movie studios, and they never understand this very simple thing: My name's going to be on it. Your name's not on it. Your point of view is as valid as any member of the audience. But it's a different thing when your name's on it, when you have to wear it for the rest of your life, when it's on a DVD and it's hung around your fucking neck. It's your albatross."[5] Fincher accepts filmmaking as a Sisyphean task: "That's the job. That's what it is. Doing cool stuff like designing shots is 1 percent of your life. The other 99 percent is holding everything together while there's total fucking chaos, maximizing the amount of hours that you have in order to get stuff, pulling shit out of your ass to

fix things, being able to work on your toes."[6] He seeks the holy grail of
the consummate shot but eventually surrenders to his own truism that
"Films are not finished. They're abandoned."[7] Fincher's notorious work
ethic and attention to detail—his reputation as a reconstructed Stanley
Kubrick demanding an ungodly number of takes—is reflected in this
painstaking anecdote from the shooting of *Panic Room*:

> I'm a movie director! I have to have meetings with a *lot* of people to
> convince them to give me even more money, and I have to be responsible
> for how that money gets spent. It's my job to prioritize where time is spent
> because time *is* money. I don't think I'm a control freak, but I have to be
> in control. Here's an example: Today on the schedule it says we have to go
> down to the kitchen and shoot this scene. And a set of knives that were
> there in an earlier scene aren't there anymore, they've been stolen. Some-
> body walked by the set and stole them. I have to be the person who says,
> "Okay, we're not doing this right now. Go find some more knives. We're
> going upstairs to shoot something else, we'll come back to this later." You
> think that should be an easy decision to make. But it isn't, because then
> you have people who go (*urgent whisper*), "You don't understand, the guy
> is here with the car and the car's rented by the day and we'll have to rent
> them some other time. Can't you shoot the scene another way without
> the knives?" And I have to be the person who either goes, "Okay, we'll do it
> another way without the knives," or who says, "No. Fuck you. Don't waste
> any more time talking about this. Get the knives; I wanna shoot the fucking
> scene with the knives." I'm not in control of the knives getting stolen, but
> I'm responsible—I'm responsible for everything. Mainly I'm responsible for
> the haemorrhaging of money it takes to keep ninety-five people employed
> for six months to make a movie. [8]

Fincher blanches at being pigeonholed as a taskmaster—"There are
a lot of people who will tell you that I like to make things more complicated than they need to be, that I like to make things hard on myself, but
those aren't the people seeing the movie in their head before it's filmed.
They're just looking at the trucking waybills."[9]—and a visual stylist—"I
don't like the idea of having a style, it seems scary. It's so weird—what
is it that makes your style? It's the things that you fuck up as much as
the things that you do well, so half your style is stupid mistakes that
you consistently make."[10] He does not rely on intertextual allusions to
other directors to define his style. While Fincher admits that *Butch Cassidy and the Sundance Kid* inspired him to pursue film as a career, he does

not recognize George Roy Hill's authorship as part of that fascination. Fincher credits George Lucas for providing further inspiration, first as a neighbor ("We lived down the street from George Lucas at the time *American Graffiti* came out. I was ten years old at the time, and I would see him picking up his newspaper when I left for school. That made me think being a director was a viable job."[11]) then as an employer when he joined ILM as a production assistant on *Return of the Jedi*, but he's quick to disavow Lucas's thirty-five-year legacy as his own: "There are plenty of people doing Joseph Campbell's *The Hero with a Thousand Faces*. That was George Lucas and Steven Spielberg's trip. I've always been more interested in noir, in seventies movies like *The Parallax View*."[12] Fincher may express an affinity for Alfred Hitchcock or Martin Scorsese, but he does not fawn over them like a J. J. Abrams. When he does reference Kubrick or Spielberg, it's to define and clarify his own balanced approach to narrative range and depth:

> I have a philosophy about the two extremes of filmmaking. The first is the "Kubrick way," where you're at the end of an alley in which four guys are kicking the shit out of a wino. Hopefully, the audience members will know that such a scenario is morally wrong, even though it's not presented as if the viewer is the one being beaten up; it's more as if you're witnessing an event. Inversely, there's the "Spielberg way," where you're dropped into the middle of the action and you're going to live the experience vicariously—not only through what's happening, but through the emotional flow of what people are saying. It's a much more involved style. I find myself attracted to both styles at different times, but mostly I'm interested in just presenting something and letting people decide for themselves what they want to look at. . . . I look for patterns in coverage, and for ways to place the camera to see what you need to see, from as far away as possible. I try to remain semi-detached; I want to present the material without becoming too involved. I'll say to myself, "Am I getting too involved in the action? Am I presenting this to someone who's uninitiated to these people, and doesn't want to be in the middle of this argument? Maybe we should be doing over-the-shoulders, as if the spectator is experiencing the scene after returning from the water cooler." My [visual] approach comes from a more voyeuristic place.[13]

Although Fincher resists being called a visual stylist, his focus on form and viewer comprehension reveals a director who wants to use the specificity of cinema to engage and manipulate his audience: "I think the first rule of cinema is that a movie has to teach an audience how to watch it. That's what the first act is, showing the audience the things they have to take seriously, the characterization and technique, laying the groundwork for point of view, and how you will or won't betray it."[14] When Fincher describes his authorship it's usually as a methodology of causality and continuity motivated by a precise application of narrative information and stylistic motifs:

> There are two things I'm responsible for. One is whether or not I'm pre-senting believable behavior, which is totally subjective. The other thing is camera position: from where am I going to see this person? People think of directing as the Big Circus: yes, 90 per cent of directing is getting the money and getting the right equipment and the right people and departments to create the right feeling out of the right context. In film we sculpt time, we sculpt behavior, and we sculpt light. Audiences only get to see what we show them at that moment, I control everything they hear and see. I'm hoping that these elements will translate into feeling. It was Louis B. Mayer who said, "The genius of the movie business is that the only thing the purchaser gets is a memory." That's what directing is.[15]

Fincher may discount his marks of authorship, but his formal disci-pline and dark worldview link all of his films from *Alien³* to *The Girl with the Dragon Tattoo*: "Entertainment has to come hand in hand with a little bit of medicine. Some people go to the movies to be reminded that ev-erything's okay. I don't make those kinds of movies. That, to me, is a lie. Everything's not okay."[16] Fincher, like the artist Banksy, remains ambiva-lent about his commercial art career and his role as a popular storyteller and image maker. Within Fincher is a drive to antagonize and alienate his audience, as he admits to Mark Salisbury in a well-known quote: "I don't know how much movies should entertain. To me I'm always inter-ested in movies that *scar*."[17] After surviving *Alien³* Fincher refused to be-come a director-for-hire, a metteur content to be part of the Hollywood entertainment complex: "A director's job is to feel like everything that they're doing is worth the amount of money, worth the cost of human life and blood, sweat, and tears. I had a meeting once with a famous com-mercial director who was running off to direct a movie, and he wanted me to join his company. He said, 'I'm going off to do this movie.' I said, 'Well, what is it?' 'Oh it's this cop thing.' I thought to myself, 'Oh my God, I don't ever want to be in a situation where I'm going off to do some 'cop thing.'"[18] From *The Game*, with its metacinematic theme of exposing the cinematic experience as a Potemkin Village of deceit and illusion to *Zodiac*, a somber dissertation on the vicissitudes of time as it turns truth into hopeless conjecture, Fincher, like his Generation X compatriot P. T. Anderson, operates like Tyler Durden in *Fight Club*, ready to make mischief, cueing you to look for that extradiegetic cigarette burn or that instantaneous phallic insert that violates the wobbly trust between filmmaker and spectator.

Fincher, like Tarantino, never attended a high-profile film school like New York University or University of Southern California. He is a throwback to the journeymen of old, developing his craft by learning the trade from the ground up, first working for small production houses and then ILM, before establishing himself as an entrepreneur with his infamous American Cancer Society spot and the creation of Propaganda Films, which led to his attention-getting music videos with Madonna, Aerosmith, and the Rolling Stones. Throughout his salad years, Fincher saw technical expertise as a form of autonomy: "I've always been a fan of people who understand kind of everything; as a director it always seemed to me that you wanted to know so much about everything that was going on so people couldn't bullshit you, so you could go, 'Here's what I want to do,' and there couldn't be some lazy fuck there going, 'You can't do that because you can't hold focus on that.' I wanted to be able to go, 'That's not true, give me a T56 on a 28mm lens and we'll be able to hold plenty into focus."[19] Fincher took his father's words to heart—"Learn your craft: it will never stop you from being a genius"[20]— and, like Ridley Scott in the 1970s, became a praiseworthy visual stylist. Ridley established his career with *Alien*. Fincher's career started less auspiciously with the same franchise.

John H. Richardson's "Mother from Another Planet" captures Fincher on the set of *Alien*[3] as a twenty-seven-year-old wunderkind at the helm of the *Titanic*. Fincher lives up to his reputation as the uncompromising perfectionist, seemingly oblivious to the fact that he is in charge of a $60 million blockbuster in perpetual development hell: "We all sat here and decided to make a china cup, a beautiful, delicate china cup. You can't tell me we should have made a beer mug."[21] Fincher's struggle to make a film out of an unwieldy high-concept franchise set the baseline for his authorial profile for the next twenty years. Fincher became another Orson Welles or Terry Gilliam, the put-upon artist who dared to put aesthetics ahead of prosthetics: "I had a spoiled existence before making that movie. When you direct a video, people give you the money and say, 'Call us when you're done.' Movies aren't like that. I think you're always in over your head on your first movie, even if it's a very small movie. All you can do is lick your wounds when it's over."[22]

Alien[3] did not break Fincher. Much like Clint Eastwood's experience languishing on the set of *Paint Your Wagon*, Fincher realized that he had to have total control over his career to avoid becoming the scapegoat for a film he never fully authored. James Kaminsky's 1993 piece "Mr. Fincher's Neighborhood" offers Fincher only by proxy, superficially pigeonholed as an enfant terrible, but upon further scrutiny a legitimate artist who, according to his associate Mark Plummer, cannot be dismissed as a music video stylist: "It's incorrect to think of him as having one distinct style. David works to arrive at a singular style for each project—often inspired by specific movies or photographs or paintings—and then he'll see it through in every detail. Lots of other commercial and video directors just try to imitate something but miss out on what made it great. David figures it out, then reconceptualizes it."[23]

Fincher himself reemerges three years late in Mark Salisbury's "Seventh Hell" with the unexpected success of *Se7en* and his audacious decision to leave Gwyneth Paltrow's head in a box. The tropes that drive every subsequent Fincher interview come together—the perfectionism and his need for control ("Do your best work. Work as hard as you can on every given day and try to live it down."[24]) and the capsule biography that gets referenced and re-referenced like a chain letter (Lucas, ILM, etc.)—but with *Se7en*, and Salisbury's piece, Fincher renews his commitment to a darker world view and an aggressive stance toward his audience: "You have a responsibility for the way you make the audience feel, and I want them to feel uncomfortable."[25] Fincher also establishes his working relationship with Brad Pitt, the Cary Grant to Fincher's Hitchcock: "On-screen and off-screen, Brad's the ultimate guy. If I could be anyone, it would be Brad Pitt. Even if I couldn't look like him. Just to be him. He has such a great ease with who he is."[26] Fincher, like Hitchcock and Kubrick, sees actors as one element among many ("Every once in a while there are actors you can defeat. . . . I hate earnestness in performance. Usually by Take 17 the earnestness is gone."[27]), but he is also dependent on a star's physiognomy to bring his images to life: "I believe in casting people whose core—that essential personality you can't beat out of them with a tire iron—has to work for the character."[28]

Ian Blair's "David Fincher Interview," Ryan Gilbey's "Precocious Prankster Who Gets a Thrill from Tripping People Up," and Jean Cooney's "The Head Master" feature a customarily distracted Fincher, shooting and promoting *The Game*, a collaboration with Michael Douglas that

Fincher conceived as a film about the narrative experience itself—the seductive allure of the suspension of disbelief even as the spectator resents
being tricked by what he or she knows is artifice and illusion: "Movies
usually make a pact with the audience that says: We're going to play it
straight; what we show you is going to add up. But we don't do that. In
that respect, it's about movies and how movies dole out information."[29]
The Game, with Douglas's association with *Wall Street* and the iconic role
of Gordon Gekko, offered an unflattering portrait of Baby Boomer las-
situde and selfishness; *Fight Club*, like Lana and Andy Wachowski's *The
Matrix*, annunciated a Gen-X call to arms, exposing America to the despair behind the slacker pose or the IKEA-boy nesting instinct. Fincher
participated in a flurry of interviews for *Fight Club*, frequently appear-
ing alongside his two young collaborators Edward Norton and Brad Pitt,
who shared Fincher's Gen-X mindset and discontent. In a number of
group interviews, Fincher would offer one insight: "There were so many
things the book's narrator said where I went, 'God I've thought that and
never told anyone.' For men today, there's an arid wasteland of information about how to live. Am I supposed to cry? Supposed to fucking break
something? Somebody just give me a hint,"[30] only to have Norton chime
in: "*Fight Club* has a generational energy to it, a protest energy. So much
of what's been represented about my generation has been done by the
baby boomers. They dismiss us: the word *slacker*, the oversimplification
of the Gen-X mentality as one of hesitancy or negativity. It isn't just aim-
lessness we feel; it's deep skepticism. It's not slackerdom; it's profound
cynicism, even despair, even paralysis, in the face of an onslaught of information and technology. . . . More than any film I've made, I pulled
very directly from my own experience for this. I'm not saying nobody
over forty-five is going to understand it. But it won't surprise me if a
great many people go, 'Huh?'"[31] with Pitt adding: "It's a pummeling of
information. It's Mr. Fincher's Opus. It's provocative, but thank God it's
provocative. People are hungry for films like this, films that make them
think."[32] Fincher, clearly empowered by Pitt's assertion that he was "pi-
loting the *Enola Gay* on this one"[33] crafted an A-bomb of subjective narration that rattled the audience's brain as hard as one of Tyler Durden's
punches: "This isn't the sort of movie you just sit back and watch. This
is a movie that's *downloaded* in front of you. It doesn't wait for you. If
you don't keep up, you're lost. It's like you've tripped and sprained your
ankle. You have to tell the rest of the audience, 'Go on. Go ahead without me!'"[34] Gavin Smith's "Inside Out," Amy Taubin's "Twenty-First-
Century Boys," and Andrew Pulver's "Fight the Good Fight" feature a

garrulous Fincher eager to play pop sociologist and cultural anthropologist, weary of a world dominated by Apple, American Express, and Starbucks. While Tarantino mastered a rococo form of postmodernism that celebrated the triumph of pop culture as America's last coherent frame of reference, Fincher confronted the ontological legacy of postmodernism—the fragmented, alienated consumer/corporate drone lost in time, space, and his own consciousness—to bemoan the dehumanizing condition of late-stage capitalism imposed on any male born after 1962: "There were people at the studio who said, 'This is evil and nihilistic.' And I said, 'No, it's not.' Because it's talking about frustration, about an inability to find an answer. It's about a guy struggling to make sense of something, as opposed to a guy giving in to the fucked way things are. So there were definitely people who didn't get it."[35]

After the Sturm and Drang of *Fight Club*, Fincher decided to make a mere movie with *Panic Room*—at least his idea of a popcorn thriller. In Daniel Robert Epstein's "Inside *Panic Room*: David Fincher, the Roundtable Interview" and Gilbey's "Four Walls and a Funeral," Fincher reverts to his filmmaking-as-masochism mantra, aptly described by Gilbey as "The Pitiful and Miserable Existence of the Modern Filmmaker." Fincher, like Hitchcock with *Rope* and *Rear Window*, conceived of *Panic Room* as a "composed film" shot entirely on a soundstage, with a rigorous treatment of unrestricted, omniscient camerawork until the final third of the film, when Fincher shifts from Kubrickian omniscience to Spielbergian character involvement. Fincher fell into a storyboard trap, composing the film so much in his head that he lost interest in its actual creation and execution once he lost lead actress Nicole Kidman and retrofitted the character psychology for Jodie Foster: "It just felt wrong, like I didn't get the most out of the actors, because I was so rigid in my thinking. I was kind of impatiently waiting for everybody to get where I'd already been a year and a half ago."[36]

Panic Room initiated a long hiatus in the 2000s. Stephan Littger's interview from *The Director's Cut: Picturing Hollywood in the 21st Century* gives Fincher an opportunity to put his career into perspective in the mid 2000s, especially his genesis from music video tyro into feature filmmaker. Nev Pierce's "Forget the First Two Rules of *Fight Club*" validates Fincher's masochistic struggle to give Generation X its cinematic due. Finally, in 2007, Fincher refashioned his author-code with *Zodiac*. Fincher became more reticent, a clue that *Zodiac* came directly from his youth, which he always associated with the Zodiac killings in the late

1960s: "It was a very interesting and weird time to grow up, and incredibly evocative. I have a handful of friends who were from Marin County at the same time, the same age group, and they're all very kind of sinister, dark, sardonic people. And I wonder if Zodiac had something to do with that."[37] Fincher always wondered if he could have been one of those traumatized kids on the school bus hijacked by the Scorpio killer in *Dirty Harry*—this was his loss of innocence, a Gen-X epiphany that no one could comprehend or apprehend this serial killer, not Robert Graysmith (Jake Gyllenhaal), David Toschi (Mark Ruffalo), or Paul Avery (Robert Downey, Jr.): "*Zodiac* is a mystery movie with no solution. This may be my particular perversity, but for me, those films are the most interesting. I don't think we'll ever know the answers."[38] Fincher granted only a handful of interviews for *Zodiac*—in Shawn Levy's "David Fincher of *Zodiac*" and Pierce's "The Devil Is in the Detail," he comes across as vulnerable, insecure that his serial killer-cum-newspaper-cum-cop film operated more on the level of Michelangelo Antonioni's *L'avventura* than Jonathan Demme's *The Silence of the Lambs*:

> I wanted the movie to take its toll on the audience, I wanted the audience to feel like they went through it, like they went through the ringer with these guys, and I didn't know how to do that because these guys didn't run across rooftops and fall off fire escapes. In their quest to bring the Zodiac to justice they followed the trail of breadcrumbs as far as it would take them, and they kept pushing and kept pushing when there were crackpots coming out of the woodwork. I felt like I didn't want to make one of those movies where you do montage/montage/montage and you get the idea that they went to the mat with this, that it took its toll—I wanted the audience to feel that. You know, in retrospect you look at it and say maybe audiences who are looking for entertainment on a Friday night don't want that toll taken on them. I felt like anything less than that would be doing the story and people involved a disservice.[39]

Fincher forces his audience to ponder how time can confound closure— there is no Eastwood dispatching Zodiac with a curt "Do you feel lucky?" only the nagging suspicion that a homely man in a hardware store could be the maniac responsible for Fincher's penchant for movies that scar.

Out of the malaise and existential sorrow of *Zodiac* emerged a more productive, confident Fincher. In rapid order came *The Curious Case of Benjamin Button*, *The Social Network*, and *The Girl with the Dragon Tattoo*.

Zodiac introduced Fincher to the possibilities of digital filmmaking, which allowed him to bring *The Curious Case of Benjamin Button* to life without sacrificing Brad Pitt's star presence:

> When you look at a great cinema performance, you're seeing somebody who knows what the camera's doing. They know where they are in the story and they dredge up something incredibly stylized to show what, at that moment, you need to hang on to in order to understand this person. Often it's not the most realistic expression of that moment. That's why we're so fond of our favorite movie stars. They give us just enough to make us see ourselves in their shoes. That's a whole different thing from acting. And it's very odd when you talk about how you interface with a computer to achieve that. But it's the beginning, not the end. Instead of saying, "Oh my god, the machines are taking over," you have to look at Benjamin and say, "Without Brad Pitt, he doesn't exist."[40]

Scott Bowles's "A Curious Case of Friendship: *Benjamin Button* Partners Pitt and Fincher Click On Set" celebrates the ongoing collaboration/ bromance between Pitt and Fincher, while Pierce's "In Conversation with David Fincher" and Salisbury's "David Fincher" showcase Fincher's technical proficiency and his congenital need to sabotage that most hallowed of Hollywood conventions, the love story: "In any love story the trick is how you keep them apart. One thing I really enjoyed about the script was that this is not codependent love. They are two fully realized people who choose for better or worse to be together. Nowhere is the choice of wanting to be there for the other person better illustrated than by her caring for him as he dies."[41] Fincher managed to make a romantic epic that, with Tyler Durden–like subterfuge, exposed *Titanic*, *The Notebook*, *Twilight*, and *The Hunger Games* as naïve sentimentality: "They aren't committed to one another out of desperation. They're not needy. I'm just tired of the ballad of co-dependency, you know what I mean? I like to see two adults in a movie deciding to live together instead of teenagers caving in."[42]

Button led immediately to *The Social Network*, which Fincher nicknamed tellingly as the *Citizen Kane* of John Hughes movies. In Emanuel Levy's "*Social Network*: Interview with Director David Fincher" and Mark Harris's "The Vulture Transcript: An In-Depth Chat with David Fincher about *The Social Network*," Fincher welcomes comparisons to his Gen-Y counterpart/protagonist Mark Zuckerberg (Jesse Eisenberg): "I know the anger that comes when you just want to be allowed to do the things that you know you can do."[43] As with *Fight Club* in 1999, Fincher once again captured the zeitgeist of his time by dramatizing the Web-based psychology of the millennials as they use Facebook to massage their narcissistic "need to be on the cover of one's own *Rolling Stone*."[44] Fincher marvels at Zuckerberg's achievement—"A lot of people have differing ideas about Mark Zuckerberg, But it's an amazing feat to scale something from a college dorm room to 350 million people. The design of it, the coding, is pretty beyond reproach. In that respect, Facebook is an *amazing* accomplishment"[45]—but he does not overlook Zuckerberg's—and Gen Y's—antisocial fixation with online "social" sites. Zuckerberg's proto-autistic self-absorption, his inability to communicate and empathize with others, brings the film to a beguiling close as he neurotically checks his Facebook account, hoping estranged old flame Erica Albright (Rooney Mara) will validate his life's work by accepting his friend request—Rosebud as an unrequited mouse click.

Rooney, that waiflike lost object of desire in *The Social Network*, morphs into Lisbeth Salander, a second-wave riot grrrl, in *The Girl with the Dragon Tattoo*, which brought Fincher full circle to another franchise only this time on his own terms: "I saw this not as a blockbuster that appeals to everyone. I saw this as an interesting, specific, pervy franchise. The only chance for something like *Dragon Tattoo* to be made in all of its perversions is to do it big. I think *The Godfather* is a pretty good fucking movie. You can start with a supermarket potboiler, but it doesn't mean you can't aim high."[46] Fincher's return to the serial killer genre allowed him to develop a close working relationship with Rooney and to cultivate a feminist strain in his work that began with Sigourney Weaver in *Alien³*. In Brian Raftery's "Heart of Darkness" and Pierce's "Chasing the Dragon," Fincher does not stray from the insidious legacy of rape in Stieg Larsson's source novel—whether from Salander's individual perspective or on a wider, more institutional level as the global 1 percent literally prey on themselves and the other 99 percent. Fincher also enjoys subverting Daniel Craig's James Bond star text with Rooney's self-reliant Salander: "Craig looks like this tough guy, not realizing that the little creature standing in front of him is a far more dangerous pit bull."[47] Rooney offers another archetypal portrait of Gen Y—like Zuckerberg, Salander is a computer hacker on the autistic spectrum who craves attention even as she hides behind her precious laptop. While Gen X lashed against the ubiquitous Apple logo in *Fight Club*, Gen Y clings to it as a last refuge in *The Social Network* and *The Girl with the Dragon Tattoo*.

The last piece in the book, Fincher Fanatic's "You Better Be Fucking

Serious: David Fincher on Directing," comes from the unofficial Fincher fan website fincherfanatic.com. The Fincher of 2002 could barely acknowledge the existence of the now-defunct Davidfincher.net ("I don't do it [check the site] religiously because it's too weird. It feels like people know too much about me."[48]). The Fincher of 2012 grants Fincher Fanatic a remarkable interview, once again denying his status as an auteur even as he explains how an auteur must behave in the twenty-first century: "I always wanted to give a lecture at film schools. You go in and you see all these fresh faces, and you say, 'You! Stand up, tell me your story. Tell me what your film is going to be about.' And they start, and you go: 'Shut up and sit the fuck down!' And if they do, you go: 'You're not ready.' Because the film business is filled with shut-up and sit-the-fuck-down. You got to be able to tell your story in spite of sit-down and shut-the-fuck-up. If you are going to let something like that derail you, what hope do you have against development executives?"[49] Keep telling yourself you are not an auteur Mr. Fincher. If that's what it takes to allow you to make a film like *Fight Club* or *The Social Network*, so be it.

In accordance with the policy of the University Press of Mississippi, these interviews are reprinted in chronological order in their original form to preserve their historical value. The purpose of any volume in the Conversations with Filmmakers series is to give the reader a sense of development as a film director attempts to define his or her work even as some journalists, academics, or bloggers revert to the same vignettes or conflicts. As with any star text, a director must tolerate repeated questions about his or her filmography and extratextual reputation regardless of his or her desire to grow and evolve. All of the pieces selected feature salient writers who want to give Fincher the opportunity to define his work on his terms, especially Nev Pierce, who, since the mid 2000s, has played the role of François Truffaut to Fincher's Hitchcock.

This book would not be possible without the support of my wife Moyenda and my two sons August and Christopher. Michael Jolls, my editorial assistant (and former student), encouraged me to embark on this book project. No one is as reliable and proficient as Michael. Trisha Collins, the librarian at Oakton Community College, never failed to honor my document requests, no matter how obscure or incomplete. Leila Salisbury, the director of the University Press of Mississippi, and Valerie Jones, my editor, tolerated my numerous inquires and idiosyncrasies with aplomb. Gerald Peary, the series editor and an old friend and mentor, worked his magic when I needed it most. Thanks to all the

contributors for their cooperation, especially Nev Pierce and Mark Salisbury, as well as Fincher Fanatic and his indispensable and definitive website fincherfanatic.com.

LFK

Notes

1. Brian Raftery, "Heart of Darkness," Wired.com, December 2011.

2. Fincher Fanatic, "You Better Be Fucking Serious: David Fincher on Directing,"
fincherfanatic.blogspot.com, 2012.

3. Simon Braund, "Hall of Fame: David Fincher, Fighter," *Empire* 155 (May 2002): 117.

4. Stephan Littger, *The Director's Cut: Picturing Hollywood in the 21st Century* (New
York: Continuum, 2006), 174.

5. Brian Mockenhaupt, "The Curious Case of David Fincher," *Esquire* 147 (March
2007): 163.

6. Fred Schruers, "David Fincher's Bizarro Game," *Rolling Stone* 757 (April 3, 1997):
52.

7. Nev Pierce, "The Devil Is in the Detail," *Total Film*, March 26, 2007, 67.

8. Braund, "Hall of Fame: David Fincher, Fighter," 112.

9. Devin Faraci, "Exclusive Interview: David Fincher," Chud.com, January 8, 2008.

10. James Swallow, *Dark Eye: The Films of David Fincher* (London: Reynolds & Hearn,
2003), 31.

11. Stephen Farber, "A Meeting of Tough Minds in Hollywood," *New York Times*,
August 31, 1997.

12. Paul Liberatore, "Director Fincher Got Taste for Film Growing Up in Marin," *Marin
Independent Journal*, December 12, 2008.

13. Christopher Probst, "Playing for Keeps on *The Game*," *American Cinematographer*
78 (September 1997): 38–39.

14. Andrew Pulver, "Fight the Good Fight," *Guardian*, October 29, 1999.

15. David Jenkins, "Pay Attention, or You're Going to Miss a Lot: David Fincher on *The
Social Network*," *Time Out*, October 14, 2010.

16. Mockenhaupt, "The Curious Case of David Fincher," 160.

17. Mark Salisbury, "Seventh Hell." *Empire* 80 (February 1996): 83.

18. Schruers, "David Fincher's Bizarro Game," 52.

19. Salisbury, "Seventh Hell," 87.

20. Littger, *The Director's Cut*, 168.

21. John H. Richardson, "Mother from Another Planet," *Premiere* 5 (May 1992): 70.

22. Farber, "A Meeting of Tough Minds in Hollywood."

23. James Kaminsky, "Mr. Fincher's Neighborhood,"*Advertising Age*, November 1,
1993, 17.

24. Mockenhaupt, "The Curious Case of David Fincher," 212.

25. Ibid, 161.

26. Xan Brooks, "Directing Is Masochism," *Guardian*, April 24, 2002.

27. David M. Halbfinger, "Lights, Boogeyman, Action," *New York Times*, February 18, 2007.

28. Jonathan Van Meter, "Playing with Fire," *Vogue* 201 (November 2011): 251.

29. Ryan Gilbey, "Precocious Prankster Who Gets a Thrill from Tripping People Up," *Independent*, October 10, 1997.

30. Johanna Schneller, "Two Heavy Hitters Put Their Muscle Behind the Controversial *Fight Club*," *Premiere*, August 1999, 71.

31. Ibid, 71.

32. Benjamin Svetkey, "Blood, Sweat, and Fears," *Entertainment Weekly* 507 (October 15, 1999): 28.

33. Ibid, 27.

34. Ibid, 26.

35. Damon Wise, "Menace II Society," *Empire* 126 (December 1999): 102–03.

36. Halbfinger, "Lights, Bogeyman, Action."

37. Ibid.

38. Tom Huddleston, "Warning Signs," *Time Out*, September 18, 2008.

39. Faraci, "Exclusive Interview: David Fincher."

40. Nick James, "Face to Face," *Sight and Sound* 19 (March 2009): 28.

41. Ibid, 28.

42. Nev Pierce, "In Conversation with David Fincher," *Empire* 235 (January 2009): 164.

43. Mark Harris, "The Vulture Transcript: An In-Depth Chat with David Fincher about *The Social Network*," *New York Magazine*, September 21, 2010.

44. Emanuel Levy, "*Social Network*: Interview with Director David Fincher," EmanuelLevy.com, 2010.

45. Nev Pierce, "Geek Tragedy," *Empire* 256 (October 2010): 115.

46. Van Meter, "Playing with Fire," 256.

47. Ibid, 256.

48. Daniel Robert Epstein, "Inside *Panic Room*: David Fincher, the Roundtable Interview," davidfincher.net, 2002.

49. Fincher Fanatic, "You Better Be Fucking Serious: David Fincher on Directing."

Chronology

1962   Born August 26 in Denver, Colorado. Son of Claire Mae (née Boettcher) and Howard Kelly Fincher.

1964   Fincher's family moves to San Anselmo in Marin Country, California.

1968–69   The Zodiac killer murders seven people in the San Francisco area. Fincher identifies this as a key part of his childhood.

1972   George Lucas moves onto the same street as the Fincher household, inspiring Fincher to pursue filmmaking as a career.

1976   Moves to Ashland, Oregon, where he graduates from Ashland High School.

1980   Works as a production assistant for John Korty's Korty Films in Mill Valley, California. Korty, a film director and animator, inspires Francis Ford Coppola and George Lucas to form their own film studios in the late 1970s.

1981   Begins work at Industrial Light and Magic (ILM). Over the course of three years, he works on various camera tech support on the films *Twice Upon a Time*, *Star Wars Episode VI: Return of the Jedi*, *Indiana Jones and the Temple of Doom*, and *The Never Ending Story*.

1984   Leaves ILM. Shoots his first commercial "Smoking Fetus" for the American Cancer Society. Directs two Rick Springfield music videos.

1985   Directs "The Beat of the Live Drum," a music video compilation/live performance piece for Rick Springfield.
Directs music videos for the Motels and Rick Springfield.

1986   Directs music videos for the Outfield and Stabilizers.

1987   Forms Propaganda Films, a music video and film production company, with Steve Golin, Joni Sighvatsson, Nigel Dick, Greg Gold, and Dominic Sena. Directs music videos for Bourgeois Tagg, Martha Davis, Foreigner, Colin James Hay, the

Hooters, Mark Knopfler, Loverboy, Eddie Money, the Out-field, Patti Smyth, and Wire Train.

1988   Directs Paula Abdul's music video "(It's Just) the Way That You Love Me" and Steve Winwood's video "Roll With It." Also directs videos for Ry Cooder, Martha Davis, Johnny Hates Jazz, Sting, Jody Watley, and Winwood.

1989   Directs Madonna's music videos "Express Yourself" and "Oh Father," Paul Abdul's "Cold Hearted," "Forever Your Girl," and "Straight Up," Aerosmith's "Janie's Got a Gun," Don Henley's "The End of the Innocence," and Jody Watley's "Real Love," as well as videos for Neneh Cherry, Gipsy Kings, and Roy Orbison. Wins Best Direction in a Video MTV Video Music Award for "Express Yourself" by Madonna. Wins a CLIO Award for Colt 45 ad "Imagination."

1990   Directs Madonna's music video "Vogue" and George Michael's "Freedom '90," as well as videos for Billy Idol, Iggy Pop, and Wire Train. Gets nominated for Best Direction in a Video MTV Video Music Awards for Don Henley's "The End of the Innocence" and Aerosmith's "Janie's Got a Gun." Wins Best Direction Award for "Vogue" by Madonna. Marries Donya Florentino

1992   *Alien³* released on May 22. Receives an Academy Award nomination for Best Visual Effects. Directs Michael Jackson's music video "Who Is It?"

1992–93 Advances advertising career with Nike commercial "Instant Karma" and a series of Charles Barkley spots (including "Barkley on Broadway"). Also directs influential Coke commercial "Blade Roller," the first ad to become part of the Museum of Modern Art's permanent collection.

1993   Directs Madonna's music video "Bad Girl."

1994   Directs the Rolling Stones' music video "Love Is Strong." Shoots a series of Dennis Hopper "Referee" ads for Nike. Daughter Phelix Imogen born.

1995   *Se7en* released on September 22. Receives an Academy Award nomination for Best Editing. Fincher's highest-grossing film overseas with $227.2 million, as well as his highest-grossing film domestically (if adjusted for ticket price inflation). Receives CLIO Gold Award for Nike ad "Magazine Wars" and a CLIO Award for Honda ad "Escape." Divorces Donya Florentino.

1996	Directs the Wallflowers' music video "6th Avenue Heartache." Wins CLIO Silver Award for Levi's ad "The Chase."
1997	*The Game* released on September 12. Wins CLIO Award for Heineken ad "Nothing."
1998	Wins CLIO Award for *The Game* teaser.
1999	*Fight Club* released on October 15. Receives an Academy Award nomination for Sound Editing.
2000	Directs A Perfect Circle's music video "Judith." Begins shooting commercials for Anonymous Content, a multimedia production company founded by Steve Golin, a former executive with Propaganda Films.
2001	Propaganda Films dissolves after the Screen Actors Guild advertising strike and the economic fallout of September 11. Produces the first five installments of the web-based series *The Hire* for BMW.
2002	*Panic Room* released on March 29. Makes a cameo appearance with Brad Pitt in Steven Soderbergh's film *Full Frontal*.
2003	Wins CLIO Gold Award for Adidas commercial "Mechanical Legs."
2004	Wins the Director's Guild of America (DGA) award for "Outstanding Directorial Achievement in Commercials" for the Nike ads "Gamebreakers" and "Speed Chain" and the Xelibri Phones ad "Beauty for Sale." Wins CLIO Gold Award for Nike ad "Gamebreakers" and Bronze Award for Xelibri's "Beauty for Sale."
2003–05	Develops a number of projects that he eventually fails to direct—most significantly *Mission: Impossible III*, *Batman Begins*, and *The Black Dahlia*.
2005	*Lords of Dogtown*, with Fincher as executive producer, released on June 3. Directs the Nine Inch Nails music video "Only." Shoots Brad Pitt Heineken commercial "Beer Run." Wins CLIO Shortlist Award for HP commercial "Constant Change."
2006	*Love and Other Disasters*, with Fincher as executive producer, released on September 9.
2007	*Zodiac* released on March 2.
2008	*The Curious Case of Benjamin Button* released on December 25. Wins British Academy of Film Television Arts (BAFTA) Awards for Best Make-Up & Hair, Best Production Design, and Best Special Visual Effects. Receives a record thirteen Academy

Award nominations including Best Adapted Screenplay, Supporting Actress, Actor, Director, and Picture. Wins for Best Art Direction, Make-Up, and Visual Effects. Grosses $127 million making it Fincher's highest-grossing film domestically; $333.9 million worldwide making it Fincher's highest-grossing film (unadjusted for inflation).

2009   Nominated for the DGA's Outstanding Directorial Achievement in Commercials for the Nike ad "Fate," the Stand Up to Cancer ad "Stand Up for Something," and the Apple ad "Hallway." Wins CLIO Silver Award for Nike ad "Fate."

2010   *The Social Network* released on October 1. Wins BAFTA Awards for Best Editing, Best Adapted Screenplay, Best Director. Wins Golden Globe Award for Best Original Score, Best Screenplay, Best Director, and Best Picture. Nominated for eight Academy Awards including Actor, Director, and Picture. Wins for Adapted Screenplay, Editing, and Original Score.

2011   *The Girl with the Dragon Tattoo* released on December 21. Receives five Academy Award nominations including Best Actress. Wins for Best Editing. Receives a CLIO Hall of Fame Award for *The Hire*.

2012   Launches Reset Content, an advertising production company, with Dave Morrison. Partners with Guy Ritchie, Jonathan Glazer, and other high-profile filmmakers. Uses Kickstarter to develop and promote Dark Horse comic book *The Goon* as an animated feature film. Produces Halo 4 launch trailer "Scanned."

2013   *House of Cards* premieres on Netflix on February 1. Fincher directs the first two episodes and oversees the entire series as executive producer. Directs the Justin Timberlake and Jay-Z music video "Suit & Tie." Wins Best Direction VMA for "Suit & Tie."

2014   *Gone Girl*, Fincher's tenth feature film, is scheduled for a fall release. *House of Cards* returns for a second season on Netflix on February 14. Announces development of an upcoming HBO series based on the 2013 British television show *Utopia*.

Filmography

ALIEN³ (1992)
Director: **David Fincher**
Executive Producer: Ezra Swerdlow
Producers: Gordon Carroll, David Giler, Walter Hill, and Sigourney Weaver
Screenplay: David Giler, Walter Hill, and Larry Ferguson
Cinematography: Alex Thomson
Editing: Terry Rawlings
Production Design: Norman Reynolds and Michael White
Music: Elliot Goldenthal
Cast: Sigourney Weaver (Ellen Ripley), Charles S. Dutton (Dillon), Charles Dance (Clemens), Paul McGann (Golic), Lance Henriksen (Bishop II), Pete Postlethwaite (David)
114 minutes
2003 "Assembly Cut" Edition (edited by David Crowther): 145 minutes

SE7EN (1995)
Director: **David Fincher**
Producers: Arnold Kopelson and Phyllis Carlyle
Screenplay: Andrew Kevin Walker
Cinematography: Darius Khondji
Editing: Richard Francis-Bruce
Production Design: Arthur Max
Music: Howard Shore
Cast: Brad Pitt (Detective David Mills), Morgan Freeman (Detective William Somerset), Kevin Spacey (John Doe), Gwyneth Paltrow (Tracy Mills), Richard Roundtree (Talbot)
127 minutes

THE GAME (1997)
Director: **David Fincher**
Executive Producer: Jonathan Mostow

Producers: John D. Brancato, Ceán Chaffin, Michael Ferris, and Steve Golin
Screenplay: John Brancato and Michael Ferris
Cinematography: Harris Savides
Editing: James Haygood
Production Design: Jeffrey Beecroft
Music: Howard Shore
Cast: Michael Douglas (Nicholas Van Orton), Sean Penn (Conrad Van Orton), Deborah Kara Unger (Christine), James Rebhorn (Jim Feingold), Peter Donat (Samuel Sutherland), Carroll Baker (Ilsa), Armin Mueller-Stahl (Anson Baer)
129 minutes

FIGHT CLUB (1999)
Director: **David Fincher**
Executive Producer: Arnon Milchan
Producers: Ross Grayson Bell, Ceán Chaffin, John S. Dorsey, and Art Linson
Screenplay: Jim Uhls (from Chuck Palahniuk's novel)
Cinematography: Jeff Cronenweth
Editing: James Haygood
Production Design: Alex McDowell
Music: John King and Michael Simpson (the Dust Brothers)
Cast: Edward Norton (the Narrator), Brad Pitt (Tyler Durden), Helena Bonham Carter (Marla Singer), Meat Loaf Aday (Robert "Bob" Paulson), Jared Leto (Angel Face), Zach Grenier (Richard Chesler), David Andrews (Thomas)
139 minutes

PANIC ROOM (2002)
Director: **David Fincher**
Producers: Ceán Chaffin, John S. Dorsey, Judy Hofflund, David Koepp, and Gavin Polone
Screenplay: David Koepp
Cinematography: Conrad W. Hall and Darius Khondji
Editing: James Haygood and Angus Wall
Production Design: Arthur Max
Music: Howard Shore
Cast: Jodie Foster (Meg Altman), Kristen Stewart (Sarah Altman), Forest

Whitaker (Burnham), Dwight Yoakam (Raoul), Jared Leto (Junior), Patrick Bauchau (Stephen Altman), Ann Magnuson (Lydia Lynch)
112 minutes

ZODIAC (2007)
Director: **David Fincher**
Executive Producer: Louis Phillips
Producers: Ceán Chaffin, Brad Fischer, Mike Medavoy, Arnold W. Messer, and James Vanderbilt
Screenplay: James Vanderbilt (based on Robert Graysmith's book)
Cinematography: Harris Savides
Editing: Angus Wall
Production Design: Donald Graham Burt
Music: David Shire
Cast: Jake Gyllenhaal (Robert Graysmith), Robert Downey Jr. (Paul Avery), Mark Ruffalo (Inspector David Toschi), Andrew Edwards (Inspector William Armstrong), Brian Cox (Melvin Belli), John Carroll Lynch (Arthur Leigh Allen), Chloë Sevigny (Melanie), Ed Setrakian (Al Hyman), John Getz (Templeton Peck), John Terry (Charles Thieriot), Candy Clark (Carol Fisher), Elias Koteas (Sergeant Jack Mulanax), Dermot Mulroney (Captain Marty Lee), Donal Logue (Captain Ken Narlow), Philip Baker Hall (Sherwood Morrill)
157 minutes
Director's Cut: 162 minutes

THE CURIOUS CASE OF BENJAMIN BUTTON (2008)
Director: **David Fincher**
Producers: Ceán Chaffin, Jim Davidson, Kathleen Kennedy, Frank Marshall, Peter Mavromates, and Marykay Powell
Screenplay: Eric Roth (based on F. Scott Fitzgerald's short story)
Cinematography: Claudio Miranda
Editing: Kirk Baxter and Angus Wall
Production Design: Donald Graham Burt
Music: Alexandre Desplat
Cast: Brad Pitt (Benjamin Button), Cate Blanchett (Daisy), Tilda Swinton (Elizabeth Abbott), Julia Ormond (Caroline), Taraji P. Henson (Queenie), Jared Harris (Captain Mike), Jason Flemyng (Thomas Button), Elle Fanning (Daisy Age 7), Elias Koteas (Monsieur Gateau)
166 minutes

THE SOCIAL NETWORK (2010)
Director: **David Fincher**
Executive Producer: Kevin Spacey
Producers: Dana Brunetti, Ceán Chaffin, Jim Davidson, Michael De Luca, and Scott Rudin
Screenplay: Aaron Sorkin (based on Ben Mezrich's book *The Accidental Billionaires*)
Cinematography: Jeff Cronenweth
Editing: Kirk Baxter and Angus Wall
Production Design: Donald Graham Burt
Music: Trent Reznor and Atticus Ross
Cast: Jesse Eisenberg (Mark Zuckerberg), Andrew Garfield (Eduardo Saverin), Justin Timberlake (Sean Parker), Armie Hammer (Cameron and Tyler Winklevoss), Max Minghella (Divya Narendra), Rooney Mara (Erica Albright), Rashida Jones (Marylin Delpy), Brenda Song (Christy Ling), Douglas Urbanski (Larry Summers)
120 minutes

THE GIRL WITH THE DRAGON TATTOO (2011)
Director: **David Fincher**
Executive Producers: Anni Faurbye Fernandez, Ryan Kavanaugh, Mikael Wallen, and Steve Zaillian
Producers: Eli Bush, Ceán Chaffin, Jim Davidson, Berna Levin, Scott Rudin, Søren Stæmose, and Ole Søndberg
Screenplay: Steve Zaillian (based on Stieg Larsson's novel)
Cinematography: Jeff Cronenweth
Editing: Kirk Baxter and Angus Wall
Production Design: Donald Graham Burt
Music: Trent Reznor and Atticus Ross
Cast: Daniel Craig (Mikael Blomkvist), Rooney Mara (Lisbeth Salander), Christopher Plummer (Henrik Vanger), Stellan Skarsgård (Martin Vanger), Yorick van Wageningen (Nils Bjurman), Steven Berkoff (Dirch Frode), Robin Wright (Erika Berger), Joely Richardson (Anita Vanger), Julian Sands (Young Henrik Vanger)
158 minutes

GONE GIRL (2014)
Director: **David Fincher**
Producers: Leslie Dixon, Bruna Papandrea, and Reese Witherspoon
Screenplay: Gillian Flynn (based on her novel)

Cinematography: Jeff Cronenweth
Editing: Kirk Baxter
Production Design: Donald Graham Burt
Music: Trent Reznor and Atticus Ross
Cast: Ben Affleck (Nick Dunne), Rosamund Pike (Amy Dunne), Neil
Patrick Harris (Desi Collings), Tyler Perry (Tanner Bolt), Kim Dickens
(Detective Rhonda Boney), Patrick Fugit (Detective Jim Gilpin), Emily
Ratajkowski (Andie Hardy), Casey Wilson (Noelle Hawthorne), Kath-
leen Rose Perkins (Shawna Kelly), Missi Pyle (Ellen Abbott)

Web Television

HOUSE OF CARDS (2013)
Season One, Chapters 1 and 2
Director: **David Fincher**
Executive Producers: Dana Brunetti, Joshua Donen, **David Fincher**,
John P. Melfi, Eric Roth, Kevin Spacey, Beau Willimon, and Robert
Zotnowski
Producer: Karyn McCarthy
Screenplay: Andrew Davies and Beau Willimon (based on Michael
Dobbs' *House of Cards*, *To Play the King*, and *The Final Cut*)
Cinematography: Eigil Bryld
Editing: Kirk Baxter
Production Design: Steve Arnold
Music: Jeff Beal
Cast: Kevin Spacey (Francis Underwood), Robin Wright (Claire Under-
wood), Kate Mara (Zoe Barnes), Corey Stoll (Representative Peter Russo),
Michael Kelly (Doug Stamper), Sakina Jaffrey (Linda Vasquez), Kristen
Connolly (Christina Gallagher), Sebastian Arcelus (Lucas Goodwin),
Boris McGiver (Tom Hammerschmidt)

Music Videos

"Bop Til You Drop," Rick Springfield (1984)
"Dance This World Away," Rick Springfield (1984)
"Shame," The Motels (1985)
"Shock," The Motels (1985)
"Celebrate Youth," Rick Springfield (1985)
"The Beat of the Live Drum," Rick Springfield (1985)
"All the Love in the World," The Outfield (1986)

"Everytime You Cry," The Outfield (1986)
"One Simple Thing," Stabilizers (1986)
"I Don't Mind At All," Bourgeois Tagg (1987)
"Don't Tell Me the Time," Martha Davis (1987)
"Say You Will," Foreigner (1987)
"Can I Hold You," Colin James Hay (1987)
"Johnny B," The Hooters (1987)
"Storybook Story," Mark Knopfler (1987)
"Love Will Rise Again," Loverboy (1987)
"Notorious," Loverboy (1987)
"Endless Nights," Eddie Money (1987)
"No Surrender," The Outfield (1987)
"Downtown Train," Patti Smyth (1987)
"She Comes On," Wire Train (1987)
"Should She Cry," Wire Train (1987)
"(It's Just) the Way That You Love Me," Paula Abdul (1988)
"Get Rhythm," Ry Cooder (1988)
"Tell It to the Moon," Martha Davis (1988)
"Heart of Gold," Johnny Hates Jazz (1988)
"Shattered Dreams," Johnny Hates Jazz (1988)
"Englishman in New York," Sting (1988)
"Most of All," Jody Watley
"Holding On," Steve Winwood (1988)
"Roll With It," Steve Winwood (1988)
"Cold Hearted," Paula Abdul (1989)
"Forever Your Girl," Paula Abdul (1989)
"Straight Up," Paula Abdul (1989)
"Janie's Got a Gun," Aerosmith (1989)
"Heart," Neneh Cherry (1989)
"The End of the Innocence," Don Henley (1989)
"Bamboleo," Gipsy Kings (1989)
"Express Yourself," Madonna (1989)
"Oh Father," Madonna (1989)
"She's a Mystery to Me," Roy Orbison (1989)
"Real Love," Jody Watley (1989)
"Cradle of Love," Billy Idol (1990)
"L.A. Woman," Billy Idol (1990)
"Freedom '90," George Michael (1990)
"Home," Iggy Pop (1990)
"Vogue," Madonna (1990)

"Should She Cry?" Wire Train (1990)
"Who Is It?" Michael Jackson (1992)
"Bad Girl," Madonna (1993)
"Love Is Strong," The Rolling Stones (1994)
"6th Avenue Heartache," The Wallflowers (1996)
"Judith," A Perfect Circle (2000)
"Only," Nine Inch Nails (2005)
"Suit & Tie," Justin Timberlake and Jay-Z (2013)

As Executive Producer

The Hire: Star (Guy Ritchie, 2001)
The Hire: Powder Keg (Alejandro González-Iñárritu, 2001)
The Hire: The Follow (Wong Kar-Wai, 2001)
The Hire: Chosen (Ang Lee, 2001)
The Hire: Ambush (John Frankenheimer, 2001)
The Hire: Ticker (Joe Carnahan, 2002)
Lords of Dogtown (Catherine Hardwicke, 2005)
Love and Other Disasters (Alek Keshishian, 2006)
House of Cards, Season One (2013)
    (David Fincher, Chapters 1 & 2)
    (James Foley, Chapters 3, 4, & 9)
    (Joel Schumacher, Chapters 5 & 6)
    (Charles McDougall, Chapters 7 & 8)
    (Carl Franklin, Chapters 10 & 11)
    (Allen Coulter, Chapters 12 & 13)
House of Cards, Season Two (2014)
    (Carl Franklin, Chapters 14 & 15)
    (James Foley, Chapters 16, 17, 20, 21, 25, & 26)
    (John Coles, Chapters 18, 19, & 24)
    (Jodie Foster, Chapter 22)
    (Robin Wright, Chapter 23)

David Fincher: Interviews

Mother from Another Planet

John H. Richardson / 1992

From *Premiere* 5 (May 1992), 62–70. Reprinted by permission of John H. Richardson.

David Fincher, a twenty-seven-year-old first-time director, was deter-mined to fulfill his creative vision on *Alien³* despite intense efforts to hold him back.

"Push some smoke up," says David Fincher, "Push it up!"

"Stand by!" says the first assistant director through a megaphone. The crew trains hoses and funnels on a silvery monster that looks like the offspring of a giant praying mantis and the Antichrist. It takes a few minutes for the crew to get the steam and smoke up to full inferno. "Here we go!"

"More fog!" cries Fincher.

The camera dollies in. The camera operator, lying on his belly, ducks under a flat pipe and curves around to shoot the alien through a scrim of chain link. The alien whips its head from side to side and starts to howl. In the movie, this moment will come a few minutes before the climax, when the indomitable Lt. Ellen Ripley and a team of religious-fanatic convicts dump a vat of molten lead on its head. Yesterday they shot the scene ten times, using black paint for lead—10,000 gallons of it over and over on the head of some poor guy in a rubber suit.

"Cut!" says Fincher, drawing a finger across his throat. The crew im-mediately starts to wet down the set for another shot.

It's December 1991, and they are shooting *Alien³* on a soundstage on the Twentieth Century Fox lot. Principle photography began almost a year ago in London, but when shooting went twenty-three days over sched-ule and untold millions over budget, Fox pulled the plug and ordered the filmmakers home. Originally scheduled to debut in the summer of 1991, then put off till Christmas, the movie is now aimed at Memorial

Day 1992. For months Hollywood has been rife with *Alien³* rumors: that it's a disaster, that it cost upwards of $60 million, that preview screenings were horrible, that Fox chairman Joe Roth hated it, that it really needed six weeks of reshoots and another $15 million and then *maybe* it would work. There's another side too—that it's visually brilliant, daring, a work of art from an extraordinary young director.

If nothing else, the movie is certainly extraordinary for the *choice* of its director. David Fincher is probably the only twenty-seven-year-old first-time filmmaker ever hired to direct a $50 million movie (Fox's official number, give or take a few million). Add that the first director was let go while sets were being built, that the line producer was fired just before the start date, that the script wasn't finished until two weeks into shooting, and you have a young man with his hands extremely full. As one of his friends puts it, "He was right out of Naval Academy School, and he got put at the helm of the *Titanic*."

Today is the seventh day of reshoots—"Not reshoots," Fincher corrects, a bit sharply, "stuff we didn't get before"—and they have been working on this one five-second shot since 7:30 A.M. It's now 4:30 in the afternoon, and they're two hours behind. Fincher is dressed in jeans and sneakers, with a grey baseball cap and a trim beard. He is calm, ironic, and exceptionally self-possessed, with some of the sly humor of Bill Murray. When a crew member makes an adjustment and tells Fincher he thinks it's good enough. Fincher calmly demurs: "This movie isn't made for people who see a movie one time, it's a movie for people who're going to see it five times."

Fox executive Michael London whispers: "That's where a lot of the friction comes. David wants it to be perfect every second." He quickly adds, "Which is what he's paid to do." It comes out only a tiny bit grudging.

Now Fincher is trying to fix a new problem—the alien is shaking its head so much that the steam doesn't seem to be coming off its body. "You know what it is," he says, "As long as it's straight up and down, it's all right, but when he picks up that left knee. . . ."

And he wants to make a lighting change. When someone asks what the change is, London shrugs: "I'm sure it's infinitesimal."

We seem to be heading straight to the door marked CREATIVE DIFFERENCES.

It takes another hour before they're ready to shoot again. "Bring up the steam," says the AD through his megaphone. "Here we go. Everybody man their stations. On your marks."

They shoot it. "Let's do it again, right away," says Fincher.

"Steam up," says the AD. "Get the lead on . . . and . . . ACTION!"

"Cut."

Fincher orders more changes and dashes over to the editing room. As he walks, he talks about how tough the shoot has been and how he's fighting to keep the film bleak. Although he's often described as arrogant, he seems merely direct. But occasionally he drops a remark that would make a studio executive with millions of dollars on the line a tad nervous: "I'm not making this movie for 50 million people," he says, "I'm making it for eight people, my friends, people who know the cameras and lighting."

That works out to a budget of just over $6 million per friend.

Back on the set, Fincher has another go at the scene. "This shot is about five times more complicated than when we started out," London says. The studio was expecting just two simple shots of the writhing alien, but Fincher has added dripping water, foreground pipes, and extra steam. Fox executive vice president Tom Jacobson and senior vice president Jon Landau have joined London and all three executives are looking over Fincher's shoulder. "Action, action, action!" cries the AD. The steam guys blast the alien with thunderclap bursts of smoke.

"Let's go again while we've got steam!" the AD calls.

"Save the steam," Fincher says calmly. "Play it back for me." He watches the playback intently. Finally he nods, satisfied. It's 6:30, eleven hours after first call. He's got his five seconds of film, his way, and it looks *great.*

Fincher: So what do you want to know about my movie?

Q: How you got involved, the production process, what happened in London, all that stuff.

Fincher: Well, it's weird, because when I got involved, it was, we have a movie to make. How do we solve these problems? How do we get this movie made? I'd love to just take the 50 million bucks and just fuckin' start over again.

Q: That's worth talking about. Maybe we can save some young director . . .

Fincher: What would you say? There's no way a first-time director can make a $50 million movie in this town with the fuckin' recession on the eve of the millennium, you know, with the panic that exists in this business right now. There's no way. You can't do it, because in the end, if you can't say, "I made *Jaws,* trust me," why should they trust you? One time,

(producer) David Giler, incredibly aggressive and pissed off on a conference call with Fox, said, "Why are you listening to him for, he's a shoe
salesman!"

Q: Meaning your Nike commercial.

Fincher: Exactly. And it's perfectly valid. What do I know? I'm a shoe
salesman.

Seven years passed between the first *Alien* and the second. Six more years
would pass before the third was ready to unreel. "It's a little like child-
birth," says Sigourney Weaver. "The first couple of years after you make
an *Alien* film, the idea of doing another one is not that appealing."

But this time it was supposed to be different. Producers Walter Hill,
David Giler, and Gordon Carroll jumped back into their *Alien* franchise
almost immediately after the second one was finished, hiring cyberpunk
author William Gibson (*Neuromancer*). They showed him a brief treatment set in a Soviet space station and asked if he had any ideas. "It was
sort of like a Cold War in space, with genetic manipulation of the alien
replacing nuclear war," says Gibson.

He set to work, but he was interrupted by the 1987 writers strike and
regime changes at Fox and finally decided to go back to work on a novel.
Only one detail survived. "In my draft, this woman has a bar code on the
back of her hand," he says. "In the shooting script, one of the guys has a
shaved head and a bar code on the back of his head. I'll always privately
think that was my piece of *Alien³*."

The second writer, Eric Red (*Near Dark*), was hired in late 1988 for a
"five-week job" intended to coax more development money out of Fox.
Working with director Renny Harlin, he turned in his draft on January
1989. As he remembers it, *he* came up with the gene-splicing idea. "In
the third film you needed a new alien. I suggested doing genetic experi-
ments on the alien." Red says that Hill and Giler were disorganized and
irresponsible. "They had no story or treatment or any real plan for the
picture," he says. Hill and Giler say the problem was Red's script; when
Harlin read it, he quit the project.

Next up was David Twohy (*Warlock*). His draft was set in a penal colony in space, and all concerned agree that it was very good. There was no
Ripley in it, since Hill and Giler planned to leave Weaver out and bring
her back for the fourth film. At that point, Joe Roth took over Fox, and
when he read Twohy's script, his response was swift and irrevocable,
says Twohy: "This is a great script, but I won't make this film without
Sigourney."

After talking it over with Hill and Giler, Weaver agreed to do the movie if she liked the script, and Twohy sat down to write her into it. Then came what Twohy calls "one of the most transparent bits of studio treachery I've ever heard of."

Back in New York, Hill saw *The Navigator: An Odyssey Across Time*, a stunning but esoteric art film by an obscure New Zealand director named Vincent Ward. Hill got Fox excited enough to call Ward. But Ward said he didn't like Twohy's script. No problem, said Fox. "So I hopped on an airplane," says Ward, "and during the flight, I had an idea that was totally different: Sigourney would land in a community of monks in outer space and not be accepted by them." The monks would live on a wooden planet that looked like something out of Hieronymus Bosch, with furnaces and windmills—and no weapons.

Ward pitched the idea to Hill, Giler, and Roth. "It was a little far out," says Giler, "but that's what we wanted, to push this thing a little bit." Ward signed on in April 1991, and Fox hired screenwriter John Fasano to work with him. "We were supposedly writing *Alien 4*," Fasano recalls, "but if ours came in first, it would be *Alien³*." Fox wanted to start the movie in October.

Across town, says Twohy, "I'm writing balls to the wall, and about two weeks before I finish, I get a call from a *Los Angeles Times* reporter. He says, 'What's this about competing drafts of *Alien³*?' I say it must be wrong. He says, 'No, I hear the director has brought on his own writer.' I call the studio, and they say, 'No, no, no, you got it all wrong. He's not writing *Alien³*, he's writing *Alien 4*. . . .' At that point, I just slapped my script together and went off to make my own film. And that's the last I've heard from them. The old adage is true: Hollywood pays its writers well but treats them like shit to make up for it."

The next screenwriter on board was Greg Pruss, hired to rewrite Fasano, who had to leave to co-write *Another 48 Hrs.* Pruss did "five arduous drafts," he says. By this time, Ward and Pruss had moved to London, where Fox was going to shoot the film in the hope of saving money. The crew was already beginning to design and build sets even as the script was being written. But now the studio began having problems with Ward, who was less interested in Ripley or the alien than in his monks. "The movie's called *Alien* because it's about the alien," says Pruss. "I couldn't get that across to Vincent. He and the studio were at odds, clear and simple, and I was in the middle."

Pruss quit, and a few weeks later, Ward was gone. Now the studio was in a real jam. It had invested somewhere between $5 million and $13 million in scripts, sets, and pay-or-play commitments (after strafing Hollywood in the press for paying its Rambos better than its Ripleys—and knowing that Roth would not make the movie without her—Weaver was able to negotiate about $4 million, plus a healthy chunk of the back end, then the highest salary paid to an actress). "My heart's like this," Weaver says, shaking her hands in the air. "I had to start working on this picture, and we had no script, and we had no director, and at best these things can be nightmares."

On their short list of potential saviors was David Fincher, a video director with a reputation as a hell of a shooter—just look at the visual flash of his Madonna videos "Vogue," "Express Yourself," and "Oh, Father"—and something of a movie savant. "Genius" is a word many use. Son of a *Life* magazine reporter, he produced a local TV news show while still in high school. As a nineteen-year-old Industrial Light & Magic employee, he shot some of *Return of the Jedi*. His first commercial was the American Cancer Society's smoking fetus. He directed his first video at twenty-one and landed a CAA agent soon after. He was a founding member of the ultra-hip Propaganda video house, which four years later was bringing in a $50 million annual gross. And he had moxie to spare—he tells of meeting Sid Ganis when Ganis was the president of Paramount and pitching him a complicated idea. "He said to me, 'Fincher, nobody is going to give you $40 million for a first picture.' And I said, 'Sid, I know that. What would I do with a forty-minute movie?'"

Hill and Giler had discovered Ridley Scott and James Cameron when they were virtual unknowns, so they were well disposed to hiring beginners. They asked Pruss, who had worked on a screenplay for Fincher, for a reference. "I said, 'Yeah, I know him,'" Pruss recalls. "'He wouldn't direct the movie in a million fucking years.'"

Fincher, it turned out, considers the first *Alien* one of "the ten perfect movies of all time." Pruss tried to tell him he was making a mistake. "I said, David, you're fucking nuts. Why are you doing this? Why don't you direct your own movie?" he recalls. "And he said, 'I don't know, there's just something about it. It could be cool. Don't you think it could be cool?'"

Q: So you've been depressed?
Fincher: I don't know. It's just . . . I don't get any sleep any more. At a certain point, I just start waking up. I wake up at two, three, four, on the hour.
Q: Thinking of things you could have done differently?

Fincher: Why didn't I do this, why didn't I do that, how do I fucking leave the country without you knowing.

Q: I can't imagine what it's like, having spent a year of your life. . . .

Fincher: Two years, my friend, two years.

Initially, Weaver was skeptical. "All I heard about him was, he's very attractive, and all the women he works with fall in love with him," she says. "He wasn't a serious contender."

Then Weaver, Hill, Giler, and Fox worldwide production president Roger Birnbaum met with Fincher in Los Angeles. Fincher came to the meeting wearing an anti-fur T-shirt, which made Weaver smile. She asked him what kind of a part he had in mind for Ripley. "And he said, 'How do you feel about . . . *bald*?'" Weaver says. "And I sort of looked at him, and I looked at Roger and said, 'Well, Roger, of course if I make the picture bald, I'll have to make more money.' At that moment, I was willing to follow him anywhere."

With Fincher signed, Fox hired Larry Ferguson, who co-wrote *Beverly Hills Cop II*, to do a four-week emergency rewrite on the script. His price: about $500,000. Ferguson knew he had to bring fresh ideas to the franchise, but he was experienced enough to know what the studio wanted. "Sequels are like Big Macs," he says. "If you went into McDonalds and ordered a Big Mac and it came out different, you wouldn't order it every time."

But Fincher didn't want a Big Mac. The plot he came up with on his own, before the studio hired Ferguson, left the suits aghast. "They said, 'My God, this is four fucking hours, it's $150 million.' And they were absolutely right." He laughs. "I was just so taken with the legacy that it had to be . . . *Apocalypse Now*."

Fincher: In the draft Larry was writing, she was going to be this woman who had fallen from the stars. In the end, she dies, and there are seven monks left—seven dwarfs.

Q: You're kidding.

Fincher: Seriously. I swear to God. She was like . . . what's her name in Peter Pan? She was like Wendy. And she would make up all these stories. And in the end, there were these seven dwarfs left, and there was this fucking tube they put her in, and they were waiting for Prince Charming to come wake her up. So that was one of the endings we had for this movie. You can imagine what Joe Roth said when he heard this. "What?! What are they doing over there?! What the fuck is going on?!"

When Ferguson turned in his draft, the movie almost fell apart. He had written Ripley so that she sounded like "a very pissed-off gym instructor," says Weaver. "I said, 'If you're going to do this, you're going to have to do it without me.'" Fox coughed up $600,000 or so for Hill and Giler to do an emergency rewrite.

Working in Hill's office in L.A., the producers quickly scraped the wooden planet and moved the action back to Twohy's prison. Since Fincher and Weaver were both taken with the religious element, they made the prisoners what Giler calls "your basic militant Christian fundamentalist millenarian apocalyptic" types. In just three weeks, they had a first draft. The studio liked it. Weaver liked it. But alas, Fincher had a few reservations. . . .

The start date was pushed back to January 14, and for the next two months, Hill, Giler, Fincher, and the studio fought over the script, the budget, the sets—even as more sets were being constructed. Hill calls the period "brutal, a real battle royal." As Hill and Giler wrote and rewrote, Fox's Jon Landau began vetting individual scenes for budgetary correctness. "It was a very unrealistic way of making a movie," says Hill. "Usually you get a script, and then you find out how much it's going to cost. Then, if that's not an acceptable figure, you decide what you don't need quite so much. But to be given arbitrary guidelines before you even have the creative work done. . . ."

Fox production president Birnbaum says he was simply hoping Hill and Giler would be "very clever" in what they wrote. "We started with a budget, and we wanted the new writing to stay within the framework of the budget, and occasionally things were being written that impacted the budget upward."

In the middle of all these battles and crises was Tom Zinneman, Hill and Giler's handpicked line producer. With Hill and Giler now functioning as writers, Zinneman was in the odd position of acting as a buffer between Fincher and the men who hired him, as well as carrying out the thousand daily details of a production that didn't know where it was going. Weaver loved him. "He's one of the best line producers I've ever worked with," she says.

But three weeks before production started, Fox fired him. "The Fox point of view is that he wasn't getting Fincher to compromise the shooting schedule and the budget," says Weaver. "He kept saying, 'You can't do it in this time for this amount of money,' and Fox didn't want to hear it. So they fired him. You know, kill the messenger."

That's certainly how Zinneman sees it. "I kept telling them—I memoed everyone—this is what's coming, these are the problems, let's deal with it, don't bury your head in the sand. We're building not a house but a high rise, *without plans*."

Birnbaum's version of Zinneman's firing is virtually identical to the other versions—with no apologies. After Fox's recent experiences with *The Abyss* and *Die Hard 2*, the studio was extremely wary of another runaway film. "Rather than rolling up his sleeves and saying, 'Okay, this is what the studio wants, let me figure out a way to do this,' he wanted us to say, 'Hey, this is what it's going to cost, let's just admit it,'" says Birnbaum. "But our strategy was to let them know right from the beginning that this was not an open checkbook—I believe in my heart that if we would have accepted a figure earlier at a higher number, we would have gone over that. And Zinneman became demoralized, so we made a change."

It is from this point that Weaver traces one of the film's major problems—that Fincher was left without a passionate ally as producer and ended up having to spend his nights fighting for his next budgetary dispensation. "We paid for *Die Hard 2* every second," she says. "The meter's been running the whole time."

And shortly after Zinneman's sacking, in a tense meeting between Fincher, Michael London, Tom Jacobson, and the new line producer, Ezra Swerdlow, Fox cut the shooting schedule down to seventy days, a loss of twenty-three days. Fincher would only get twenty-five special effects shots, less than half what *Aliens* had. Weaver thought the shortened schedule insane. The filmmakers ended up working eighteen-hour days and six-day weeks to try to meet the stop date, a grueling pace that she says caused actual physical danger—at one point, when an explosion effect backfired, five crew members got burned, one badly enough to go to the hospital. "The first *Alien* took sixteen-and-a-half weeks, and the second one took eighteen weeks," says Weaver. "Why did they think they could make the third one in thirteen weeks?" Birnbaum's reply: "We were trying to manage the cost of the picture, which was not Sigourney's responsibility. She was not paying for this movie or line producing this movie."

Once more last-minute fight cost Fincher the goodwill of his producer-writers. Over the Christmas holidays, Hill and Giler were going to take a ten-day vacation, and a writer named Rex Pickett was hired for one more bit of rewriting. Fincher took Pickett out to dinner and told him all the problems he was having with the script. "I said, 'Am I crazy? Am I totally insane?'" Fincher recalls. "And he said 'No, this makes sense. Maybe you're just not communicating it well.'"

It all blew up when Pickett wrote a memo savaging Hill and Giler's script, and Zinneman somehow got hold of it. "I was furious," says Zinneman, who brought it to Hill.

He and Giler read the memo and exploded. "I was pissed, absolutely furious," says Giler. Hill says the thrust of the memo was "that we were fools not to recognize the merit of the ideas the director had." Although Pickett's pages were thrown out (he wouldn't comment), the irate producers left London and never came back. "They fired Zinneman," says Hill, "they hired another writer behind our backs, they were being in our opinion, very unrealistic about certain economic realities, and our conception of what a producer is had already been nullified. If they weren't going to do anything we were telling them to do, what was the point in being there?"

The blowup rocked the London set. "It was electrifying news," says one of the crew. "It basically stopped the production."

Then shooting began, and things got worse.

Q: I heard Landau and you were at each other's throats.

Fincher: We have had amazing, amazing bouts, with screaming and spitting, cat scratching, the whole thing. It's his job to control costs and my job to get the shots. It was a bloodbath—a constructive bloodbath.

Q: So how did he pound you?

Fincher: It's all a random and bloody blur. Ask Muhammad Ali, "How much do you remember?" I can't really form the words because I'm so brain-damaged.

Q: So did he actually call "Cut"?

Fincher: No, he tried to fucking wrap before we'd shoot stuff.

Q: Like at the end of the day, call "Wrap"?

Fincher: Yeah, like, "Okay, it's 6 P.M. and we have to get out of here."

Q: So what would you say?

Fincher: "There's no point in trying to force it before it's done. It's a guy in a rubber suit. If it looks like a guy in a rubber suit, we're fucked."

Q: And you'd say it in that calm tone of voice?

Fincher: Absolutely. Constantly. That's one of my most irritating qualities.

On the first day of shooting, Sigourney Weaver was lying naked on a table, covered only by a sheet. She was wearing a contact lens to make her eye look bloody, leaving her almost blind. Fincher called over the production's bug wrangler, who was carrying a cup full of . . . lice. "David said, 'Just sprinkle a few bugs on her forehead,'" says Weaver. "And my eyes are open and I'm talking, and all these bugs drop down on my face. They went into my ears and my eyes, and I—who pride myself on having worked with gorillas and everything and being a good trouper—I went *nuts*. You realize what it's like to be naked and blind and have bugs thrown in your face? It was the worst beginning with a director I could imagine."

But the lice turned out to be cute baby crickets, and from there things went relatively smoothly (even though the studio didn't finalize the budget until a few days into shooting, and the writers didn't deliver a "final" script for two weeks). They began with the dialogue sequences, saving the action scenes for later. Fincher won Weaver back completely a few weeks later when they shot a scene in which she does an autopsy on the dead Newt—the girl she spent the entire second movie saving—to make sure no alien is hidden inside her.

"To me it's the most emotionally charged scene because you are doing something absolutely despicable to the person that you love more than anybody in the world, and I was terrified because that scene was so important to me," says Weaver. "If David had been insensitive, it would have been a nightmare. But he was great, incredibly sweet and supportive. You do find out what people are like when you shoot. He's not only brilliant but also a very good guy."

Line producer Swerdlow, who has worked with Woody Allen, Mel Brooks, and Mike Nichols, was also impressed with Fincher. "A lot of directors just tell you what they want the end product to be but not how to get there," he says, adding that "David is a world-class visual-effects expert and seems to understand lighting very scientifically."

Fincher was particularly happy to be working with Jordan Cronenweth, the cinematographer of *Blade Runner* and one of his all-time heroes. "When Cronenweth works, it's like he's playing 3-D chess and the rest of us are playing Chinese checkers," he says. "The tonal range is amazing. It's like Ansel Adams." But Cronenweth worked slowly (in part because of the language barrier, according to Fincher), and Fox began pressuring Fincher to let him go. "I think they felt the two of us were in cahoots," says Fincher. Finally, after yet another transatlantic phone call, Fincher reluctantly fired his hero.

With a new cinematographer, things picked up. They even had some fun—Weaver says that as far as laughs on the set go, this was her favorite *Alien*. But when they started shooting the big action scenes late in February, things started slowing down again. The pace was brutal—days typically started at 7 A.M. and continued till 1 A.M. Fincher was supervising four units and spending his nights and Sundays working on script changes. "Thank God he's young," says Weaver.

By this time, Swerdlow was becoming convinced that Zinneman had been mostly right about the schedule. "Fox wasn't thrilled to hear it," he says. The exchange rate had shifted against the dollar, and shooting in London was getting more expensive by the day. Often, Swerdlow and Fincher would get on the phone together to argue with the home office.

But the biggest and longest-running fight was over the ending. Hill and Giler (who continued to consult long-distance on the movie after Fox threw in another hundred grand or so) wanted a clear-cut, good guys/bad guys ending. The argument reached a climax in early February during the "shoe salesman" conference call. Hill and Giler left Birnbaum's office with Fox on their side—or so they thought. But the next day, Giler says, "we had a kind of extraordinary meeting, where Roger basically said, 'You guys are sophisticated writers. You've conned us to your point of view with the force of your ideas and logic, but basically we want to go with Fincher's idea.'"

Birnbaum says he doesn't remember the incident quite that way, "David and Walter wanted the scene to go one way, and they made all the sense in the world. But when Fincher came up with his point of view, it made sense to us, too. So I said, 'If both arguments hold water, I'm going to go with the guy who's shooting.'" That was the last straw for Hill and Giler, who then severed all contact with the production.

As shooting continued into May, Fincher passed the targeted stop date. When the production went about ten days over, Jon Landau showed up and took over from Swerdlow. "I wasn't totally unhappy with it, because the stakes were getting very high," says Swerdlow. But Weaver was incensed. "Jon came over with instructions to cut this, slash that, and there was an inference that David was this enfant terrible going mad. It was very contemptuous of the effort we were putting in to come in and say this isn't necessary or that's not necessary."

By now they were shooting the climatic scenes—the same scenes they would partly re-shoot a year later. The work was enormously complicated. "You're talking about a creature that is ten effects guys, and the close-up head is eleven guys, and the fucking steam effects is, like, twenty guys," says Fincher, "and just to turn the steam on took ten minutes, and we've got five or six cameras rolling, and you rehearse the whole thing, and a Louma crane is up on a fucking twenty-five-foot platform, and it's got to go through these chains, and the chains have to be in the right place. That kind of choreography takes time."

And Fincher was meticulous about getting the effects he wanted. "Jon couldn't push David as a director," says Swerdlow. "He could push crews, but the shot itself had to be the shot David wanted. If something was wrong in the art direction or the mechanical effects, he would wait, and that was something you couldn't push him on. You just couldn't."

After watching for two weeks, with the film still unfinished, Landau pulled the *Alien³* plug. The sets were put in storage and the filmmakers ordered home.

Weaver tried to use her clout and called Joe Roth directly, but it was too late. "In the end," she says, "it came to a showdown between the director's vision and a dwindling amount of cold, hard cash."

Roth says he couldn't be sure that Fincher wasn't wasting film on unnecessary effects. "It's really hard to tell on science fiction," he says. "Fincher had shot a long time before he came back, and I felt it was important to see the movie at that point and reconstruct what needed to be finished."

Besides, Birnbaum adds, Fincher's background was in commercials, and commercial directors tend to shoot and shoot. Fox had already spent upwards of $40 million. "The artists want to make a piece of art, and I have to take every piece of art and put a price tag on it," he says. "It's the squirrelly part of our business, but there it is."

For most of the cast and crew, the end came none too soon. "It was a general relief for everyone," says actor Charles Dutton.

Ironically, Fincher had shot ninety-three days—three days less than Zinneman had originally predicted.

Q: What did you do when they pulled the plug?
Fincher: As upset as I was, I was so exhausted, I was glad to get back on the plane. We were told they were going to hold the sets until Joe could take a look at the picture, but they decided it was more cost-effective to cut the film and see exactly what was needed—what's laughingly known as the surgical strike. So we assembled it—and it was like two hours and seventeen minutes—and we showed it to them. It was quite a sobering experience.
Q: I saw a list of your reshoots that was seven pages long.
Fincher: No, no. You must have seen the wish list. . . .
Q: So to this day there's still a dispute over how to handle the ending?
Fincher: Oh, yeah. Absolutely. In my most depressed moments, people

say, "You know, they didn't know how they wanted to end *Casablanca*."
Hopefully this is *Casablanca*.

A few weeks after returning to L.A., Fincher showed his rough assemblage to Hill and Giler, who came back to the project in postproduction, and to Fox. "Everybody could see there were certain problems," says Hill. Roth says his notes were basic first-screening notes—"too long, could be paced better, needs to be more like a traditional horror film."

For the next year, Fincher labored in the editing room. He made about $250,000 for *Alien³*, not much more than a DGA minimum. Fox ultimately decided to keep him in L.A. and to cut down his "wish list" from almost six weeks to a mere eight days (at a cost of about $2.5 million extra). Weaver remembers his response when the studio started pressuring him to bolster the horror side of the film. "He said to them, 'We all sat there and decided to make a china cup, a beautiful, delicate china cup. You can't tell me we should have made a beer mug.'"

But as the film approached final cut, people's spirits started to pick up. Weaver and Fox and even Hill and Giler started praising the film. "It really stands on its own as a brilliant *Alien* picture, very unusual and very provocative," says Weaver, who is not given to hype. And it's clear just from the script that what Hill and Giler wrote and what Fox agreed to do is a very ambitious movie with a stark and brooding quality that smells of art—brilliant or failed, it will certainly not be your average monster movie. Fox was even happy enough to kick in six more days and another million or two to shoot one of Fincher's pet scenes—the birth of a baby alien. "There's no question we've had our dark hours," says London, "but in the end, Fincher's vision and his talent are all up there on the screen. David doesn't see it this way, but I think all the battling actually helped it get there."

None of this seemed to make Fincher much happier, though. He just saw the things he could have done, the things he could still do.

"Here we go!" cries the AD. "Steam! Steam!"

A raging orange fog sweeps through the set, a tangle of chains and pipes that looks like the intestines of some martial god. The floor is gleaming wet, the puddle contained by an artificial lakebed of plastic edged by one-by-twos. This is the last day of reshoots—at least that's what they're saying now—and they're shooting the climax of the movie.

"Faster with the smoke," Fincher calls out. He's happy with his shots and tells the AD to order all of them printed.

"Get that fucking tail out of there," he tells the alien-effects guy, Alec Gillis. "It looks like a fucking coat hanger."

He's in a good mood today. He's wearing the Spielberg uniform again, jeans and baseball hat. When the take is over, he ribs Gillis. "I'll take out one of your thumbs next time that happens."

Gillis ribs back: "Yeah? I'll have to take it out of my ass."

A few minutes later, when someone mentions a company run by Mormons, Fincher asks, "Is that a Ma and Ma and Ma and Ma and Pa outfit?"

He's impatient. "What's going on, are we perforating our own film?"

The suits are still around in force. Later, Fincher starts setting up an odd shot—on the other side of the soundstage, he's placed pipes on the floor. The alien is "climbing" the horizontal pipes while the camera shoots its reflection in a huge mirror propped up at the end of them, making it appear that the alien is climbing vertically. "David wanted to build a whole set," says London. "We said no; then he got creative."

Tom Jacobson comes to look over Fincher's shoulder. He tells him it's a great shot. "It's all done with mirrors," Fincher says dryly.

Jacobson asks another question. Maybe he's just making conversation. "The planet," he says, "is that being done in camera?"

Fincher shrugs. "We didn't plan it that way. We haven't found the right planet. We have location scouts out."

Mr. Fincher's Neighborhood

James Kaminsky / 1993

From *Advertising Age*, November 1, 1993, 17. Reprinted by permission of James Kaminsky.

When Gaston Braun, head of production at Ayer/New York, first sat down with director David Fincher earlier this year to pitch him on an ambitious new campaign for AT&T, he was more than a bit anxious. "If anything worried me, it was the pessimism," he recalls. "Fincher's world view is mainly made up of tough, nasty, and unsentimental things—everyone knows the man is not an optimist. This was a big-image account, all about futurism and technology, and absolutely nobody does those things better than Fincher. But we didn't want *Blade Runner*. We had to make sure that he wasn't going to take us to a cold and dark place. But then, out of nowhere, Fincher said to us, 'Remember *The Wizard of Oz*? Well, the way I see it, these spots need to have a Yellow Brick Road—something nice and friendly and optimistic to walk on.' My colleague and I looked at each other. Was this guy really David Fincher?"

Indeed it was. Ever since he first exploded on the commercials scene in the mid-eighties, Fincher has defied any kind of easy categorization. Those who have worked with Propaganda Films' superstar director—who, by the way, doesn't give interviews—say he is, by turns, cynical and idealistic, gregarious and enigmatic, technology-obsessed yet humanistic; an intimidating enfant terrible and a witty work-obsessed pro experienced far beyond his years. "You really can't pigeonhole David," says Michael White, a production designer who works frequently with the director. "Agencies never quite know what kind of ride they're in for once they hire him, but they do know that they're going to wind up with a very distinctive visual style and attitude."

"My God, he really puts you through your paces," says Charlotte Moore, a copywriter at Wieden & Kennedy who worked with Fincher on last year's Nike women's campaign. "Working with David is an exhausting and invigorating creative process. It's a nonstop debate, an endless argument, a continuous sparring match. There's nothing else quite like it—you either love it or you hate it."

Only thirty-one years old, Fincher seems to already have had at least five distinct careers. First there was the precocious special-effects whiz kid from San Rafael, California, tapped by George Lucas for an Industrial Light & Magic staff job while barely out of high school. Then came the high-powered music video director who co-founded Propaganda Films at twenty-four and instantly became its reigning icon. Next up was Fincher as the ultimate crossover artist, who merged rock video style with high-impact imagery to create a new advertising vernacular: an edgy, complex, densely layered look that helped give birth to the newest directorial label, that of the visual stylist.

And then there was *Alien³*. With a budget eventually hitting $50 million, it was by far the largest film ever entrusted to a first-time director. A troubled two-year production marked by pitched studio battles and crew dissension, it was widely perceived as Fincher's Waterloo: a remarkably downbeat artistic vision that was a critical failure and a major commercial disappointment in the U.S. (Even so, Fox claims the film made $175 million globally.)

Now Fincher finds himself in a brave, new post-*Alien* world. "Here's a guy who changed the face of advertising in the eighties—for better or worse—more than any other single director, and he did it all before he was thirty," says a former Fincher colleague. "When he left to do the movie that was a void, and lots of other directors stepped in to imitate his style. Now Fincher wannabes are all over the place, and that rebellious, expensive 'Propaganda look' is everywhere. He isn't the only game in town anymore. So what the hell does he do for an encore?"

What he's done for an encore, it seems, is throw himself back into the commercials scene with a vengeance. These days the normally picky director is, by some accounts, being sought after by a broader range of clients than ever before. In addition to his AT&T work, he has also shot for Chanel and Budweiser (a job that wrapped production late last month) in addition to his frequent forays for Levi's and Nike.

Fincher's re-emergence comes at a time when more and more directors are aspiring to the ranks of the visual stylists, a rarefied plane occupied by directors like Tony Kaye and Tarsem Singh. Still, says Wieden's head of production Bill Davenport, "I see a lot of people trying to duplicate Fincher's look but they all come up short. He's probably the most creative director I've ever worked with: he takes control over every part of the process, from the earliest concepts to the last minute of post. It's a densely packed, dramatic style with incredible attention to detail: not just cinematography but styling, production design, all of it. Some agencies brand him as a rock video guy, but that's off the mark.

"In fact," he adds, "Fincher is one of the two guys who stand out as this industry's top creative talents, along with Joe Pytka. They're the most versatile directors in the business, and both can be an incredible pain in the ass to work with. But style-wise, they're total opposites. Joe is more human, a little warmer, with more of an emotional quality that's authentic without being sappy. David brings something else entirely: an edge, both conceptually and visually. He'll push a concept as far as it can go. He has more of a cynical outlook—he's not a warm, happy guy, and he generally doesn't make warm, happy spots."

One thing Fincher shares with Pytka is a stylistic versatility that runs the gamut from the slick visual flash of such videos as Madonna's "Vogue," to the stark simplicity of his first commercial, the chilling "smoking fetus" PSA for the American Cancer Institute. Somewhere in between falls the sophisticated noir-surrealism of his spot for Colt 45 (starring Billy Dee Williams and some snarling Dobermans, this spot, Fincher's second, won the Clio for Best Director back in 1989), to his more recent "Blade Roller" Coke spot, and a hilarious forties musical spoof for Nike dubbed "Barkley on Broadway."

But according to Mark Plummer, a DP who works regularly with Fincher, "It's incorrect to think of him as having one distinct style. David works to arrive at a singular style for each project—often inspired by specific movies or photographs or paintings—and then he'll see it through in every detail. Lots of other commercial and video directors just try to imitate something but miss out on what made it great. David figures it out, and then reconceptualizes it.

"For example," he adds, "when we did the 'Barkley on Broadway' spot, we studied footage and stills from old Busby Berkely musicals, and had long discussions on what made them look the way they did. Then we took the elements of that lighting and visual style that we liked—brighter sets, more front lights—and ignored others. It ends up as a pastiche, something new and old at the same time."

The son of a *Life* magazine reporter, Fincher developed an early fascination with film and video. While still in high school he produced a local TV news show, and, at eighteen, he and some friends invented innovative computer special effects and animation for a startup company called Korty Films. The work landed him a spot at ILM, where he honed his high-tech mastery on such films as *Return of the Jedi*, barely out of his teens.

"He's probably the only commercials director out there who could step in and take over anyone's job on the set, from the cameraman, to the stylist, to the editor," says White. "As a result, he's incredibly demanding on the entire crew. He pushes you to do your best work, and he knows exactly what that is. And there are some who crumble under the pressure."

By many accounts, working on a Fincher set can be a trial by fire. When the going gets tough, the director can be witheringly sarcastic, quietly emotional, and above all, uncompromising with crew members and agency creatives alike. Says White: "He comes to the set knowing exactly what he's looking for in every shot; everything is thoroughly thought out in preproduction and completely storyboarded. And he's pushing the edge technically, aesthetically and conceptually. Inevitably, working at this level can get tense, and it often leads to conflict. When things go wrong, it's one of the ugliest sets you can be on.

"I know how to steer clear of David when he's having one of his moods," he continues. "You have to know how to play Fincher: be in his face when you need to, avoid him when he's in a brooding moment. Those are moments when you want to stay in the loop, but avoid getting too close. But however intense it can get with crew members, it's nothing compared with the pitched battles he's had with agencies."

"We've certainly had more than our share of run-ins at the creative level," agrees Davenport. "It can get nasty, but it has never been a disabling problem. Good as he is at digging his feet in the sand, he knows how to compromise. He's very smart, very persuasive, and a bit arrogant. It's an intimidating combination."

For Moore and her partner Janet Champ, the challenge was how to merge their distinct vision of Nike's award-winning women's print campaign with Fincher's equally strong point of view. While the finished b&w spots reflect the poetic, lyrical feel of the print campaign, Moore recalls that "there were incredibly heated debates over the visuals, and at times it seemed like a stalemate: nobody wanted to give up any ground. But in the end we learned to pick our battles. With David, it's a bit like child psychology: if you want something really badly, then don't ask for it. I certainly wouldn't call it an easy shoot, but when we weren't fighting we were laughing."

Cinematographer Plummer agrees that Fincher can be an intimidating force during production, but adds, "There are certain guys out there who are abrasive in an offensive way. David isn't. If he raises his voice, it's for good reason. He has a reputation as a terror on the set; I've seen that side, but the rap is overblown. David keeps the energy and tension level of a set very high. If he feels strongly about something he'll fight for it."

And while he's usually described as obsessive about pre-planning his shots, he's not inflexible, either. Doug Biro, a group CD at McCann-Erickson Hakuhodo in Tokyo, worked with Fincher on the Coke "Blade Roller" spot, which has run in Japan and other Asian countries. Set in some unspecified city in the year 2021, the spot is a stylistic homage to *Blade Runner* in which a band of renegade rollerbladers defy curfew to skate daredevil-style through the deserted rain-slicked streets. They stop only to break into a store and liberate some icy cold bottles of the real thing, which they quaff on the go. In the closing frames, one of the skaters tosses a bottle to a small boy, who gazes on with *Shane*-like adoration.

It was, recalls Biro, a difficult shoot, given the acrobatic stunts required and the seven successive nights of rain and cold that pelted the crew. Shooting in a desolate section of downtown L.A., the agency team and Fincher worked despite the weather, using the rain to add to the stark mood of the piece. A problem arose with the final shot, where a lone skater tosses his bottle to the kid.

It's the emotional payoff of the whole commercial, and they almost didn't get it. A fifty-foot, backlit prop sign, which was supposed to be in the background of this shot, providing an eerie neon-like effect, had blown down the night before.

Fincher and his crew were reduced to cruising the streets of Hollywood in a camera car with a skater, in costume, fastened on the hood, trying to find the right spot to shoot it. Almost out of time, Fincher finally got the shot needed with an improvised lighting arrangement while at his final setup. "And this from a guy who doesn't like to improvise." Biro says. "He came up with the solution at the eleventh hour."

While the Coke shoot was yet another Fincher epic—as is the Chanel spot he did at the start of the year, which has run in Europe—Biro says the director has an unfair rap for only being able to handle big jobs. In fact, the director shot two fairly low-budget spots for Biro and Levi's after the Coke project. And Fincher's Levi's Loose Fit "Keep It Loose" campaign, shot earlier this year for FCB/S.F., is a goofy, upbeat teenfest of hip-hopping kids matted over static backgrounds.

All this aside, the basic Fincher job is still high concept, all the way around. If anything, says Davenport, Fincher's absence from the commercials scene has "made him bigger and bolder, and he's gotten a hell of a lot more expensive. Not just his own fees, but his entire style of working: it's extremely crew heavy and equipment heavy. A lot of times these days, he prices himself out of the running for our ads. We wouldn't even consider him for a tight-budgeted account.

"Of course, now that he has more experience under his belt," Davenport adds, "he's even better at transforming a good shot into a great one. In certain respects, there's still no one else like him."

Seventh Hell

Mark Salisbury / 1996

From *Empire* 80 (February 1996): 78–85, 87. Reprinted by permission of Mark Salisbury.

David Fincher is a man back from the dead. With two stories to tell. First, of his hellish new movie *Se7en*. Second, of the hellish time that produced his debut *Alien³*. Hollywood turned its back on him after that, but now, says Mark Salisbury, it had better sit up and listen.

David Fincher's first feature was a dark, moody, malicious piece, dripping in atmosphere and oozing in menace. It was released in a blaze of glory in 1992 and sunk with barely a trace at the US box office. Critics hated it. The public scorned it. Fincher's name was mud.

Fast forward three years and Fincher's second film (*Se7en*), even more so than his debut, is a dark, moody, malicious piece, dripping in atmosphere and oozing menace. This time the critics loved it. The public came in droves. To paraphrase Laura Dern in *Blue Velvet*, it really is a strange world.

As the director of *Alien³*, the much maligned second *Alien* sequel, Fincher was on the receiving end of abuse from both critics and fans of the monster movie franchise who felt his morbid, gloomy approach had contributed to the film's lukewarm box office reception and therefore had effectively kicked the series into touch as far as its commercial viability was concerned.

Unlike *Alien³*, however, *Se7en* has a coherent script and no baggage. The result is an extraordinarily gripping, and totally terrifying story of a serial killer murdering his victims according to the seven deadly sins. Thanks to *Se7en*'s $80 million box office bonanza, Fincher has gone from being Hollywood's favorite whipping boy to arguably the hottest director in town. After the critical savagery that greeted *Alien³*, the success of *Se7en* must be sweet revenge.

"No," muses the thirty-three-year-old filmmaker in his office at

Propaganda Films in Los Angeles, "No one's harder on my work than I am. I didn't think I was treated unfairly. However much I didn't like the color of the carpet that was rolled out, I didn't blame the critics."

You might not know Fincher's name but if you've ever watched MTV you'll know his work: as one of the founding fathers of Propaganda, Fincher was *the* pop promo director of the late eighties/early nineties: Aerosmith's "Janie's Got a Gun" and Madonna's "Vogue" and "Express Yourself" are just three of his award-winning canon, not to mention his countless TV commercials.

With his slick visuals and witty, inventive, cinematic approach to the medium, Fincher carved himself out a striking niche, and one that had the executives at Fox offering him the shot at directing the second sequel to *Alien*. Expectations were high. The financial returns were low. And by the time the reviews came out, Fincher had pretty much gone to ground.

"It was a very tough experience to go through," he muses pragmatically of his time on *Alien³*, "and I just don't know of a twenty-seven-year-old who is going to turn down a $50 million movie."

"I'd probably do it again—at least I'd be smarter how I'd play stuff politically—but I'd probably get more of what I wanted on the screen. But it's a very difficult situation when you're dealing with a huge movie studio with a hell of a lot to lose."

The negative effect of the whole *Alien* experience was so profound that Fincher wasn't even sure if he wanted to make movies anymore.

"It was just miserable," he insists. "I don't do the trained dog act, I'm not there to shepherd somebody's idea through. I get very involved in the commercial work I do and rewrite and reconceive a lot of stuff. You make it your own, and I didn't really get to do that in two years of working on *Alien³*. It was like 'We like your idea, but see if you can do it for $15,000 instead of $150,000?' I had never been a traffic cop and I didn't know how to do that. I don't respond well to people saying 'Get more coverage.'"

So Fincher went back to the world of pop promos and commercials, reading the scripts that were sent his way, but never finding one that motivated him enough to want to pick up the feature megaphone again. Then *Se7en* arrived on his doormat and suddenly Fincher was excited.

"I didn't know what was going to happen at the end" he recalls of reading Andrew Kevin Walker's script, "or I kind of thought to myself, 'Well maybe this could happen but they'll never do that, they'll never do that to these guys in this movie, it's just not the Hollywood way to do it . . .' I like the fact that the movie was so ruthless. I got twenty pages into it and I thought, 'Oh God, it's just a buddy movie, and it's like I'm the last person in the world to do one, because I don't understand them, but them all of the sudden it took this turn, and I found myself getting more and more trapped in this kind of evil, and although I felt uncomfortable about being there, I had to keep going."

If you haven't yet seen *Se7en*, dear reader, then may I suggest you stop reading this at this point and skip to page 88—the very next story—because the following ten paragraphs in particular may seriously jeopardize your enjoyment, if that's the word, of the film. You see, Fincher was enamored of the script's ending. . . .

"The icing on the cake was when John Doe (the killer) gives himself up. I was holding the script so I knew how many pages were left in the movie and I thought, 'Holy shit, if I'm sitting in a theater, this movie could go on for another hour, this could be the middle of the movie.' It made me very uncomfortable."

Indeed, *Se7en* has probably the most depressing ending to any mainstream Hollywood film. Fincher hoots with laughter when I mention this.

"Excellent," he trills, "most movies these days don't make you feel anything so if you *can* make people feel something. . . . I just felt so much at the end, and I also felt the movie hearkened to these kind of weird movies of the early seventies, it just sort of reminded me of *Klute* and *Vanishing Point* and to have this sort of we-don't-know-exactly-what-we're-doing-but-it-could-be-a-movie kind of attitude to it."

It's an ending that very nearly didn't make it to the screen at all.

"I called my agent and said, 'This movie, are they going to make this? I mean, have you read this thing?' and he said, 'Yeah, I read it.' And I said, 'There's this fucking head in the box at the end, it's just amazing. Are they really going to do this?' And he said, 'No, you've got the wrong draft.' So they sent me the right draft and there was this big chase at the end to get to the bathroom where the wife's taking a shower and the serial killer's crawling through the window."

Fincher, you can tell, wasn't much impressed with ending number two.

"I said, 'This is just crap, the first one is much better.'" And so Fincher went to bat for the script's original climax. The one with the head in the box. "I went in to talk to (Michael) De Luca (from New Line) and said, 'The head in the box, that's the cool ending,' and he said, 'Yeah, I thought so too, let's go make that version.'"

Having convinced the studio, the only other person left to persuade was the film's producer, Arnold Kopelson.

"He said, 'There's no way that there will be a head in the box at the end of this movie, there is absolutely no way that that will ever happen, don't even talk to me about that,'" laughs Fincher, "and I said, 'Arnold in fifty years from now, there's going to be a bunch of twenty-five-to-thirty-year-olds at a party and one of them is going to say, 'Remember when you were like fifteen and that movie was on TV, I don't even know who was in it, but at the end there's this head in the box and the guy drives up in the middle of the desert,' and everybody's going to go, 'Oh yeah, I loved that movie.' That's how this movie is going to be remembered, so how can you cut the head in the box?' And he said, 'You're right.' He thinks in terms of like immorality."

If someone asked you to think of a serial killer movie, chances are you'll probably come up with *The Silence of the Lambs*. It's all about a serial killer, after all, but the comparisons end there. *Silence*, as good as it is, never strays out of thriller territory. Moreover, there is something perversely appealing about Anthony Hopkins' Lecter. He may be a mass murderer, but he's a charming one. He may escape custody at the end, but he's off to murder the person you least like in the film, so that's all right then. It's a cinematic escape valve.

Se7en, on the other hand, has no escape valve. No opportunity for the audience to let off steam.

"I wanted it to be tough," insists Fincher. "First you thought it was gonna be a cop movie, then you thought it was gonna be a thriller, and then at the end it's really a horror movie—It's the fucking *Exorcist*, you don't have any control over this, you're just along for the ride."

"From the time he fucking opens the box and Morgan's running to Brad and the killer, it's like you realize that the end of this movie's been written in stone and it's been there for like eight or nine hours and you don't have any choice. All of a sudden it became a horror movie, it's like how do you deal with circumstances way beyond your control?"

"You're in the water and there's a shark and you can't swim faster than it can, or you're in a spaceship and there's a fucking monster running around and you can't go outside. And here's a man and the fate of his wife has been decided and it's just a question of how he's going to deal with it. It started off being a buddy movie, in the middle it becomes a thriller but they never really get in front of the train, and they thought the thriller ending was going to come and you just totally sucker punch 'em and hit 'em with a horror movie and I thought that was cool . . . just kind of fuck with their ideas of what entertainment should be."

Entertainment? *Se7en?* Surely the two words are anathema. "I don't know how much movies should entertain," muses Fincher. "To me I'm always interested in movies that *scar*. The thing I love about *Jaws* is the fact that I've never gone swimming in the ocean again. I was like twelve when I saw *Jaws* and I was like, 'Good God!' It was amazing."

With *Se7en*, Fincher manages to fuck with your mind, and your pre-conceptions, from the word go. The opening credits are like a demented pop video, scored by David Bowie. It's an amazingly apt portent.

"The only way to do that in two minutes was to do something that was fucking really abstract, made up. It had to travel a pretty good distance 'cause you had to establish, basically, that somebody was out there and they were pretty fucked up. Also we wanted people to know that this was not *Legends of the Fall*. If you thought this was *Legends of the Fall* you were in the wrong theater."

Ah yes, Brad Pitt, who proves once and for all that he's not just a pretty boy but a rather fine actor, too—even if he is blown off the screen by Morgan Freeman's world-weary seen-it-all-before cop on the verge of re-tirement. Pitt, Fincher recalls, wasn't his immediate choice in the role of the young detective.

"I had always seen somebody who was more sort of a fuck-up," ex-plains Fincher, "and CAA said you should just meet with Pitt, he's really interested in this. We had lunch and he definitely saw the guy that way too, but he also had this amazing ability to say anything and you don't hold it against him.

"He was incredibly enthusiastic and I told him, 'This is not a major thing. This is a minor movie for everybody involved—and that's how we've got to keep looking at it. It's a little, tiny minor movie and it's just an experiment to let everybody do what they do and everybody invest in these people, and hopefully we can trick an audience into loving them or being fascinated by them, but it's going to be gritty, little, hand-held, fucked-up, scrungy cop movie . . .' and he was like, 'I'm in. I want to do it.'"

In the pivotal role of Pitt's wife, Fincher cast Pitt's real-life girlfriend, Gwyneth Paltrow, who he had first seen starring in *Flesh and Bone*.

"She was my first choice, and everybody said, 'You'll never get her—she's too picky, she doesn't want to play the cop's wife, she's not inter-ested in doing this stuff, this is too dark.'

"We tried to get a costume designer that I had worked with before and she said no, I won't be involved in this movie, and a lot of agents said I'm not going to send this to my client because it's evil and misogynistic and everybody kept saying, 'Gwyneth's not going to do it.'

"We saw probably a hundred people for it and had a couple who were really fine and finally Brad called her and asked her to come in, not to read, but to meet and I remember telling Arnold to watch this girl. He hadn't seen *Flesh and Bone* and she came in and she sat down for about two seconds and said, 'Do you have a rest room?' and she walked into the restroom and closed the door and Arnold said, 'She's perfect. . . .'"

In retrospect, directing a $50 million sequel to two of the most influential and well-loved science fiction films of the last twenty years probably wasn't the easiest option as a debut movie. Especially one that went through more writers than the Bible. But it was the personal attacks that riled Fincher most.

"Probably the most difficult thing about the savagery was that it wasn't really a personal vision anyway," recalls Fincher. "It's not like somebody said, 'Here's $60 million, you can do whatever you want,' and that's what I came up with. It was people going, 'Here's $30 million and we really like your ideas but we don't want to do any of them because they sound too expensive, and they all sound a little questionable, and that's not what we want, we want something that looks and reads and smells like a sequel.'"

Looking back, what does he think went wrong? Was it to do with the script not being right, him being young, or too many producers interfering?

"It's *all* that stuff," sighs Fincher. "It was like the Gulf War. You've got to have cast iron balls to make those kinds of movies. That's why most producers don't do $50 and $60 million movies that are sequels that have stunts and monsters and special effects. If we didn't have to live up to the other two movies, they wouldn't have spent that much money because we would have been much freer, but there was an expectation level on every single thing. . . . You suddenly have seven people in a room and they all have to agree on, 'Yeah, that's bigger than what we did last time, and that's better,' and any time you have to get seven people in a room to make a decision about what happens in a movie you're going to end up with something mediocre, because seven people in fear of their jobs are only to agree on what they know works and what they've seen before."

Woah. Let's backtrack a little here—the Gulf War?

Fincher nods in the affirmative.

"It was a very strange thing, because none of the studio executives wanted to fly over to see what we were doing, they tried to control what was going on without actually knowing what was going on. They were sort of taking the word of a lot of people who were very terrified that they were going to lose their jobs if this thing went over budget and yet they were all sort of trying to cover their arses over the phone. So none of the people from Fox were really there, they were making these kind of blanket policy decisions about what would happen without actually knowing. 'If that's going to cost $138,000 then you can only have half of it.' 'Well, I can't shoot the scene with only half the set.' 'Then you're going to have to figure out a way. . . .' It was all that kind of stuff."

So what was the worst horror story?

"They're all horror stories," he sighs. "The most horrifying thing about doing *Alien³* was realizing that the more you cared, the more they fucking had you. It was a very tough lesson to learn. The game that you have to play when you're dealing with that kind of money is that you have to be able to walk away and go 'Fuck it.' Then if it doesn't work out, it doesn't work out. Say, 'I don't give a shit.' Then you really are in a position of power. I was totally powerless because I was so possessed to do something that would live up to the other two movies."

Rewatching *Alien³*, it's not as terrible as you might remember. It's still a bad *Alien* film, but as a movie divorced of its two prequels it's an interesting piece of work. Talking to Fincher, it's a pity his ideas didn't make it to the screen.

"The story I told them, that got me the job, was cool. It was a fucking David Lean movie. It wasn't about tough guys in outer space, it was about pedophiles in outer space. It was a huge movie and it was very complicated and political. There were three Lance Henriksens running around, Paul McGann was a serial killer, and at the end of the movie you had the alien running around and you've got three thousand storm troopers on their way. It was massive and strange and the idea of it was great. I went, 'They gave me the work, so they're going to let me make this movie.' Then it was like, 'We can't do that, we can only have eighteen guys show up at the end.' 'Well, they should have some amazing kind of contraption.' 'Well, we can't afford that.' And so at a certain point they cut the fucking balls off the thing."

Fincher grew up in Marin County, California. Down the street from George Lucas. It was, he says, a "very sunny and happy and very safe environment, although for about six to eight months, the Zodiac Killer was around so we were all being followed by the Californian Highway Patrol in our little yellow school buses, but that was kind of the only thing to break the idyllic patina. It was a beautiful place to grow up."

This is important because Fincher's two movies are both set in such gloomy, depressive, dark milieus, one could easily see them as a reflection of a deeply depressed childhood.

"You're not going to make a fucking *Alien* movie that has like a bunch of carousels and people selling balloons," he grins. 'You're going to make a fucking *Alien* movie that takes place in the bowls of some hideous joint. And when you start doing research on serial killers these people don't prey on senators, they pick off the weak and the stragglers and the runaways and the prostitutes and the people hitchhiking, and people unfortunate enough to be at a 7-Eleven at two o'clock in the morning. It takes place in a very dark world, and so it just seemed like the darkness was more in keeping with making a horror movie."

What about the fact that it's always raining in *Se7en*? Is that a reflection of six months living in England while he was making *Alien³*?

Fincher laughs. "No, that was really a completely pragmatic decision based on that fact that we had fifty-five days with Brad Pitt and then he was going on to Terry Gillian's movie (*Twelve Monkeys*)—there were no ifs, ands, or buts about it. So, it was raining in L.A. at the time and we knew we would have to match in the exteriors stuff that was being shot interiors. Also, it was a way to make it kind of not look like Los Angeles, 'cause Los Angeles is always seen in the sun."

From the age of eight Fincher wanted to be a film director. "That's all I wanted to do," he says. The film that got him hooked was *The Empire Strikes Back*. "Fuck man, the coolest stuff being done, the most interesting application of all the processes involved in filmmaking—painting and sculpting and making models and rubber creatures—the most interesting place to get experience of that kind of stuff was at ILM."

So rather than go to film school, Fincher started working at an animation company, loading cameras, learning the craft of filmmaking from inside out.

"I've always been a fan of people who understand kind of everything, as a director it always seemed to me that you wanted to know so much about everything that was going on so people couldn't bullshit you, so you could go, 'Here's what I want to do,' and there couldn't be some lazy fuck there going, 'You can't do that because you can't hold focus on that.' I wanted to be able to go, 'That's not true, give me a T56 and a 28mm lens and we'll be able to hold plenty into focus.' So I figured the best place to be would be at a special effects place."

At eighteen Fincher went to work at Lucas's multi Oscar-winning special effects facility Industrial Light and Magic (ILM). He stayed for four years, working on *Return of the Jedi, Indiana Jones and the Temple of Doom*—"When they started work on *Starman* and *Explorers* is when I split"—before leaving to make TV commercials. His first was shot at weekends for the American Cancer Society and featured a fetus smoking a cigarette. He then formed Propaganda and a career was born. What was the favorite pop video he directed?

"I don't like any of them. I did that stuff for very selfish reasons. I wanted to play with a certain piece of equipment or I wanted to do this little gag or that little thing. They're like my Da Vinci sketchbook, you use to kind of fuck with something, you got to kind of play, I take everything very seriously when I'm doing it, but my attitude has always been I do my job and then try to learn to live it down."

Se7en is a film Fincher shouldn't need to live down. The question is, will he make another?

"I just want to do it really well and I want it to be stuff that I give a shit about. It's hard to find those things that I can spend a year thinking about, but I have a couple of things that I'm interested in doing and we'll see. . . ."

David Fincher Interview

Iain Blair / 1997

From *Film and Video* 13 (October 1997): 15–18. Reprinted by permission of Iain Blair.

Of all the young hot shots who've emerged from the music video and commercial scene, director David Fincher seems the most likely to fulfill the promise once held by every contender and succeed as a major Hollywood director.

After making his (reportedly unhappy) feature debut at the helm of *Alien³*, Fincher hit his stride with the stylish dark thriller *Se7en*. Now he's back with another twisted tale, *The Game*, which stars Michael Douglas as Nicholas Van Orton, a mega-rich but emotionally numb businessman whose brother Conrad, played by Sean Penn, involves him in a bizarre—and ultimately life-and-death—game of role playing that includes Christine, a sexy and mysterious waitress played by Deborah Unger.

Here, in a rare interview, Fincher talks about making *The Game*, working with stars Douglas and Penn, and composer Howard Shore.

Iain Blair: Is it true that this script was pretty much fully developed six years ago, and that all that time since has been spent agonizing over the last three pages?

David Fincher: That's true to an extent. Originally, Michael's character kills Christine and that drives him over the edge and he throws himself off the building. And originally the guy who brings him the game was a college buddy, and those were the two elements we kept saying, "There's not a big enough emotional hook here for what has to happen." It had the whole father back story and the rest, but I didn't see why killing this woman who's lied to you at every turn would make you commit suicide. So it was more of a tone thing for me, a lot of little changes. For instance, Nicholas was more of a Gordin Gekko type, more of a player, and I liked the idea of him being more like Scrooge, this emotional miser cut off from the world.

IB: How many drafts did you do?
DF: About five.

IB: So not that many.
DF: It's a lot for me. I have a very short attention span, coming from music video (laughs).

IB: Michael Douglas is an accomplished filmmaker whose own company recently produced the blockbuster *Face/Off*. What kind of input did he have?
DF: He's a classic enabler. He gets off on people who have an opinion and point of view and passion for what they do, so when you go in and go, "No, it has to be this way because of that," he likes that. He didn't even have to hear the reason. He just wants to hear you say "No." Because most of directing is just limiting choices. There are infinite choices you can make and with today's technology you can do anything, so the question is deciding what it is you're going to do. What helps the psychology of the storytelling.

IB: What about Sean Penn, who's also directed, and who's got a reputation for doing it "my way or the highway"?
DF: I didn't run into any of that. He's like, "OK, I'm here. Where do I go?" So you tell him, "OK, you come in, sit down and you guys do what you're going to do at the table." "Can I smoke?" "Yeah, but I don't think we should see the cigarette before he says 'I thought you quit." 'OK.' So those are the only specific things we knew we wanted to do in a scene like that. The rest of it was, "It's written very cold, play it even more distant." It would have been a very different scene with another actor, because Sean gives you the feeling that he's fucked up and he's trying to ingratiate himself. A different actor would have probably been more like, "Well here I am and there's no love lost and I've found this great thing."

IB: So he was very cooperative?
DF: Yeah, I don't know what anyone's talking about.

IB: He said you're a true intellectual.
DF: Hmm. That's probably true, in that I'm more concerned with how things track in terms of the thinking on it as opposed to the emotional. I kind of leave that up to the high-priced talent.

IB: Wasn't Jodie Foster originally slated to play the Sean Penn role?

DF: When she expressed interest we didn't have Michael or a final script. She just wanted to be in it, and I said, "I think it's a little distracting for the waitress to be played by a two-time Oscar winner." So she called back and said, "What if I play the brother's part? Would you rewrite it for me?" I thought that was very interesting, especially as I have two sisters, so that made sense to me. Of course, everyone else like Michael and Sean and producer Steve Golin have brothers, and when Michael and Sean got involved they're all going, "How could you ever see it any other way? It's definitely a brother battle." So I said, "OK, I believe you."

IB: So where did the "Jodie as Michael Douglas's daughter" idea come from?

DF: We were looking for anything to make it work, but we never really did any work on the script in that sense. It never got that far because we got into some pretty severe scheduling problems with the Sheraton Palace Hotel in San Francisco. It was an enormously expensive location and we had to work around stuff they were doing. So if we'd been able to fit it in before she went off to do *Contact*, so she could do the three weeks that Sean did, we'd have had to have started shooting on the final scene with the air bags, and Michael didn't feel comfortable with it. You've got to walk around in those loafers for at least a couple of days before you do a scene like that.

IB: What were the main problems of pulling this off?

DF: First, finding an actor who'd be able to play someone who's so unlikeable. And then trying to cast the Sean Penn part, who to do that. It took a long time. Then it was a long, long shoot—over a hundred days—so it was a matter of keeping everyone's morale up because everyone was exhausted. There were a lot of night shoots, a lot of locations, and it was just grueling. And intellectually really exhausting too, because everyone's playing so many roles in it, so it was a question of keeping it all clear. Is Deborah playing the first lie of being the bad waitress? Or the second lie of being the girl who doesn't know what's going on? There are so many different lies going on it was difficult to keep track.

IB: Because of the shifting nature of the film's game, continuity must have been a nightmare.

DF: And the script supervisor (Jamie Babbit) did a fantastic job. It was hard, but when you break things down so minutely in order to put a schedule together, it gets broken down to its cellular level so keeping it organized isn't so tough. The most difficult thing was trying to keep focused on what the lie you're telling at any given moment is. What's the one that's out front? What's the one people are supposed to be concentrating on?

IB: Did you ever consider shooting in continuity?
DF: Yeah, but there wasn't a chance. As it ended up, we shot the climactic air bag scene about three weeks in. But at least that gave us a couple of weeks to get up and running.

IB: Like *Se7en*, this is intensely atmospheric and San Francisco is a major visual element. At what point do you start deciding on such elements?
DF: It came out of a lot of discussion. The first thing is, why San Francisco? Because shooting there added probably $3 million just to go up there. So there was an enormous amount of pressure to bring the movie back to L.A. or take it to Chicago which is cheaper. So we said "OK" and started scouting Chicago, but there were no mansions in town. They were all too far away, with too much travel to his house, so it didn't seem like it had the same storybook quality. It had the old money, but not the prettiness or magic. So then we looked at Seattle, and it just seemed like new money, and there wasn't the same financial district. The script was written for San Francisco and we finally just decided, it's a detective town, it's an obsession town because of *Vertigo* and *The Maltese Falcon*, you've got all that history, let's do it there.

IB: Did you feel any pressure to equal the success of *Se7en*?
DF: No, because that'd make you crazy and there's no calculated way to do that. When we finished *Se7en* and showed it for the first time, the lights came on and three people whispered, "This is a disaster." And somebody turned to me and said, "How could you take a perfectly good genre movie and turn it into a foreign film?"

IB: Talk a bit about working with DP Harris Savides, who's shot various videos and commercials for you.
DF: I've worked with him for the past five or so years, whenever I can get him, because he's incredibly in demand—probably the most sought-after commercial cameraman in the world. I offered him *Se7en* but he'd just finished *Heaven's Prisoners* with Phil Joanou and he said he never

wanted to make a movie again. So then I got Darius Khondji but that was a real nightmare with visas. Anyhow, Harris did some second unit stuff for me on *Se7en* and then I got him for this. He's very collaborative and always has great ideas. I didn't storyboard a lot of it because things changed so often.

IB: How important is music to your films?
DF: I like to say that everything is 50 percent of the movie—the picture, the sound, the performances, the music—and hopefully it all adds up to more than 100 percent. I look at the shadows as being as important as the light, and the production design to be as telling as the costumes or acting. The actors are telling you this is their character, but the lamp should be telling you something else, and the tie they're wearing should be telling you something.

IB: Do you use music when you cut the film?
DF: No, I don't have any of it. I think we had just three cues when we previewed the movie.

IB: This is the second film you've done with composer Howard Shore, who's also scored such films as *The Silence of the Lambs*, *Naked Lunch*, and *Mrs. Doubtfire*.
DF: He did a fantastic job on both this and *Se7en*, and in fact we used three cues from *Se7en* when we previewed it—a cue when Michael goes to Christine's house, one at the Hotel Nikko scene, and one for the home movie sequence at the start. So I don't think in terms of music. I make the film and then show it to Howard, and hopefully he's a helluva lot smarter about it than you are, and he goes, "I want to do this," and you just kind of go, "Fine."

IB: The film's score and music is used in a very interesting way.
DF: And it all ties in with how I approached making this movie. I said to myself, "Look, this isn't about how it looks. It's about whether or not you believe these people are lying to you. So cast the best people you can and present it as simply as possible." It was a matter of creating a stage for these characters to simply tell you their stories, and then my job was to go, "OK, I believe that take." I didn't want it to feel like it was being engineered cinematically, with a close up of the keys or whatever. I didn't want to underline stuff and have the ominous music cue come in, because I didn't want people to feel like it's a movie. We use a lot of

tricks to imbalance the expectations of the movie-going experience. For instance, in the cab scene there's no music. That was a very conscious decision as you expect music when it's a big moment in a film. So when there isn't, does that make it a movie or make it real?

IB: So there's a lot of manipulation going on.
DF: Absolutely. There's another music cue that goes all the way through as Michael's character goes to the hotel and then to see his ex-wife and finally ends up in Chinatown, and which literally disappears on the frame where the carjacker comes in. So it's as if the carjacker also carjacks the movie and interrupts everything that's going on. So we were playing with all those ideas.

IB: Do you still like shooting videos and commercials?
DF: Absolutely. I did the Wallflowers' "Sixth Avenue Heartache" while I was prepping *The Game.*

IB: What do you still get out of it?
DF: It's fun. To me directing is creating a context for understanding, and music videos are an interesting manipulation, certainly for the Wallflowers because you're creating a context for something that didn't exist until then. The idea was, Let's make a video that looks like liner notes from songs from The Band's *Music from Big Pink.* Here's a band that just got their guitarist eight months ago, so you're trying to create an understanding for this style of music that might be considered anachronistic today, and you're doing that through pictures that hopefully evoke some kind of emotional response.

IB: Was *Se7en*'s success a vindication for you after the problems of *Alien³*?
GF: Not really. I'm in this for the long haul, for a career. Hitchcock made seventy-five movies, and six of them are amazing, while thirty-five no one will ever speak about again. Unfortunately we live in a day and age when it takes two years to make a movie. I guess I'm just slow, but I will never make seventy-five movies.

Precocious Prankster Who Gets a
Thrill from Tripping People Up

Ryan Gilbey / 1997

From the *Independent* (London), October 10, 1997. Reprinted by permission of Ryan Gilbey.

Brussels is not the brightest of places. This we know. Pea-green and cadaver-grey, it spurns all but the most resilient tourists. The director, David Fincher, is here to promote his latest film, and if his last two are any indication of the man's outlook and temperament, then Brussels should suit him down to the ground. We are not talking knockabout fun for all the family. His first feature, *Alien³*, was like being locked in Strangeways prison for two hours, although it now feels like a Radio One roadshow compared to last year's follow-up, *Se7en*. That film is the reason why at least three people in your social circle still sleep with the light on. Ask around.

Those acquaintances will be relieved to hear that *The Game*, Fincher's latest thriller, is less hazardous to your well-being. Which is not to say that it's an easy ride. But it is an enjoyable one. Michael Douglas plays the arrogant tycoon who enters into "the game," a real-life adventure tailored to fit the life and challenge the weaknesses of the fat cat who has everything. What it does for Douglas is disrupt the San Francisco he knows and challenge the validity of everything from the city's emergency services to his own ethical beliefs. From the moment his signature dries on the consent form, the basic principles of his world collapse. It's something like Woody Allen's joke about the man whose sister tells him that he's really a dwarf. "Everything in the house has been made to scale," she reveals. "You are only forty-eight inches tall."

However, Brussels has not been amused by *The Game*. "The reaction here has been interesting," says Fincher. As expected, "interesting" turns out to be a euphemism for "hostile and bewildered." "A couple of people here have said: 'So you made a really good movie last time. Why would you go and make a movie like this?' People who don't like to be tricked by the films they watch tend to hate *The Game*."

The film is a hybrid of morality tale and conspiracy thriller, with enough little practical jokes to have Jeremy Beadle running for the exit crying tears of blood. On a literal level, we know that nothing which happens in the picture is real—because we're watching it on a cinema screen. But in the world of the film itself, we must determine whether the illusion has gone off the rails, like *Westworld*, or if the chaos is all part of a carefully orchestrated facade. It is likely to leave you in need of a quiet lie-down.

Both *The Game* and *Se7en* suggest that, like Hitchcock, Fincher derives a lot of pleasure from wrongfooting the audience. "Those films have gimmicks in them which challenge the responsibility of the storyteller in the venue of a motion picture theatre," he explains. "For me, the best trick in *Se7en* was the killer showing up on page ninety-five. 'Cause you sit there in a movie theatre and go: 'What? This doesn't happen! You don't chase somebody for this long only for them to go and give themselves up. Woah, something really bad's gonna happen now.' You didn't know if you were in the third act, at the end of the second act, or halfway through.

"There are a couple of good gimmicks in *The Game*. You spend the first thirty pages of the script establishing how rich this guy is. Then he goes: 'Why are they doing this to me?' Duh. And there are lots of red herrings that your brain naturally catalogues because you don't know what will turn out to be relevant. Movies usually make a pact with the audience that says: We're going to play it straight; what we show you is going to add up. But we don't do that. In that respect, it's about movies and how movies dole out information."

At just thirty-four years old, Fincher has quickly established himself as one of the American cinema's most precious and precocious talents. But you don't get that far without ruffling corporate feathers. Fincher knew the way he wanted things done right from the start. By the age of eighteen, the young Californian was a Lucasfilm employee, working on *Return of the Jedi* among other things, before landing a job in the music video division of "a really shitty commercial company." The company prevented its promo directors from straying into its commercials wing, which didn't irk Fincher too much because the output was pretty pathetic—breakfast cereals, models holding bars of soap next to their face, all that nonsense. And then they rubbed him up the wrong way.

"They said to me: 'You have to make a commitment to doing lower-budget videos because that's where the industry's going," he recalls. "I just sort of lost it with them. I thought: 'You guys are morons if you can't see that the music business is ego-driven, and that if there's lucre out there, there's gonna be some to spend on how to package and market these artists.'"

In his frustration, he co-founded Propaganda Films in 1986.

"Basically you'd set the tone for what people wanted to see with music videos, then sell the ideas back to commercial companies for ten times the money—'We did this video and we can tell you exactly how much it's going to cost to do it for your client and their stupid soft drink.'" His client list provides unequivocal proof that he wasn't some arrogant college kid bluffing his way into the executive bathrooms of the rich and famous. There were commercials for Nike, Coca-Cola, Chanel. And promos for Madonna, the best of which was "Express Yourself," the one that looked like *Metropolis* remade in the style of gay porn.

He remains convinced about what makes a good music video. "The best ones don't tell the story of the song, but offer an alternative way of thinking about what's being sung. They're jumping-off points for other ideas, things which, while being singular, don't become the definitive interpretation."

Fincher hasn't lost his admiration for the modern music video. While the immaculate production design and constant sense of foreboding in his films recalls the best work of Walter Hill or Alan Rudolph, the kinetic, disorientating style hints at his own past. "Music videos are probably the most creative filmmaking being done right now," he says boldly. "They're also close to true directing—creating context for the understanding of an idea. I still feel that films are nowhere near as abstract as they could or should be, and I know there's an audience out there who would understand those abstractions. It's too bad so many movies end up being so literal."

As our conversation draws to a close, I try asking Fincher about his experience on *Alien³*, a notoriously difficult production during which the director was rumored to be all but exchanging gunfire with representatives of Twentieth Century Fox. In no time at all I discover why the subject rarely gets discussed in interviews.

Is it true that Fox were unhappy with the film's bleakness?

"Oh yeah."

Is that an understatement?

"Oh yeah."

Did you get a lot of flak?

"Oh yeah."

Finally, he chooses to elaborate. A bit. "I was contractually obliged to be there, yet no one wanted me to be doing it. It was a bad situation."

He pauses.

"But I learned a lot," he says, his dry laughter bristling with sarcasm. "My motto is: I just do my work and try to live it down."

The Head Master

Jenny Cooney / 1997

From *Empire* 101 (November 1997): 128–134. Reprinted by permission of Jenny Cooney Carillo.

"Can I please have more fucking smoke on set," barks director David Fincher from the dark grubby corner of soundstage twenty-two on the Sony backlot, Culver City, Los Angeles, the clipped notes of his command cutting through the general hubbub and chaos of his movie set. Across from him is his star, the stocky, indelibly chinned Michael Douglas, patiently waiting to begin shooting his next scene with Canadian actress Deborah Unger. As precious minutes tick by, a crew member scurries away in search of someone who can find out why the smoke machine is not creating San Francisco on a foggy night. "It doesn't seem like much to ask," Fincher grumbles to no one in particular, "just a bit more fog. . . ."

Fog has become something of a motif for the thirty-four-year-old Fincher. The stuff damn near buried his career on the ill-fated *Alien³* as he devised art and atmos on a grungoid prison planet but forgot to include the bugs-bugging-Ripley stuff. But, to quote an irrepressible Hollywood saw—you're only as good as your last film—and the pea-souper effect was back with a vengeance in a dark crime drama called *Se7en* which despite a sensitivity as black as *Alien*'s gullet was the stand-out shocker of the year. Not bad for the former ILM effects wizard turned music director who started out on Aerosmith and Madonna videos before he co-founded Propaganda Films ten years ago. Now, though, there is *The Game*, a psychological thriller of sorts. And the fog is back.

"I was always the kind of person who didn't like being victimized by other people's expertise," Fincher reveals, having taken a break from his technical complications to perch on a sofa in a nearby log cabin set. Speaking quietly between bites of a burrito, he is assessing his back-door entrance into filmmaking (Fincher has never been near a film school).

"I don't like being in a situation where you go, 'I would like to do this' and somebody says, 'You can't do that because you have to do this, this, and this.' And I never want to be victimized by not knowing whether or not they were telling me the truth, so I always wanted to learn as much about everything as I could. Videos were like—how do you learn how to play basketball? You go to the local playground, so for me it was the playground. . . ."

Around the time of *Alien³*, Fincher first read the John Brancato/Michael Ferris script for *The Game*, but waited to take it on until he had sideswiped the critics with the brilliant *Se7en*.

"We probably did four of five rewrites with different people and finally, after I did *Se7en*, we did about six weeks of just changing the tone and trying to make the story work," he explains. "Initially, the person who perpetrates 'the game' was a university chum of his and I just didn't feel there was enough backstory. So it was a pretty obvious change to make it into a brother, played by Sean Penn."

As if to compound the various incarnations the script has taken, Jodie Foster flirted briefly with the script, causing a right old rumpus when she eventually fell out of the film.

"She wanted to be in it and we were going to rewrite the brother for her but she also wanted to make *Contact* and we could never work out the scheduling," Fincher says sheepishly, skirting the issue completely.

The tale of the film's turbulent conception is suddenly interrupted as Douglas plants himself besides Fincher on the sofa and boldly declares: "I think that the only thing that's important to know is that this is the best script I've seen in I-don't-know-how-many years!"

"Since when?" Fincher interrupts curiously, much to his surprise.

"Since one of the last pictures I've done," Douglas returns, perturbed that he is entering into a debate with his director rather than *Empire* opposite. "But really, it was a great, great script that was really well thought out and I was a big fan of David—*Se7en* was pretty amazing, it was very, very effective."

The very, very effective director, however, is the model of modesty when asked about the technique that has led him to be regarded as a "visual stylist." Whatever the hell that means.

"I just get out of the way—cast the right guy and get out of the way," he shrugs with embarrassment. Douglas, seeing a chance for payback, jumps in.

"In the early stage you're thinking, yeah, music video, commercials, yeah right, this is one of those 'visual directors' . . ."

Fincher clutches his chest: "Oh, drive a stake though my heart!"

Douglas, though, is on a roll: ". . . and just when you think that, you are all of a sudden totally surprised at how well he watches performances. A lot of times we talked about the characters and I look at them in two ways. You either paint on a character like a clown's mask, or you spend all your time wiping away the make-up, trying to wipe it away and this is one that's kind of closer to wiping it away and trying to be more trusting. When you have a good director and a really good script, it gives you much more confidence."

"In fact," he adds, warming to his theory of the young man with the half-grown goatee staring embarrassedly back at him, "I could only think of two other directors who had such strong concepts as David—it's so rare when you watch a director who has such as good idea of where you are at all times in the picture—and one was Milos Forman who was like that on *One Flew Over the Cuckoo's Nest* and the other was Paul Verhoeven on *Basic Instinct*."

"Actually, Michael," interjects Fincher, unable to sit still while his leading man waxes lyrical about him, "I wanted to talk about that scene we shot earlier—that didn't seem to work out at all!"

They both break into laughter.

Beneath the laughter and the good vibes, however, Fincher is struggling with the part of his job he likes least.

"I never feel comfortable on set," he offers as Douglas is called away. "I don't know why I do it—honestly, I don't know. It's the most unpleasant part of the whole thing—collecting all the stuff and going through it like the military part of an operation where you have to show up early and marshal the forces and shoot stuff and argue with people and cajole and cheat and do whatever you have to do. . . ."

So, what is it you actually like about directing?

"I like the initial design and rehearsal, all the possibilities," Fincher responds cheerfully. "Then when you go back to shooting, it's, 'We can't put a wide enough lens on,' or, 'We can't get the wall further back.' That's always so unpleasant and has not gotten any easier."

But surely the actual bossing around of the actors must offer some perverse joy?

"No, it's a series of problems and problem-solving," he says matter-of-factly. "Then the arguments ensue. . . . Although most of the time I don't think Michael and I ever really disagree. I've worked with people who don't understand what it is you're asking of them—or to whom you are unable to explain it in terms that are active enough—but ultimately the actors have a really lonely job because they're up there in the dark and somebody has to be their gauge and they have put themselves in your hands and hopefully you won't betray them."

Any heads in boxes this time around?

Fincher shakes his head, looking up as Douglas returns to the sofa.

"I remember people talking about *Se7en*," the star begins as if he had never left the conversation, "saying, 'God, that picture is so violent—how could he do that head in the box at the end?' And I said, 'But you never saw the head in the box.' And they thought about it and said, 'Shit, you're right. . . .'"

"We just ran out of money," claims Fincher with a smile. "We had a head and we set out to re-shoot it. . . . Er, that was meant to be funny. . . ."

In *The Game*, Douglas plays a wealthy stockbroker who has everything but feels nothing until his black-sheep brother Conrad (Penn) enrolls him in a so-called "game" on his forty-eighth birthday that will mysteriously show up in his life when he least expects it.

"I always saw the movie as a kind of modern-day Scrooge," Douglas begins. "The story of a man who found his soul again. This is a man haunted by the fact that his father had committed suicide in his forty-eighth year, so he was beginning to have some suicidal thoughts, whether he liked it our not, and was out of touch and divorced and living in his family's home and having a midlife crisis and his brother shows up and gives him a gift certificate to this company that creates life games."

"It's fairly sadistic fun, but it's fun," adds Fincher with relish. "I hope the audience walks out of the theatre and go, 'What would my game be?' Or go next door to eat and go, 'I know what yours would be—it involves some kind of crashing jet liner. . . .'"

"Look, you're taking a hell of a ride and you're not driving," Douglas booms. "That's all I can say. It's like getting in a car in traffic with a Grand Prix race driver and all of a sudden being totally surprised. You think it is going to be one thing and you go off on something else."

"We hope," Fincher adds nervously, before being whisked away to his revived smoke machines, leaving the press-friendly fifty-two-year-old Douglas hanging around anxious to offer a few more words.

"David is a strange combination because as shy as he is, I think it's a little put on. I tease him a little bit because as shy as he is in interviews that's how forceful and committed he is when he's on the set. When he sits in the chair, he has the stamina and energy of—well, my father Kirk, comes to mind. He sits there and watches the video and is the first one there and the last to go home and he's a perfectionist and talented."

"What that little crazy thing is back there in David," he adds pointing an index finger at his forehead, "God only knows. I met his father, nice man. Mother seems very nice. So, it's difficult to know, but it reminds me again of how great it is to work with talent. . . ."

Inside Out

Gavin Smith / 1999

From *Film Comment* 35 (September/October 1999): 58–62, 65, 67–68. Reprinted with permission from *Film Comment* and Gavin Smith.

It's tempting to describe David Fincher's stunning, mordantly funny, formally dazzling new movie *Fight Club* as the first film of the next century and leave it at that. It certainly suggests a possible future direction for mass-appeal cinema that could lead it out of the nineties cul-de-sac of bloated, corrupt mediocrity and bankrupt formulas. Indeed, its vertiginous opening credits shot—a camera move hurtling backwards from the deepest recesses of its main character's brain, out through his mouth and down the barrel of the gun that is inserted into it—could almost be a metaphor for the cinema viewer's predicament.

Adapted from Chuck Palahniuk's novel by Jim Uhls, *Fight Club* is ostensibly an anti–New Age satire on both the dehumanizing effects of corporate/consumer culture and the absurd excesses of the men's movement. Its main character is a twentysomething wage slave (Edward Norton) whose voiceover discloses a sardonic, dissenting, but impotent interior life beneath his subdued exterior conformity. Finding relief from chronic insomnia by attending multiple self-help group meetings under false pretenses, he leads a pallid, vampiric half-life, feeding vicariously on the catharsis and suffering of others. He reluctantly shares his perverse addiction with Marla, a despised fellow misery "tourist" (Helena Bonham Carter, whose damaged-goods-with-attitude turn is something of a revelation). In the course of his travels as a "recall coordinator" for a major car manufacturer (a job that deeply implicates him in the casual cynicism and corruption of corporate America), this unnamed protagonist encounters and falls in with an elusive, slightly outrageous trickster individualist called Tyler Durden (Brad Pitt).

For all his ironic distance, the nonconformism of Norton's character pales in comparison. Durden, with his outlandish self-presentation and ersatz-Nietzschean pronouncements, is everything our narrator isn't. He answers to nobody, sees through the hypocrisies and agreed deceptions of modern life, is given to casually mentioning, say, the recipe for making nitroglycerin out of soap, and in his part-time job as a movie projectionist amuses himself by splicing single frames of pornography into family movies. In his best work to date, Pitt, who's always good when he takes risks as an actor, relishes every juicy moment.

The two men seal a kind of unspoken pact with a spontaneous fist-fight—something that becomes a regular activity. Before long, other men begin to participate, and a club is founded for weekly one-on-one fight sessions. Durden also takes up with Marla, to our narrator's disgust. In sharp contrast to the drab ambiance of the narrator's prosaic daytime world of offices, hotels, and public spaces, Durden inhabits a disorderly realm of eccentric dilapidation that suggests a shadowy subconscious hinterland. As Durden's influence on him grows, the protagonist becomes an accomplice in his escalating program of antisocial pranks and subversive mischief, until they take an abrupt left turn with the formation of a quasi-military all-male cult with an expressly antisocial, revolutionary agenda—a kind of surreal prole insurrection against bourgeois values.

For all their emphasis on hard surface, vivid texture, and sensational effect, Fincher's previous films staked out suggestively dreamlike psychic/narrative spaces: Ripley's rude awakening from cryogenic suspension in *Alien*[3] (92), Somerset going to sleep to the tick of a metronome in *Se7en* (95), the living nightmare of *The Game* (97). A tale told by an insomniac who doesn't know when he's asleep, *Fight Club* takes things one step beyond into new realms of dissociation and movie mindfuck. Suffice to say viewers might wonder just what they can trust: Is Tyler Durden projecting this movie? And just how reliable is this flipped-out narrator anyway?

To be sure, this film is the culmination of a recurrent Fincher scenario: repressed, straight white masculinity thrown into crisis by the irruption of an anarchic, implacable force that destabilizes a carefully regulated but precarious psychosocial order. In *Alien*[3], a shaven-headed, celibate, all-male penal colony of killers that anticipates *Fight Club*'s "space monkey" cult of violent, obsolete masculinity, is disturbed first by a woman, then by a libidinously destructive organism. In *Se7en*, locked in an endgame with a killer who's equal parts deranged artist and Old Testament avenger, Morgan Freeman's troubled, paternal detective seems to act with the stoic understanding that an older civilization of culture, values, and reason that he defends has been all but submerged in a Bosch-like world of corruption and chaos. The sterile, controlled universe of Michael Douglas's uptight millionaire tycoon in *The Game* unravels until he is stripped of everything he relies upon to define himself—though in the end, masculine power and privilege remain intact, indeed reaffirmed, by the ordeal. In *Fight Club*, sweeping through the main character's tidy, airless life like a tornado, Tyler Durden is a galvanizing, subversive force dedicated to revolt against the inauthenticity and mediocrity of modern life, seeking a nihilistic exaltation of disenfranchised masculinity through abjection and destructive transgression.

Fincher's films seemingly repudiate the values he's paid to uphold in his TV commercials. All his features, *Fight Club* especially, seem to be reactions to or commentaries upon the seductive, fabricated realities, spectacles of consumption, and appeals to narcissism and materialism of commercials. The dreamlike suspension, relative freedom from conventions and formats, and formidable technique that distinguish Fincher's sensibility have been honed or acquired from commercials and music videos, with their routinization of spectacle and "style," conceit-based construction and permissiveness in terms of breaking down film grammar conventions. (Fincher's 1989 Madonna video "Oh Father" demonstrates the potential aesthetic discipline and integrity of the form at its best.) His features apply these qualities to more complex, rigorous aesthetic strategies: the starkness and fragmentation of *Alien³* with its minimization of wide shots and spatial resolution; the gliding, hollow sleekness of *The Game*; the luxuriating in painstaking degradation and gloomy decay of *Fight Club* and *Se7en*.

Fight Club belongs to a distinct moment of both dread and rupture in American mainstream cinema, also manifested in *The Matrix* and traceable at least as far back as Verhoeven's *Starship Troopers*. The acceleration and dissolution potentially ushered in by digital cinema are only a partial manifestation of this. There's a kind of dissociative hyperrealism operating in Fincher's film, and a mocking sense of flux and liminality in its attitudes and values both formally and conceptually. Its recourse to evident digital imagery has less to do with expanding the boundaries of what can be visualized than with a derangement of or insolence toward cinematic codes and conventions concerning authenticity and the narrative representation of space and time. (In an early, defining scene, Fincher's protagonist, ironically contemplating his consumerist lifestyle, moves through his condo as it transforms around him into a living IKEA catalog with prices floating in space.)

Is *Fight Club* the end of something in cinema, or the beginning? Zeitgeist movie or cult item? Whether you find the state-of-the-art cinematic values of this current moment liberating or oppressive, radical or specious, of lasting significance or entirely transitory, as the little girl in *Poltergeist* says: they're here. —G.S.

Gavin Smith: What did you set out to do with this film?
David Fincher: I read the book and thought, How do you make a movie out of this? It seemed kind of like *The Graduate*, a seminal coming of age for people who are coming of age in their thirties instead of in their late teens or early twenties. In our society, kids are much more sophisticated at an earlier age and much less emotionally capable at a later age. Those two things are sort of moving against each other.

I don't know if it's Buddhism, but there's the idea that on the path to enlightenment you have to kill your parents, your god, and your teacher. So the story begins at the moment when the Edward Norton character is twenty-nine years old. He's tried to do everything he was taught to do, tried to fit into the world by becoming the thing that he isn't. He's been told, "If you do this, get an education, get a good job, be responsible, present yourself in a certain way, your furniture and your car and your clothes, you'll find happiness." And he hasn't. And so the movie introduces him at the point when he's killed off his parents and he realizes that they're wrong. But he's still caught up, trapped in this world he's created for himself. And then he meets Tyler Durden, and they fly in the face of God—they do all these things that they're not supposed to do, all the things that you do in your twenties when you're no longer being watched over by your parents, and end up being, in hindsight, very dangerous. And then finally, he has to kill off his teacher, Tyler Durden. So the movie is really about that process of maturing.

GS: Is the narrator a kind of everyman?
DF: Yeah, definitely. Every young man. Again, *The Graduate* is a good parallel. It was talking about that moment in time when you have this world of possibilities, all these expectations, and you don't know who it is you're supposed to be. And you choose this one path, Mrs. Robinson, and it turns out to be bleak, but it's part of your initiation, your trial by fire. And then, by choosing the wrong path, you find your way onto the right path, but you've created this mess. *Fight Club* is the nineties inverse of that: a guy who does *not* have a world a possibilities in front of him, he has *no* possibilities, he literally cannot imagine a way to change his life.

GS: Like *The Graduate* it's also a satire.

DF: A stylized version of our IKEA present. It is talking about very simple concepts. We're designed to be hunters and we're in a society of shopping. There's nothing to kill anymore, there's nothing to fight, nothing to overcome, nothing to explore. In that societal emasculation this everyman is created.

GS: Tyler says, "Self-improvement is masturbation. Maybe self-destruction is the answer." That's a pretty radical statement.

DF: I totally believe in that. I love the way it was couched. In the book, Tyler's already been on the journey. He's waiting impatiently for the narrator to make the same trip he has. And that was a thing we consciously got rid of. One of the things that Brad brought to it—and I think it was really smart—was, you don't want to be pedantic. You don't want to have a guy going, "No, don't you understand, this is bullshit." You have to have a guy that's going, "Well, I can see your point, but it seems to me. . . . You can look at losing all of your stuff both ways. Yeah, it's all of your stuff; yeah, it took you years to collect; yes, they were all tasteful, interesting choices. But there's another side to it, and the other side is, you don't have any of the responsibilities to that. Or to dig deeper, you find responsibilities to that image of yourself. But it's up to you—maybe I'm wrong."

GS: You have the impression that he's making it up as he goes along.

DF: Kind of saying, "We're both on the same path together, there's something in me that says it might be interesting if you just hit me. I don't know where it's going, it's no big deal; if you really don't want to do it, you don't have to."

GS: Were you involved with the adaptation from the start?

DF: Yeah, pretty much. A lot of the typical development-speak was being thrown around: "You can't have it all in voiceover because voiceover's a crutch." The first draft had no voiceover, and I remember saying, "Why is there no VO?" and they were saying, "Everybody knows that you only use VO if you can't tell the story." And I was like, "It's not funny if there's no voiceover, it's just sad and pathetic." I remember having a conversation early on when we were discussing what the feel of the first act should be. I was saying, "It's not a movie, it's not even TV, it's not even channel-changing, it's like pull-down windows. It's like, *pffpp*, take a look at it, *pffpp*, pull the next thing down—it's gotta be downloaded.

It's gotta move quick as you can think. We've gotta come up with a way that the camera can illustrate things at the speed of thought."

And that's one of the things that was interesting to me, how much can you jump around in time and go: Wait, let me back up a little bit more, okay, no, no, this is where this started, this is how I met this person. . . . So there's this jumping around in time to bring you into the present and then leaping back to go. Let me tell you about this other thing. It's almost conversational. It's as erratic in its presentation as the narrator is in his thinking.

GS: I think maybe the possibilities of this kind of temporal and spatial freedom point to a future direction for movies.
DF: Well, I kind of do too in a weird way—just in the amount of freedom over content, and also how those different things are apportioned. You don't necessarily have to make everything so concisely, narratively essential. There are a lot of scenes that, although they feel narratively redundant, are part of a thematic build.

GS: What was the thinking behind the opening shot?
DF: We wanted a title sequence that started in the fear center of the brain. [When you hear] the sound of a gun being cocked that's in your mouth, the part of your brain that gets everything going, that realizes that you are fucked—we see all the thought processes, we see the synapses firing, we see the chemical electrical impulses that are the call to arms. And we wanted to sort of follow that out. Because the movie is about thought, it's about how this guy thinks. And it's from his point of view, solely. So I liked the idea of starting a movie from thought, from the beginning of the first fear impulse that went, Oh shit, I'm fucked, how did I get here?

GS: What was your attitude towards the use of CGI to accomplish these impossible camera moves?
DF: To me it was a selfish means to an end. It wasn't about, Oh it would be cool to try something like this. In the book there are these long passages of description about how nitroglycerin gets made, and what could have happened to cause the explosion at the narrator's condo, and we were going, How do we illustrate that? "The police would later tell me the pilot light could have gone out, letting out just a little bit of gas"—but you can't just cut to a stove, you've got to become the gas. I always loved the threatening nature of the telephone in Scorsese's *After Hours.*

Every time the phone rang, the camera rushed right at it as somebody picked it up, and you didn't *want* to find out who was going to be on the other end. Well, if we were talking about how this tea smells, we'd just push in so we knew we were talking about the tea, and show you the steam coming up, and then follow the steam and see that there's other people in the room, and end up on somebody sniffing. There's a way to tell that story as a narrator's telling you that stuff. That's what makes Chuck's writing so funny—there's this cynical, sarcastic overview, and at the same time when he gets into detail about how things are done, it's sort of wonderfully compulsive. Here's something you need to know, here's the recipe for napalm.

GS: It's the visual equivalent of stream of consciousness.

DF: That's it, that's what the movie is, it's a stream of consciousness. And that's the thing that makes it so fun to follow. Because he's just doling out information as he thinks of it. We take the first forty minutes to literally indoctrinate you in this subjective psychotic state, the way he thinks, the way he talks about what's behind the refrigerator, and you go there. He talks about the bomb, and you zip out the window and the camera just drops thirty stories and goes through the sidewalk, into the underground garage, through the bullet-hole in the van, and out the side. We take the first forty minutes to [establish], This is what you're gonna see, this is what he's gonna say, those two things are inextricably tied, this one comments on that one. And then we get to a point where we go: Oh yeah—remember where we were taking you and showing you this whole thing? You only saw this much of it—the other side of it is, this is what was going on. [WARNING: If you haven't seen *Fight Club* yet and want to have an optimal viewing experience, skip over the next section.]

GS: I have to say I didn't see the twist coming.

DF: You can't. I've had this argument with people who go, Yeah, well, I knew. And I go, Bullshit, how could you possibly know? We spent tons of money to get two different people to make sure that you wouldn't know. The point is not whether you're stupid or smart because you didn't see it coming, the point is that that's the realization that this guy comes to. But if you trick people, it's an affront, and you really better be careful about what you're doing. A wise friend of mine once said, "What people want from the movies is to be able to say, I knew it and it's not my fault." And it's so true. I've had this argument with a couple people we've shown the movie to. Like, "Fuck you man, this is like *The Game*, you're just looking for some way to dick with me." It's not about tricking you, it's a metaphor, it's not about a real guy who really blows up buildings, it's about a guy who's led to feel this might be the answer based on all the confusion and rage that he's suffered and it's from that frustration and bottled rage that he creates Tyler. And he goes through a natural process of experimenting with notions that are complicated and have moral and ethical implications that the Nietzschean *übermensch* doesn't have to answer to. That's why Nietzsche's really great with college freshman males, and unfortunately doesn't have much to say to somebody in their early thirties or early forties. And that's the conflict at the end—you have Tyler Durden, who is everything you would want to be, except real and empathetic. He's not living in our world, he's not governed by the same forces, he is an ideal. And he can deal with the concepts of our lives in an idealistic fashion, but it doesn't have anything to do with the compromises of real life as modern man knows it. Which is: You're not really necessary to a lot of what's going on. It's built, it just needs to run now. Thank you very much, here's your Internet access.

GS: Is the Edward Norton character ever named?
DF: In the screenplay we call him Jack. In the credits it says "The Narrator."

GS: Did you see him in terms of the literary device of the unreliable narrator?
DF: Oh, he's totally unreliable.

GS: How does that affect the staging—how do you hint at it?
DF: We had tons of little rules about Tyler. Tyler is not seen in a two-shot within a group of people. We don't play it over the shoulder when Tyler gives him an idea about something that's very specific, that's going to lead him. It's never an over the shoulder shot, it's always Tyler by himself. There's five or six shots in the first two reels of Tyler, where he appears in one frame, waiting for Edward Norton's character. When the doctor says to him, You wanna see pain, swing by First Methodist Tuesday night and see the guys with testicular cancer, that's pain—and, boop, Brad appears over the guy's shoulder for one frame. We shot him in the environment with the people, and then we matted him in for one frame, so that Tyler literally appears like his spliced-in penis shot, just dink, dink. You can see it on DVD. We did a lot of that stuff. When Edward's on the airplane and

they have that little promotional Marriott television loop, when they're showing all their banquet facilities, there's this shot of all these waiters going "Welcome!" and Brad's in the middle of those waiters.

GS: I didn't know what the flash frames were but I took them to mean that the movie we're watching has been tampered with by Tyler Durden. **DF:** True. Same thing. At the end, when the buildings blow up, we spliced in two frames of a penis.

GS: Do you see links to *The Game* in which he goes on this journey where everything is stripped away and nothing is what it seems? **DF:** He's humiliated. Yeah, they're cousins. It's a *Twiliight Zone* episode. That's all it's supposed to be. In *Fight Club* it's even worse—having to contend with somebody who's powerful and you look up to them and his ideas become all too questionable, but then to find out that they are indeed your ideas, that this is your mess, that you are the leader.

GS: What did you envisage in terms of style? **DF:** Lurid was definitely one of the things we wanted to do. We didn't want to be afraid of color, we wanted to control the color palette. You go into 7-Eleven in the middle of the night and there's all that green-fluorescent. And like what green light does to cellophane packages, we wanted to make people sort of shiny. Helena wears opalescent makeup so she always has this smack-fiend patina, like a corpse. Because she is a truly romantic nihilistic.

[Cinematographer] Jeff Cronenweth and I talked about Haskell Wexler's *American Graffiti* and how that looked, how the nighttime exteriors have this sort of mundane look, but it still has a lot of different colors but they all seem very true, they don't seem hyperstylized. And we talked about making it a dirty-looking movie, kind of grainy. When we processed it, we stretched the contrast to make it kind of ugly, a little bit of underexposure, a little bit of resilvering, and using new high-contrast print socks and stepping all over it so it has a dirty patina.

GS: What's resilvering? **DF:** Lower-scale enhancement. Rebonding silver that's been bleached away during the processing of the print and then rebonding it to the print.

GS: What does that do?

DF: Makes it really dense. The blacks become incredibly rich and kind of dirty. We did it on *Se7en* a little, just to make the prints nice. But it's really in this more for making it ugly.

We wanted to present things fairly realistically, except obviously the Paper Street house—there are no Victorians with eighteen-foot ceilings on the West Coast. [Production designer] Alex McDowell and I looked at books of [photographer] Philip-Lorca diCorcia because it just felt like the motel-life world that you see. Marla's apartment, which was a set, was literally like photographs of a room at the Rosalind Apartments in downtown L.A. We just went in and took pictures of it and said, "This is it, build this." As much as possible we tried to incorporate real office buildings, just went down and said, "All right, put some cubicles in and we'll shoot." Kind of a low-budget approach.

GS: Where did the IKEA catalog scene come from? That was the moment where I knew I'd never seen a movie like this before.
DF: In the book he constantly lists his possessions, and we were like, How do we show that, how do we convey the culmination of his collecting things, and show how hollow and flat and two-dimensional it is? So we were just like, Let's put it in a catalog. So we brought in a motion control camera and filmed Edward walking through the set, then filmed the camera pan across the set, then filmed every single piece of set dressing and just slipped them all back together, then used this type program so that it would all pan. It was just the idea of living in this fraudulent idea of happiness. There's this guy who's literally living in this IKEA catalog.

GS: Did you have a sense of biting the hand that feeds you, given that you direct commercials?
DF: Well, I'm extremely cynical about commercials and about selling things and about the narcissistic ideals of what we're supposed to be. I guess in my heart I was hoping people are too smart to fall for that stuff. But it's unfortunate that it had to be presented in such a low-budget way. I would have loved to have done a whole sequence of it.

GS: What gets you going as a director?
DF: I don't want to be constrained by having to do something new. I look at it as: What are the movies that I want to see? I make movies that other people aren't making. I'm not interested in *The Hero with a Thousand Faces*—there's a lot of people that do that. A friend of mine used to say there's a pervert on every block, there's always one person in every

neighborhood who's kind of questionable. You're looking for that one pervert story.

GS: What's the most creative part of directing?
DF: Thinking. It's thinking the thing up, designing all the sets, and it's rehearsals, and then the creative process is fuckin' over. Then it's just war, it's just literally, How do we get through this day? It's 99 percent politics and 1 percent inspiration.

I've had days of shooting where I went, Wow, that's what it is, that's what it's like to be making a movie. Everything's clicking, people are asking questions, and the clock's ticking, but you feel like you're making progress. But most of the time it isn't that. Most of the time it's, How do you support the initial intent of what it is you set out to do, and not undercut that by getting pissed off and letting your attention get away on that? It's priority management. It's problem solving. Oftentimes you walk away from a scene going, Wasn't what I thought it was gonna be. Often. But it's also knowing that you don't have to get it exactly the way you see it.

You want to be able to provide something, and you're pissing down a fucking well. It will suck you dry and take everything you have and, like being a parent, you can pour as much love as you want, and your kid still says, "Just let me out right here, you don't have to take me all the way." You're working to make yourself obsolete. I'm not going to make *Persona*—my movies are fairly obvious in what the people want and what it is that's happening; it's not that internalized. What's internalized is how you process the information from the singular, subjective point of view. And that becomes the subtext of it.

I'm not Elia Kazan; I'm probably not going to reinvent an actor for the audience or for themselves. But I pay meticulous attention to getting the environment right so that the people have to do less work to pretend to be that person. It makes sense—seeing them next to that desk, and with that light. Michael Douglas and I went through this on *The Game* a lot. He would say, But you need to be able to make this turn, so that later on you can do this. And I would say, "You know what? That may be narratively essential, but I don't believe that somebody would do that at this point. So go ahead and take the producer cap off and be the selfish actor and make me deliver what's around it to make it make sense. You don't have to help me tell my story. You don't have to get riled over here. You don't have to let people know what your potential is for losing control." There are times when you, as the director, need to say to the actor, "Be selfish, make me do this. Create a hurdle for me to jump over instead of me creating a hurdle for you."

GS: Any example where something turned out the way you wanted it?
DF: No. [Laughs.] I think the master in *Se7en* where they walk in and see big Bob on the table with his face in spaghetti—that was what I thought it was going to be.

GS: What about in *Fight Club*?
DF: I went into it thinking, Grow up, stop trying to fucking control everything and just let go. Try to give the guidance where you can and be smart editorially about what you allow to happen—directions that you allow things to go in, so you don't create a fucking morass for yourself. But don't try to over think it, because it's the kind of thing that's got a lot of truths in it, and those truths are going to come through no matter what you do. You have a responsibility to the schedule and the budget and those things, but you're not really responsible for making everything happen. Create a good environment, cast the thing as well as you can, and get the hell out of the way of those people. This is a movie about twenty-six-to-thirty-four-year-olds, and I think that there's a definite generational division between Brad and Edward. They're definitely about a different kind of thought process. I thought, There's a thing that Edward Norton's going to bring to this that's going to be really important, and he's safeguarding his generational input, he's the caretaker of that.

GS: Apart, from the fact that directing pays the bills and you enjoy it—
DF: I don't enjoy it at all.

GS: Okay. So what need does it satisfy in you?
DF: Filmmaking encompasses everything, from tricking people into investing in it, to putting on the show, to trying to distill down to moments in time, and ape reality but send this other message. It's got everything. When I was a kid I loved to draw, and I loved my electric football sets, and I painted little things and made sculptures and did matte painting and comic books and illustrated stuff, and took pictures, had a darkroom, loved to tape-record stuff. It's all of that. It's not having to grow up. It's four-dimensional chess, it's strategy, and it's being painfully honest, and unbelievably deceitful, and everything in between.

When I was a kid I would spend hours in my bedroom drawing. I could never get my fucking hands to do it the way I had it in my head. I used to always go, Someday you'll have the skill to draw exactly what you see in your head, and then you'd be able to show it to somebody, and if they like it, then you will have been able to transfer this thing [in your head] through this apparatus to this, and then you'll truly know your worth. And I gave up drawing and then painting and then sculpture and then acting and then photography for things that were that much more difficult—to get that idea in your head out there.

It's kind of a masochistic endeavor. I know that if I can put all this together, record the sound the way I want to hear it. . . . You know, we had such a hard time getting the timbre of Edward's voiceover, because it has to sound like a thought. We ended up using five different microphones trying to get this sound. You listen to it and it doesn't sound like a thought, it sounds like a guy talking to you. The voiceover in *Blade Runner*, if you listen to it, sounds like a guy reading prose while he's sitting on the john. How do you avoid that? So it's all those things, it's so challenging.

Twenty-First-Century Boys

Amy Taubin / 1999

From *Village Voice*, October 19, 1999. Reprinted by permission of Amy Taubin.

Fight Club director David Fincher doesn't think his film is pervy or so-cially irresponsible. Others, ranging from the absurdly influential Lon-don critic Alexander Walker to the *New Yorker*'s David Denby, disagree. In his review, Walker indicted Fox owner Rupert Murdoch. "If he had to blow dust, it might as well be in that direction," says Fincher, speak-ing on the phone from L.A. just before the pre-release controversy took on a nastier tone than anything in the film itself. "I understand Edward Norton's character *Fight Club*'s protagonist so well that I think what he's thinking is what everybody's thinking. It's not like wanting to fuck somebody's leg brace."

The leg brace reference has to do with the comparison floating around between *Fight Club* and David Cronenberg's *Crash* in which James Spader lusts for Rosanna Arquette's heavy metal accessory. Fincher says that he doesn't mean to slight *Crash*; it's just that his film is less specialized.

If *Crash* seemed like the last movie of the twentieth century, then *Fight Club* could be the vertiginous, libidinous preview of the twenty-first. Both films share an outrageous sense of humor; they make punch lines of things that are supposed to be no laughing matter. Walker trashed *Fight Club* for being "anti- capitalist, anti-society, and, indeed, anti-God," which is exactly what it is.

Fight Club levels a Swiftian attack on our consumerist, designer-label-worshipping society and the alienation (Fincher calls it "emasculation") of its citizens.

Adapted from Chuck Palahniuk's manic first-person novel, *Fight Club* explores the symbiotic relationship between an alienated yuppie (Norton) and the glamorously nihilistic Tyler Durden (Brad Pitt), whose motto is "Self-improvement is masturbation; self-destruction might be the answer." Fight Club, in which guys strip off their shirts and shoes and go mano-a-mano, is the strangely liberating manifestation of this philosophy. But when Tyler turns Fight Club into a terrorist network that blows up buildings, the Norton character has to think about how he can separate from a guy who's so much a part of him.

The film seems dangerous because the Fight Club scenes are extremely seductive—the adrenalized rush of head-banging feels like an answer to the mind-body split. But then the worm turns, and the film becomes a critique of the blood-letting it made so erotic. What Fincher said about the people who attacked his similarly controversial *Se7en*—"they slow down when they pass an accident, just like everyone else"—applies here as well.

Fincher read Palahniuk's novel while he was editing his previous feature, *The Game*. His immediate reaction was, he says, "Awesome. Where do I sign?" To his horror, Fox had already bought the book. Fincher had had a bad time with Fox on his first movie, *Alien³*. Although the studio never officially took the film away from him, he says that the version that was released was only 25 percent of what he had envisioned. The experience so traumatized him that he claimed at the time to prefer "having colon cancer to making another studio movie." But the success of *Se7en*, which he directed three years later for the mini-major New Line, put Fincher in a better position to call his own shots.

"Because of the horrible *Alien³* thing, every time I hear the name Fox, it just makes me shrivel. I lose circulation in my hands and feet and I think I'm going to become a quadruple amputee. But I felt this was something I had to follow through with. So I met with Laura Ziskin, head of Fox 2000. I said the movie I see isn't *Trainspotting*. The real act of sedition is not to do the $3 million version, it's to do the big version. And they were like, 'Prove it.'"

Fincher gave copies of the book to Pitt and Norton. He worked with screenwriter Jim Uhls for about eight months after Uhls turned out a first draft that Fincher felt was far too linear and eliminated the inner-voice narration, which was what had attracted him to the novel in the first place: "It was like taking the voice out of Dashiell Hammett." He put together a schedule, storyboards, a budget. "I went back to Fox with this unabridged dictionary-sized package. I said, 'Here's the thing. Sixty million. It's Edward, it's Brad. We're going to start inside Edward's brain and pull out. We're going to blow up a fucking plane. All this shit. You've got seventy-two hours to tell us if you're interested.' And they said, 'Yeah, let's go.'"

Fincher's starting point was the narrator, whom he dubbed "IKEA boy." Nameless in the novel, he's referred to as Jack in the film. Fincher says he knew Jack's world and his plight because he once was an IKEA boy too—and not just because he learned how to make films by directing Nike commercials and Madonna videos.

"At some points in my life, I would say, 'If I could just spend the extra money, I could get that sofa, and then I'd have the sofa thing handled.' I was reading the book and blushing and feeling horrible. How did this guy know what everybody was thinking? It's funny how everybody has this sense of propriety about this material but in slightly different ways. Edward, who was twenty-nine when he read it, sees it as about his generation—not slackers, but numbed and befuddled and with this pent-up rage. Art Linson, one of *Fight Club*'s producers, who started making movies in 1972, says that he felt all these things. And Brad, who you wouldn't expect to identify with this feeling of impotency, said, 'I know this guy.' It was like a call to arms."

Casting Pitt as the charismatic Tyler Durden, the embodiment of pure id with a little Nietzsche thrown in, was a no-brainer. "The narrator idolizes Tyler, he wants to become him. And if I were to choose to become someone else, it would be Brad Pitt." Casting the IKEA boy was more complicated. "It's not Matt Damon, it's not Ben Affleck. It has to be someone who wears that self-doubt and yearning for the right way as Edward did in *The People vs. Larry Flynt*."

That Norton's presence echoes Dustin Hoffman's in *The Graduate* also seems to be a factor. "Brad, Ed, and I were talking and we realized that one of the reasons we'd gotten into movies was Katharine Ross. If you could work in a business where you could meet Katharine Ross that would be the ultimate. So this movie owes something to *The Graduate* in many ways."

Fight Club is a doppelganger movie with a strong homoerotic undercurrent. It's not just there in the intimacy between the Norton and Pitt characters, but also in the Fight Club sequences, shot in a wet-dream half-light that turns the men's bodies opalescent as they pound each other into the cement. And, of course, it's there in Pitt's presence, which seems more feminine the more it's butched up. Fincher doesn't pull back from the homoeroticism, maybe because he seems not to be conscious that it exists. "I think it's beyond sexuality," he says. "The way the narrator looks up to Tyler and wants to please him and get all of his attention doesn't seem to me to have anything to do with sex."

Opening with a shot that twists through the protagonist's brain to end on a gun stuck in his mouth, *Fight Club* is a psychodrama for cyberpunks. The disorienting special effects, the muffled whispery sound of the voice-over, the way the narrative backs up, leaps ahead, turns corners in a flash—all these elements make it difficult to keep a comfortable distance from the film. "We didn't set out to leave the audience in the dust but we wanted to move at a clip," Fincher says. "We wanted to be random access."

Fincher can also do the Hollywood thing and make the film sound like a straightforward journey, although he can't help laughing at his own doublespeak.

"The narrator was captivated and seduced by the manifestations of very perverse and extreme concepts of masculinity to the point that he was involved in some pretty severe destruction of public property. But he comes to a place where he realizes that although there are parts of what Tyler is selling that are important and right, there are other parts that are based on ideas of domination and power that are unhealthy, and that, as an empathetic, not totally guilt-free human, he can't live with."

In the wake of Littleton, Fox became so nervous about *Fight Club* that they pushed its release back four months and tried to pass it off with bland, silly posters as a goofy Brad Pitt comedy. "We always had that Alfred E. Neuman 'What me worry? I read *Mad*' concept about Tyler Durden," says Fincher.

"But I do think the promotional materials are a little light. And although the book was written five years ago, I think the movie's about Littleton in more ways than anyone would care to address. Do I think that people who are frustrated and disenfranchised should blow up buildings? No. Do I care if people who are consenting adults have this Fight Club? I have no problem with that. I'm no sadomasochist, but it seems more responsible than bottling up all this rage about how unfulfilling their lives are. I think the movie is moral and it's responsible. But the scariest thing about Littleton is that two eighteen-year-olds would say, 'Okay, I'm going in and I'm not coming out,' that they would give up their lives to make a statement, that they would die because of such trivial frustrations. And no one wants to look at that."

Fight the Good Fight

Andrew Pulver / 1999

From the *Guardian* (London), October 29, 1999. Copyright Guardian News & Media Ltd 1999. Reprinted by permission.

Four feature films down the line, David Fincher knows he's not making friends. "Listen," he says, "I've been just as trashed for *Fight Club* as I was for *The Game*; as I was for *Se7en*; certainly as I was for *Alien³*. It comes with the territory." As a director who deals so remorselessly with the bleak and tortured regions of the human psyche, Fincher, even at the relatively tender age of thirty-seven, has had time to become thoroughly accustomed to the sound of flying brickbats. "Every time," he continues, "you make a product that's designed to be consumed by twenty million people let us all hope you're opening yourself up to other people's interpretations, and other people's feelings. In choosing to go in and say, I'm the guy to make this into a movie, and here's what I see; in choosing to muster that enthusiasm and push that rock up a hill you've made your bed, basically."

Fight Club, though, is something special, even for someone with Fincher's record of critic-riling. Adapted from Chuck Palahniuk's satirical novel of yuppie disillusion, *Fight Club* has become the latest plaything of self-appointed guardians of America's moral conscience, who have accused the film of everything from glamorizing fascism to encouraging the production of home-made napalm. "I didn't expect people to take it so seriously. I didn't expect people to be so offended. Listen, I like *Fight Club* like I like *Peter Pan*. I read Chuck's book, and it just fundamentally reorientated my shit. Chuck is a pinball machine of ideas, there were things bouncing around, and stuff lighting up. If you're going to make a film that has that many ideas in it, you don't really have total control over it. But I never saw anything fascist about it. I never understood that as a criticism, when people say it is fascist entertainment. How can a movie that is a proponent of no solution whatsoever be labelled as fascist? It's just fundamentally opposed to the idea of fascism.

"Listen, I knew (*LA Times* film critic) Kenneth Turan would hate it, but that's not reason enough not to make a movie. But I didn't expect some of what happened. I walked out of the premiere in LA, and overheard two women who work at CAA, my agency, just going off, saying, 'This shouldn't have been made, who do these people think they are? This is socially irresponsible, this is exactly what's wrong.' It reminded me of the moment in *The Rocky Horror Picture Show* when Susan Sarandon is looking at the monster and says, 'Too many muscles.' Tim Curry turns to her, and says, 'We didn't make it for you.'"

Hate it the influential Turan certainly did, describing *Fight Club* as a "witless mishmash of whiny, infantile philosophizing and bone-crunching violence," and calling Fincher "one of cinema's premier brutalizers." Other critics have weighed in too, on both sides of the Atlantic. Rex Reed, in the *New York Observer*, critiqued *Fight Club* as "a load of rancid depressing swill from start to finish," while in the UK, *London Evening Standard* critic Alexander Walker declared, "The movie is not only anti-capitalism but anti-society, and, indeed, anti-God."

In person, however, Fincher is disarmingly ordinary-looking—a far cry from the sharp-suited style merchant his track record might suggest. He wears a grubby black T-shirt, a well-worn baseball cap, and a stubbly young-Spielberg beard—an only slightly grown-up version of the student filmmakers in *The Blair Witch Project*. It's hardly surprising, then, that Fincher should feel such affinity for Palahniuk's novel, and use it as the basis for his first assault in the territory of the message movie. *Fight Club* pairs Edward Norton, as a beleaguered corporate drone, with Brad Pitt, his anarchic, nihilistic antithesis, Tyler Durden. As he delineates *Fight Club*'s central thesis, Fincher begins to get animated: "It's a tale of maturity," he insists. "It's about someone who says, 'I followed my pre-programming, I've opened my desktop, and it's not for me, I need something else—I'm looking for some other specific software that will make me feel alive. The stuff I was given, that came with the package, just doesn't cut it.'

"To me," he continues, "the story is more like *The Graduate* than anything else. But instead of it being 1967, with a guy in his twenties and a world of opportunities ahead of him, it's 1999, he's thirty years old, and he's a guy who has bought into the whole thing, and he's looking to kindle some kind of passion. It isn't about having a world of opportunities, it's about having no opportunity; and someone comes along and says here's the other path. You know, Tyler's Mrs. Robinson, the catalyst that allows you to see your own destiny."

Fight Club also taps into a virulent skein of rage that's been dominating American protest politics for years, the dehumanizing effect of an all-pervading corporate culture. "I don't have anything against Starbucks, per se," Fincher says, deadpan, "because finally there's good coffee in LA, but do we need three on every corner? Should there be corners that have something other than Starbucks? But, to me, the material is so far away from being political; it's way more about the DNA's need for defining itself, and making itself singular. Tyler takes it too far, yes, but he's filling a need for these people. There's a lot of lost people out there."

As you'd expect, Fincher has nothing but outspoken praise for his cast. Norton, veteran of *American History X* and *The People vs Larry Flynt*, is genuinely exceptional in the pivotal role. "His contribution is that he's exactly that guy; you can believe he is overthinking his whole situation, and creating this whole problem for himself" while Pitt does his best work since *Se7en*, his last collaboration with Fincher. "Brad," according to his director, "doesn't want to burn himself out; doesn't want to overanalyze stuff. He's an intuitive—he's like a reactive chess player. You make your move, he's going to see what it is, what you're doing, and he's going to make his move. He's not one of these guys who come in with a fucking game plan; his whole process is all about creating a happy accident, fucking it up to a point where there's a little moment where the truth comes through." Helena Bonham Carter, too, excels, and seems finally to have cast off her increasingly oppressive Merchant Ivory tag. "We called her agent," explains Fincher of his approach. "Her agent in LA said, 'Fantastic,' her English agent I think was appalled. Anyway, I met her and she was perfect: she chain-smoked, she's a total neurotic, she's exquisite to look at, and she was very caustic and funny."

But it's one thing to talk the talk; it's another to walk the walk. Fincher's reputation doesn't merely rest on the unrelieved gloom and restless paranoia that has infected all his films to date; he's also demonstrated a cinematic ability of stunning audacity and imagination, and his films are littered with visual set-pieces of unparalleled brilliance. Ripley's slow-motion suicide dive in *Alien³*, for example, more than offsets the confused plotting and awkward characterization—a legacy of well-documented behind-the-scenes interference.

Se7en floats from one hellish vision to another in its nightmarish descent into urban foulness. *The Game* treads with exquisite skill along a knife-edge of plausibility. *Fight Club*, too, offers its battery of stylistic

triumphs: from the soon-to-be-legendary sequence when Edward Norton steps into a living IKEA catalogue, Brad Pitt's projection-room lecture, illuminated by a single moment of self-reflexive hilarity.

Fincher's beautifully crafted title sequences are another key indica-
tor of his dedication. *Se7en*'s opening credits are justly renowned, while
Fight Club's computer-generated vision of neural pathways in the cere-
bral cortex ("the movie is about thought, the deterioration of thought,
the organization of thought, so it seemed right to start the movie in his
brain") are equally praiseworthy.

"Listen," he says, "you're dealing with the most plastic medium there
is. Now there are computers that can make anything look real, and make
anything happen, so you have to be very careful about what you show
an audience. I think the first rule of cinema is that a movie has to teach
an audience how to watch it. That's what the first act is, showing the
audience the things they have to take seriously, the characterization and
technique, laying the groundwork for point of view, and how you will or
won't betray it.

"It's all about bringing the audience to realizations at the same time
as the characters—it's impossible to do it perfectly. Oh, maybe it's been
done perfectly two times, *Rear Window* being one of them. You watch
Rear Window, you think, fuck, that's it, can't be done much better."

Despite Fincher's obvious filmmaking panache honed through an ap-
prenticeship of high-profile music promos (Madonna, Aerosmith) and
commercials (Nike), he's unnervingly uncertain of his own gifts. By the
time *Se7en* was finished, he says, "I never thought it was scary at all. I
turned to the editor and said, 'My God, what have we done? We've totally let people down in the fucking terror department; we need to go
shoot some dismembered bodies. Go and see if you can get someone
from a morgue and chop 'em up.'" The same process repeated itself on
Fight Club. "Right up to when we finished, I just didn't think it was violent enough. I was like, 'We've got a movie called *Fight Club*, we might
as well call it *Glee Club*.' I still don't understand all this most-violent-
movie-ever stuff. My biggest worry when we previewed the movie was
that everybody would say, 'What's this? There's not enough fighting."

"I find," he explains, "when I read interviews with directors I love,
that they often say, 'I had the whole movie in my head.' Well my hat's
off to you, pal, because I don't know how the fuck you do that. I can
barely keep four and a half seconds of screen time in my head at any
given time. At the start, there's the excitement of all the possibilities;
then as you define it, you crush all the life out of it. You're picking paint

samples and deciding where the stains on the ceiling are, you're working on minutiae; then you go shoot the fucking life out of it; and then you cut it and say, 'Oh, that's not what it's supposed to be.' You eventually get to a point when you're simply relying on technique—relying on truisms. Like, if in doubt, hold on to the business card, so the audience can really read the guy's name."

Upstairs, it seems, Fincher is working on an adaptation of James Ellroy's novel *The Black Dahlia* ("I can't get a script that's under three hundred pages").What Fincher, with his acute eye for human wretchedness, will make of Ellroy's forties-set tale of obsession is enough to set the nerves jangling already.

Whatever emerges, Fincher's talents are restless enough to ensure that he'll never be content simply to mark time. "The thing is," he concludes, "if I ever put a tape of *Se7en* on, I'll just be, 'Oh God, you fucking idiot, what were you thinking?' You never have the perspective to truly assess what it is you've done until it's too late."

Four Walls and a Funeral

Ryan Gilbey / 2002

From the *Independent* (London, England), April 19, 2002. Reprinted by permission of Ryan Gilbey.

I experienced so much pure, uncontaminated pleasure at David Fincher's new thriller *Panic Room* that when he tells me he associates the picture with dread and anxiety, I'm not sure whether to reproach or console him. I find it hard to hear a bad or even ambivalent word said about this movie, in which Jodie Foster plays a divorcee whose first night with her young daughter (Kristen Stewart) in a regal New York brownstone is disrupted by a trio of burglars who want something that's in the hidden safe. The bad news for them is that the safe is in the "panic room," an impenetrable steel chamber in which the homeowner can take sanctuary while waiting for the police to arrive. So begins a torturous series of attempts to squeeze mother and child out of their hiding place. I'm happy to accept that the movie veers close to being *Home Alone* with excessive, bone-crunching violence, if only because the worst thing about those comedies was that they stopped short of excessive, bone-crunching violence.

But my endorsements count for little. When I say how snappy *Panic Room* feels for a film confined to several rooms and a staircase, Fincher eyes me suspiciously. "Does it? Does it move fast?" he asks, half-hopefully, half-skeptically. "That's interesting." He makes "interesting" sound like a euphemism for "crap."

Nothing I can say is going to dent his memory of the production's difficulties. He doesn't seem especially vexed that his original lead, Nicole Kidman, dropped out due to injuries sustained on *Moulin Rouge*, and he seems now to consider it inevitable that the original cinematographer, Darius Khondji (who shot *Se7en* for him), would leave the shoot because the rigid choreography left frustratingly little scope for creative maneuver. The banal daily compromises and frustrations trouble him most.

"There was absolutely nothing fun about making the movie." He gives the matter a little more thought. "Nope," he finally decides. "Nothing."

As it happens, I think that's the point with David Fincher. He's one of life's complainers. Which isn't to suggest that he hasn't got something to complain about, just that he likes to make things tough for himself. I'm not sure he would know what to do without the problems and paraphernalia involved in a typical David Fincher picture. For a while, he was set to make a comedy about celebrity chefs—a nice little film, no special effects, no violence—only it got abandoned when the budget started ballooning. I wonder if he was secretly pleased at the prospect of being released from a movie that might not have tested his physical endurance. This theory isn't based so much on the notoriously traumatic production of his 1992 debut feature, *Alien³*, during which he was all but exchanging gunfire with Twentieth Century Fox, but on the fact that whatever direction our very enjoyable conversation takes, he always manages to steer it around to one subject: The Pitiful and Miserable Existence of the Modern Filmmaker.

"I don't think it [directing] is fulfilling," he says cheerfully. "I enjoy the stuff that's like a high-school play, when the actors come in and put on their make-up. I like choosing the costumes. But when you get down to it—urgghh!" He makes a sound like he's just seen Gwyneth Paltrow's severed head in a box. "It's horrible. Because the only thing you're doing is prioritizing to cover the downsides. 'That great thing you wanted to do, that cool shot—forget it, it's not happening.' You're not able to do what you want. You never are."

I decide that we're not going to mention the production again. It's too easy for him; he slips into descriptions of his various on-set dilemmas with such ease and nonchalance ("Then we have to do a close-up, then re-light, that takes forty-five minutes, then we have to pull the wall out and do a two-shot, and then . . .") that I suspect those tales are something of a comfort blanket.

So we talk about the movie; the finished movie. And even there it seems we see things differently. A few weeks ago in these pages, David Thomson remarked that he could detect "no ulterior meaning" in *Panic Room*. He meant it as a compliment: like *Jaws* or *Speed* or *The Wages of Fear*, it is lean and nasty and relentless. But while it's an exemplary "Boo!" movie (with a dash of B-movie thrown in for added spice), that is by no means all it is. Right, David? "It's a movie," he says softly. "That's what it is. That's all."

Well, I say, I don't think that's all. He looks intrigued. He has already described it as a film about divorce: the way in which this beautiful house is gradually and systematically destroyed in the hunt for material wealth, as well as the violence doled out to mother, daughter, and errant father, all point toward a metaphor for the brutality of marital break-down. "If there is a thematic underpinning to the movie, it's that," he concedes. "Bad things do happen to good people in that situation. But really I just wanted the film to be an alternative. There are so many mov-ies out there that tell the audience: 'We don't want to make you uncom-fortable 'cause this is your Friday night.'"

To this end, he cranked up the menace from which David Koepp's screenplay had shied away. In the script, the child gets slapped by one of the burglars, but Fincher needed something more. "I wanted to see her get really smashed," he grins. "I wanted people to know this was not a movie that was going to play nice." Then there was the reinforced steel door to the panic room. "In the script, there was all this stuff about the door, the safety mechanism, the fact that no one could ever get caught in it. I said to David Koepp: 'How can you have nine people talking about how dangerous the door is, and then we don't sever any limbs?' He said, 'We can't have someone get a hand or a leg caught—they'd just sit in the background whimpering for the rest of the movie.'" Fincher's eyes light up. "I said, 'Yeah! What's wrong with that?'"

For me, the brilliance of *Panic Room* goes even deeper than Fincher's fearlessness. Like *Rear Window*, it's about the passivity of the audience, and how one audience member—James Stewart in Hitchcock's film, Jodie Foster here—graduates spectacularly from observer to participant. When she's hiding in the panic room, monitoring the intruders' move-ments on television screens, Foster is like us: she's the viewer, rendered impotent by her voyeurism, and unable to influence the outcome of what she's seeing. In one scene, she has to watch someone being sav-agely beaten, while one of the attackers, who knows she is watching, helpfully "lights" the scene for her enjoyment by shoving a lamp in the face of the semi-conscious victim.

The rest of the movie catalogues the emancipation of Foster's charac-ter, and the means by which she takes control of the "movie." It won't spoil your enjoyment to reveal that by the time the credits roll, she has not only busted out of her cinema seat, but she's tearing around the film set, adjusting the lighting, dishing out props and generally turning into David Fincher. Now try telling me it's just a movie.

"Hmm," says Fincher thoughtfully. "Maybe I should've thought about it some more. I thought I did. I guess I didn't have enough time. One day, we spent eight hours rehearsing a shot, lighting it, blocking the actors, only to find we couldn't do it, so we scrapped the whole day's work, and then. . . ."

Inside *Panic Room*: David Fincher, the Roundtable Interview

Daniel Robert Epstein / 2002

From DavidFincher.net, 2002.

Daniel Robert Epstein: Let's talk about logistics. I heard the challenges, the difficulty, and that you didn't realize the enormous undertaking of making *Panic Room*.

David Fincher: Its deceptive because you read a script and it reads like, these guys are doing things downstairs and it's being seen on video monitors then you cut to the room where two people are trapped and they start talking. No script is really written in stone. There are things that you want to change or have the actors riff on. But you have to commit to what's on the video monitors behind the two actors in the panic room that you shot days before.

A lot of times when you think it's really simple you realize that you don't have enough footage to play on those monitors while the two actors talk so you have to cover that stuff now. What was one setup now becomes three setups. Another example is when Dwight [Yoakam who plays Raoul] starts smashing the ceiling to get into the panic room, so he's smashing the plaster. Now you have to replace the plaster for every take, it's a forty-five minute reset time, the plaster weighs eight hundred to nine hundred pounds, you have to build steel rails to get it up there. Also, you need to cut take three with take eleven so the smashed ceiling has to look the same from each and Dwight is actually breaking it so he needs to do it correctly. You're shooting something that's an eighth of a script page long, it should take half a day to shoot, instead it takes two days.

DRE: Does that stuff interfere with getting what you want from the actors?

DF: Not really. It becomes an added element that has to be juggled.

DRE: In retrospect would you do it another way?

DF: Maybe on a houseboat [laughs] to make myself more miserable. Well it probably would have been easier to do it all with all specials effects with green screens. In retrospect that would probably be less expensive than what we ended up doing.

DRE: Your movies look somewhat the same even though you use different cinematographers. But do you consciously think about maintaining your signature style?

DF: No. Everything has to funnel through what one thinks it is aesthetically correct. Quite honestly, I don't like to justify sources of light in the shot so you end up doing toplighting. You end up solving problems in similar ways because you have the same criteria for them. I also make movies that take place at night so you can't put people next to windows. That won't help you.

DRE: What is it about night that you like?

DF: I think almost everybody in life has been afraid of the dark. I don't think this movie would be very scary if it took place during her lunch break.

DRE: I loved that shot with the camera traveling into the keyhole; most directors would just show the lock turn. How do you decide which shots you're going to stylize?

DF: That was described in the script and it seemed to fit. I think [screenwriter David] Koepp was trying to establish a really specific relationship between the windows and the burglars, the predators, were looking through. It's kind of like with fishbowls when cats press their noses up against them. Also since in one stylized shot where we float through the entire house, it established the geography. That's why the bad guys could have a conversation on the first floor and Jodie and her daughter can't hear them because she's so far away and we've shown that.

DRE: You are very aggressive in your techniques in eliciting emotion from the audience.

DF: I think that it's always a balance between subjectivity and omniscience. That's always the thing you are trying to balance. This movie in the first two-thirds we try our best to establish a distance. The camera is completely unencumbered while the people are. The people run up, hit a door, and fall back. They can't get through the wall, and then the camera just goes right through it. I think that there is something about that that tells the audience, "scream all you want no one can hear you. You can only watch."

DRE: Did you realize that you were hiring three directors as your actors [Jodie Foster, Forest Whitaker, and Dwight Yoakam]?
DF: Oh yeah. I thought of Forest and Dwight initially and at the time Nicole Kidman was cast in the movie. When she was injured and Jodie became available it was right after I met with her that I thought, "This is great, these people will know why I'm so neurotic."

DRE: Did they have a lot of suggestions for you?
DF: That's the thing, if you've directed before the one thing you know is to just shut up and act. You do have to work to the audience's eye. That's what's funny about movie acting is that it is completely silly looking. The way people have to move around each other in a two shot. If you saw people behaving like that in real life you would ask what the hell their problem is. But through the camera's lens, it works. When I asked these actors to do something they never said, "I don't think my character would do that." They just did it.

DRE: Tell us about how Nicole actually hurt herself.
DF: She was running up steps or down steps. She said, "Ouch!" We thought maybe she had hyper-extended her knee or something like that. She started limping and my initial reaction was, "Oh, she wants to leave early." But then her doctor came in and shot some x-rays. She had a hairline fracture of the bone beneath her knee joint.

DRE: So she just wouldn't be able to handle all the physicality of the movie?
DF: Well I didn't think the movie would end up being so physical but certainly all the actors have the bumps and bruises to prove me wrong.

DRE: How far along in the shoot were you when that happened?
DF: About eighteen or nineteen days.
    Jodie was available because her next movie that she was going to direct, *Flora Plum*, had fallen apart while we were shooting with Nicole. After Nicole got hurt, I told the studio to shut it down and collect the insurance, they would have made a $3 million profit from it.
    But they wanted this movie. So I told them it would cost like $10

million more to shut down and gear back up. They wanted it so we sent the script over to Jodie and we met in the bar at the Four Seasons Hotel and she agreed to do it.

DRE: How much time did Jodie have to prepare?
DF: About nine days.

DRE: Alan Parker said that when Jodie Foster was eleven years old she had very specific ideas about how *Bugsy Malone* should be directed. Has she grown up?
DF: Mellowed maybe. We've all mellowed since we were eleven years old.

DRE: What happens to a movie when you switch a major role like that?
DF: It's very odd. There were a lot of things that I wouldn't think would need to change that did. We were working on two different sets basically, the panic room and the main floor. You have all the physical stuff that has to happen pretty well set. But when we shot things with Jodie that we had already shot with Nicole I found that as a presence just a different vibe, not just what they have to say. Certain lines did have to be rewritten. In my opinion Jodie Foster can play anything, but helpless is asking a lot of the audience to believe because she just isn't. The character was originally written more helpless.

For example, the scene where Jodie was eating pizza with her daughter [Kristen Stewart] was already shot with Nicole. So when we went to re-create it with Jodie, it just didn't work, it was weird. So we had them switch sides and do different things. People just carry different vibes with them.

DRE: What about Jodie's pregnancy, how did you shoot around that?
DF: That was a problem. We shot all the wide stuff, then the medium stuff, and then the close-ups.

DRE: Well there is a lot of action, how did it work with her being pregnant?
DF: Well, Jodie's stunt double, Jill Stokesberry, who is really amazing, does most of the action stuff. Because it would be really irresponsible to throw a woman who is six months pregnant around. Jill would step in for most of it, then Jodie would do the close-up and I would yell "More violent, more violent."

DRE: Did you feel doomed because of all the problems?
DF: Yeah, it was cursed.

DRE: Since you're neurotic already what did this do to you?
DF: You do feel a little persecuted by the forces.

DRE: Well not only did you switch actors you also switched directors of photography. What happened, why did you replace Darius Khondji with Conrad Hall Jr.?
DF: Y'know it just wasn't working. We also switched kids.

DRE: Were you trying to find a kid that looked more like Jodie?
DF: No, we switched kids in rehearsal with Nicole.

DRE: That kid in the movie is amazing. She actually reminds me of a young Jodie Foster.
DF: Well when we hired we didn't think she looked like Nicole but like Jodie Foster actually. It's funny that it worked out that way.

DRE: What do you think about this kind of film, the thriller?
DF: I don't think there is any kind of importance to this kind of film. It is truly the guilty pleasure genre of moviemaking.

DRE: Doesn't that have importance?
DF: Yeah in a lurid, kind of fear-based entertainment. Comedies are probably more important to the human psyche than movies that scare people. But it's nice every once in a while. One of the reasons I made this movie is because I like scaring people.

DRE: Well, like *Fight Club*, I think *Panic Room* is very much a black comedy.
DF: It's got its humor and there is a bit of sadistic relish especially with Dwight Yoakam's character. We talk so much about this door [to the panic room] that won't close, the door this and that. So I have to see this door close on someone's hand. Koepp was like, what is going to happen, this person is just going to scream and thrash through the whole scene. I said, "Oh yeah. People will just enjoy that scene so much."

DRE: Any second thoughts about making Dwight's character punch the kid in the face?
DF: None. You want a movie villain that people want to spit at.

DRE: There was a big gasp at the screening.

DF: The fact is that the horrible reality of child abuse is that it isn't back-handed slaps. He is supposed to be an appalling character and you have to in some way get the kid out of the picture.

DRE: Is Jared Leto tired of getting the crap beaten out of him in your movies?

DF: He's perfect for it, isn't he? If there is any guy you want to see get his face burned off it's him.

DRE: He's just so damn pretty.

DF: We love that.

DRE: When you cast this movie did you intentionally cast three guys who were very different types from one another?

DF: Raoul was originally written as a giant scary hulking guy. But I thought what if he was this wiry mean kind of ex-con, white-trash kind of guy, I remembered *Sling Blade* and I thought Dwight Yoakam would be cool. Burnham [played by Forest Whitaker] was sort of glib and was originally the guy who designed the panic room. I didn't buy talking that guy into breaking into a house. I think we had to make him the guy who installs them, the blue-collar guy. I loved the idea of Forest Whitaker; you can't get someone more physically imposing than him. Then I turned into a CAA agent, "who could I get to be in the middle?" It's got to be someone little and glib. Who has aspirations to be Latrell Sprewell? Jared Leto, original gangster. Jared came in, he had the gold teeth and he was doing this whole rap thing. I said, "I'm not too sure about that." So he went away, came back with cornrows in his hair. I thought it was awesome because it speaks so much to him being a wanna-be hard guy, a fuckin' OG.

DRE: Your DVDs seem special. *Fight Club* in particular is kick-ass. It goes beyond the films, and into the context of it.

DF: We needed to do that with that movie because the ball was dropped with it so radically. The marketing was so botched; we wanted to tell people that it wasn't intended to be offensive, if it was. It was intended to be a black comedy, a satire. We fought really hard to get that DVD packaging. We had to make a deal for the studio to use that hideous green and purple photograph of Brad Pitt. They wanted Brad's face as big as they could make it. We said we could use that but the DVD has to look like a brown package, like pornography. They agreed.

DRE: One of your missions is to place your films in the right context then.

DF: Yeah and you can do that through DVD. The DVD, whether we like it or not, will place it in historical perspective.

DRE: When you talk about people liking to be scared, there are few things that come up like ghosts or monsters. But your movie is different; we all have that fear of people breaking into our home.

DF: Right, it's based on neuroses as opposed to the supernatural. We all have the power to make things worse for ourselves than any supernatural force could do. The fact that more people lock their doors and turn the lights on when they are alone, not because of ghosts but because of the human element.

DFN: How indebted are you to Alfred Hitchcock, especially for this sort of film?

DF: I saw a lot of Hitchcock when I was a kid; there were very few people who were that specifically true to their ideas and proclivities. So he was and is a very interesting filmmaker. His movies are so mainstream and so personal at the same time. But we didn't do much research on this. I sold the studio on this by telling them this was a cross between *Straw Dogs* and *Rear Window*. But that was as far as it went. We didn't screen the movies or anything.

DRE: You didn't say it was a slasher version of *Home Alone*.

DF: We tried that. [laughs]

DRE: They were puppeteers in the credits. What did they do?

DF: When the husband's [played by Patrick Bauchau] collarbone was sticking out, we needed five guys to make it move.

DRE: How is *Rendezvous with Rama* going?

DF: Nothing yet. We're trying to get a script together fewer than three hundred pages.

DRE: What's it like having a screenwriter as your producer?

DF: It's good. If he's good at both then it's good.

DRE: Some people might consider you an auteur and having the screenwriter there all the time might not be good.

DF: I'm just a hard-working interpreter. I like David Koepp and I liked his writing on this, I thought it was really terse. He has a concept and a conceit. He has something that he wanted to do. Not just in terms of cinema, David doesn't write for the money. The highest compliment that's he's paid since he saw the movie was "that you weren't afraid to make it a genre movie." I said there was no reason for me not to, the script was good.

DRE: You don't exactly do genre films.
DF: I do. I think *Se7en* is a subversion of a genre movie, I don't know which one. But this is a piece of entertainment designed around eliciting certain responses from the audience either by playing on their expectations, subverting or crushing them. [laughs]

DRE: *Panic Room* is definitely more of mainstream project than *Fight Club*.
DF: I think most movies are. [laughs]

DRE: Will the success of this film bring us another similar project as *Fight Club*?
DF: *Fight Club* was just one of those opportunities that came along that you just can't turn down. I couldn't believe the studio even bought it.

DRE: So was it a conscious decision to do a more mainstream project?
DF: Well, how many *Fight Clubs* are going to come along? The projects that make you want to kill to get involved with.

DRE: Well, Bill Mechanic [former head of Twentieth Century Fox who championed *Fight Club*] lost his job over it and he is happy that it is out there.
DF: I don't think Bill Mechanic lost his job over it. I think that that is a glib thing to say.

DRE: Well, he said it.
DF: I think that that is even especially glib for him to say. I would wear that as a badge of honor. Bill Mechanic supported us in the making of that movie in a way that I have never seen. Michael De Luca [former President and Chief Operating Officer of New Line Productions] went to the mat for *Se7en*. When we needed eighteen more days to reshoot on *Se7en* and Phyllis Carlyle [producer of *Se7en*] was saying, "We need to fire this

guy. He's a music video guy. He doesn't know what he's doing. We need to redo the ending. The head can't be in the box." When all that shit was going on, Mike De Luca was watching my back. When we went to Bill Mechanic we told him we were having a problem with the ending [of *Fight Club*]. We said, the tone of the movie had shifted radically. It's a lot goofier than we thought it would be and we need the ending to be more visceral. We need to take a week off and it's going to cost a million dollars more and we had already spent $62 million. He said okay.

I don't know many people that would do that. So I am eternally indebted to Bill Mechanic because every step of the way he and Arnon [Milchan] were there to help us with our problems. Sony, with *Panic Room*, has been that way as well but they got very nervous when the shooting went over a hundred days.

DRE: You've said that people use "music video director" as a put-down but you still do music videos like "Judith" for A Perfect Circle. What is it about them that you still like to do them?

DF: Music videos are fun. You're not encumbered by a narrative. There's nothing more gratifying than shooting, cutting, scoring, and mixing a scene that works. It has a beginning, a middle, and an end. When you watch that scene with an audience and they react to it, it's amazing. You've gotten to them, you've touched them. It's also an amazing thing to be able to take a piece of music and put pictures to it that may or may not be related to the lyrics and to create this whole other thing. You kind of force abstraction.

DRE: In many interviews George Lucas has said that he desperately wants to go back to doing abstract experimental films.

DF: That's what he says. Well, he should do it. How much fucking money does he need?

DRE: You have the chance to do it with music videos.

DF: Well why not, some of the most interesting and most talented people I have ever worked with are musical artists.

DRE: Well, for the features you use composers. You don't really use songs or pop songs in your movies.

DF: It depends. Obviously Howard Shore makes a lot of sense for *Panic Room*. But we used the Dust Brothers [composers for *Fight Club*] because we wanted something that was more. We didn't want anything that was thematic or that would tie the beginning of the movie to the end. I wanted it to be like you were changing stations on the radio. I didn't want any "Darth Vader's March." No cues to fit the characters. What we decided we wanted was to use something that was current, that couldn't be tied to any songs. We couldn't tie it to Beck or the Beastie Boys.

DRE: Well, to talk a little about Howard Shore; it took him this long to get an Oscar nomination [for composing the score to *The Lord of the Rings: The Fellowship of the Ring*]. What did he bring to the table?
DF: Howard Shore is one of the best, most fearless, collaborators you could ever work with. He is completely undaunted by what you are trying to achieve, totally pragmatic, and will tell you what does not work with the scene and how to fix it. He's a guy who will help you tell your story.

DRE: He's worked with David Cronenberg on nearly all his features and scored big Oscar winners like *The Silence of the Lambs*. Why do you think it took him twenty-five years to get an Oscar nomination?
DF: He's a little outside the norm.

DRE: *Crash* is still one of the best soundtracks ever made.
DF: It is amazing.

DRE: Is there anything that didn't get into the movie that will be on the DVD?
DF: I don't know. We start working on that in a couple of weeks.

DRE: Was Jodie the second choice after Nicole Kidman?
DF: Jodie was never on the list because she wasn't available and when I read the script I talked to Nicole about it. At one point Nicole wanted to do *Fight Club*. We had talked about that but we weren't able to do it for a number of reasons. I think she is amazing. I hadn't seen *The Others*. I was busy during all that. There was no list.

DRE: Andrew Kevin Walker had a cameo as the "Sleepy Neighbor" in *Panic Room*. Did he do any rewrites?
DF: No, he and Koepp are best friends. But even if he did, if you're a professional screenwriter in Hollywood you get rewritten all the time. I would tease David all the time: "Andy's coming down. Just for a fitting!"

DRE: They're saying that after September 11 movies are going to change. Is it going to change the way you make movies?
DF: I don't know. I've never wanted to make movies about terrorists.

DRE: Well, I think they want to change the amount of violence in movies. Certainly *Straw Dogs* wouldn't be able to come out now. It's still banned in Britain.
DF: That's ridiculous.

DRE: You're a very technical director. You know so much more than the average director. Could you do the job of director of photography?
DF: No, I have a working vocabulary of what it is they are doing. That's an art form all its own and it's something I probably won't ever have enough expertise to do. I have way too much respect for them to try to do that job.

DRE: How much writing do you do on your films?
DF: I don't do any writing. I consider myself sort of an editorial gadfly. I move scenes around and move dialogue about. I'm really doing more of what an actor would do, asking questions about the material or how can I help the material translate properly. I don't write. I come up with ideas for lines and stuff.

DRE: Would you ever generate your own screenplay?
DF: No.

DRE: So you wait for screenplays to come to you?
DF: Or you develop stuff. I'm always doing that.

DRE: What's the dumbest rumor you've heard about yourself on the Internet?
DF: I heard that I just had a son.

DRE: Congratulations!
DF: Right. I can't believe I missed that. A friend of mine called me and congratulated me. Never believe anything you read on the Internet.

DRE: Do you ever visit davidfincher.net?
DF: I don't do it religiously because it's too weird. It feels like people know too much about me.

DRE: What's the hold music thing you were doing stuff with?

DF: There was hold music that was generated by these directors who were represented at Anonymous Music who did a CD of different kinds of hold music. It got sent to me with a note saying I should listen to this. I wanted to do a music video of it. That was it.

DRE: What about working with Fred Durst?

DF: I love Fred. I think he is a hilarious guy, and really smart and creative. We talked about doing a movie called *Runt*. I just didn't think that it would be the best situation for his first film. There wasn't enough money; the guy who was producing was never sure what he wanted. I just wanted to help him out with it, literally just sitting down with him and going through it scene by screen.

As smart as Fred is, he is a pretty impetuous guy. He's all over the place. I was just curious because I wanted to be able to provide a service for him as a friend that was never provided to me. Helping him circumnavigate the waters and know some answers even before the questions are presented. There was a lot of violence at the end involving kids shooting in a high school.

DRE: Last question, might you be doing *Mission Impossible 3*, or is that horseshit?

DF: It's not horseshit.

DRE: Thanks again.

DF: Thank you.

David Fincher Interview

Stephan Littger / 2006

From *The Director's Cut: Picturing Hollywood in the 21st Century* (New York: Continuum, 2006). Reprinted by permission of Stephan Littger.

David Fincher: I grew up in a sort of middle class, very bedroom community in the San Francisco Bay Area in Marin County. I lived there from age three to fourteen, from the late sixties to the seventies. It wasn't as affluent as it is today, but it was a nice sort of suburb and part of a relatively liberal collection of small towns. I would describe it as more hippieish than more conservative places like San Raphael and Terra Linda.

Because of the time, the art of making movies was sort of everywhere and classes in middle school, high schools, and grade schools had access to Super 8 movie equipment. It was cheap and readily available and there were a lot of filmmaking courses available to very young kids. I remember taking my first Super 8 filmmaking class when I was in third grade. By the time I was eight years old, I had pretty much decided that I wanted to be a director—that was that for me.

My mother worked in mental health and substance abuse. My dad was a writer and journalist who wrote for *Life* magazine for a few years and then freelance for magazines and stories—he was sort of a science writer. He was a big movie buff and used to take me to films every weekend—it was sort of our time together. And he would take me to see his favorite movies. So from the time I was six or seven years old, I was watching, you know, *Singin' in the Rain* and *2001: A Space Odyssey*. It was an eclectic smattering of influences.

Stephan Littger: Did you tell your father you wanted to be a director?
DF: Yeah, yeah—he probably thought kind of the same thing I'm thinking now when my daughter says to me that she wants to be an actress—or that she wants to be a doctor, and I say, "That's great!" So he was trying to be encouraging.

But I remember watching that making-of documentary that was on network television that had director George Roy Hill talking about the process of making *Butch Cassidy and the Sundance Kid*. I remember watching this documentary and thinking . . . because it never occurred to me that movies weren't made in real time, you know. If a movie took two hours, it maybe took a couple days to film because you had to go from one place to another—but it never occurred to me that it took months.

I was eight then. They showed this sort of gypsy life of going from one place in Montana to some place in Wyoming, then shooting a train sequence maybe somewhere else. And then they were building full-scale trains and blowing them up. I just thought: "This is fantastic, what a great gig. You get to build stuff and blow it up and hang out with Katharine Ross and travel around." And I kind of thought, "That's it!" Then my parents let me go see the actual movie *Butch Cassidy*. And I ended up going every weekend for probably like five weeks just to see that movie. I just loved it; also because I had sort of peeked behind the curtain—well I sort of knew more about it. And I remember appreciating it, because all of my ideas of how movies were made had been kind of dashed by this documentary.

And suddenly, I saw this whole other discipline. Also, my father had bought the screenplay which was available in this little paperback that also had a bunch of photos in it. So I read this book over and over again. I sort of started getting this idea that all that stuff was intended—like all these moments: they didn't just happen. These words were given to these people, and these people were selected because of their chemistry and their abilities and then they were sort of made part of this process that looked so much like it was happening for real. And this kind of did me in.

SL: Did you try to reshoot sequences of *Butch Cassidy* with your own Super 8 camera or what kind of films did you make?

DF: Oh, they were insane. This was a pretty violent time, you know? So I like to think my mother was often extremely disturbed by the films that I would make [chuckling]. They would always involve somebody getting you know. . . . *The Sting* was a big movie and we always loved that moment in it where the hit woman Loretta gets shot in the forehead. The movies were more of excuses really to have friends shoot at other friends.

Most of the material was based on television; detective stuff. It's funny, I remember seeing Spike Jonze's "Sabotage" video going, "Oh my God, those are all the movies we used to make," with fake mustaches and fucking sunglasses and kids running around shooting cap guns at each other. It was very silly.

SL: Tell me a favorite story you did?

DF: I don't remember it too well. I think we did our own versions of *The Six Million Dollar Man*—anything that we could do so we could run it in slow motion and be bionic. Or there was that whole series of commercials back then in stop motion. It was all that sort of "Yay-physics" kind of stuff: "Isn't it amazing? They are here and then they're gone—"

SL: When did you realize that in order to keep on doing the "silly stuff," you would need a serious strategy to follow it through?

DF: You know I never really figured out a strategy until I was like in high school. As luck would have it, there was a big house up the street from us—like two driveways down. It was purchased in '72 or '73 by George Lucas. So he moved in up the street. There was a lot of stuff going in Marin County at the time. John Korty had his studios there, and Michael Ritchie was cutting in Lucas's basement, and *The Godfather* was being filmed in the Marin Art and Garden Center. I remember in second grade, kids would come to school with shaved heads, 'cause they were extras in Lucas's *THX-1138*.

So, there was a lot of stuff going on. It didn't seem like Hollywood, which was physically centered around a particular place. I mean, we had a very different idea what filmmaking was, because people here were *doing* it—it was extremely prevalent.

SL: So you could hardly wait to be doing it yourself?

DF: My goals initially were extremely unreasonable, because I wanted to be the guy who was in charge of everything and I didn't really know how to do that stuff.

And I do think of the director's job that you should be the guy who not only knows how it's all going to go together, but also who sort of knows how you are going to get the material for it all.

In high school, I thought I'd work at ILM for a while, then try and direct television commercials and from that I would make features. It seemed like a logical kind of progression to me. And everybody just said, "You can't just go from working at a factory like ILM to directing TV commercials." It was too big a leap it seemed. And then, "You can't go from TV commercials to directing features," which is rare that people get that opportunity. But I went sort of, "But hey, you *can* make this step."

So I sort of knew that it was going to be a long road, because I didn't want to be the guy who's loading the magazines for the guy who was shooting the scene for the guy who had the whole thing in his head. I wanted to be the guy who had the whole thing in his head.

I mean, a lot of my work ethic was based on a saying that my father had: "Learn your craft: it will never stop you from being a genius." It's a valuable thing to know what everyone's doing. And from a fairly early age of making stupid little student movies, it was amazing to me how nobody really wanted to push the dolly, nobody wanted to operate the camera; no one wanted to light the scene. Everyone either wanted to act in it or they wanted to go "cut" and "action."

So I assessed my skill set and tried to set myself reasonable goals, given what I was capable of. I eventually went to the sort of bogus film school in Berkeley in the summer of '80—

SL: Why bogus?
DF: It was an extremely Northern California operation. It was very what I would call "the Resentful Indie."

SL: In reaction to the mainstream?
DF: Which is really healthy. But there are people who, I think, take it to an extreme. My experience there turned out to be very valuable, though, because I met some really good people. But ultimately, it was a very Berkeley experience.

Then John Korty was hiring. ILM wasn't hiring, and US Effects didn't exist at the time. Also, I didn't live in San Francisco and I didn't want to work there. And I didn't want to be a freelance guy, schlepping around from documentary to documentary. I simply didn't want to be that guy. I wanted to sort of find a place to perch and to watch.

I remember meeting Korty when I was eleven or twelve. My younger sister did voice-over for some of his cartoons that he was doing for *Sesame Street*, and I remember coming with her when she went to do it, seeing his studio on Miller Avenue. He had flatbed editing equipment in the house. He was very much invested in the local filmmaking scene. So I thought this was sort of a good place to perch for a while.

SL: What was your job there?
DF: You know, I did fucking everything. I started out as a PA, schlepping Xerox machines up and down the street, cleaning up. Then I helped the kind of technical systems guy there—I had some kind of background

in electrical work and I helped with wiring stuff, just PA stuff, just fucking around. Then I did some assisting camera work there, loading cameras. And then I moved over to the dark room, where I was for about nine months, maybe a year—it seemed like five years. It was sort of fun, though.

SL: Maybe a bit dark for your taste?
DF: Very dark. I mean it was good. I learned about printing and things—on a big scale. You are making trans-lights that are four feet across every time you make an exposure, burning a couple thousand dollars worth of film sheet. So you got to be good at it and know what you're doing. And dealing with the different artists; different animators—among them Henry Selick and Carl Willat.

SL: Was that helpful in any way?
DF: It wasn't so much contacts that I made. I mean you know it's people that I still speak with and check in with from time to time. You know animation is its own kind of weird subset of filmmaking because the intention has to be so specific. So when you come from animation, your thing is about, "What am I trying to solve in these fourteen frames," or "these sixty-four frames." You're not thinking in terms of, "Well let's just see what happens"—you're thinking in terms of, "It's gotta be moving left or right in order to keep the momentum," or, "The cut has to be moving at a pretty good velocity, the camera should be panning with it." There are all these things that make you think in terms of staging. Staging becomes extremely important in terms of how you get the idea across. Also, looking at performance in kind of fractal time—time *between* time. So you're dealing with, "When does this person blink—and how long is the pause before that person blinks and at what point do they say their line," and "Can I take this dialogue track and make this funnier by having a longer pause?" And to me the people who did that for a living were incredibly valuable. Although at the time, I probably wasn't thinking to myself, "Oh great, let me find a company that's doing cut-out animation and roost there for a couple of years." It was more that I knew Korty's reputation, I liked Mill Valley, I lived nearby, I could commute easily, it was a beautiful serene setting although enormously carcinogenic, given all of the dyeing techniques and things that they were using at the time. And it was this giant sort of clapboard house that had animation stands in it and artists and graphic designers and motion-control designers. It

was a really interesting time—and a very odd and special movie: special as in "Special Olympics" I mean!

It was a very strange experience but it was also valuable because you just met all the weirdest, most interesting talented people under this one roof. And I had to sort of interface with all of them because I was in sort of the place doing all the still photography.

SL: When did you professionally find yourself behind a film camera for the first time?

DF: The first thing I ever got to direct was when I swindled my way into a commercial for the American Cancer Society. It was in motion-control: a puppet that was smoking a cigarette in utero—it's a very odd little thing.

I was working at ILM at the time and I was kind of fed up and tired of being the special effects lettuce picker, the itinerant laborer. There were seasons at ILM—you know like, "Oh the new *Star Wars* movie is ramping up." I was assistant camera or working in various departments or whatever I was doing.

SL: ILM hired you as what actually?

DF: As assistant cameraman, loading mags. I did the cancer thing in my spare time. There was my friend Kirk Thatcher who was in Monster Shop, working with Phil Tippet and Tony McVey and several others. Then there was a friend of mine that I had known since I was five and that went to State with him. And we were all sitting around going, "We should just do commercials, 'cause at least we'd be doing our own stuff and we wouldn't be so neurotically waiting for what's going to happen at ILM next. Let's have some kind of say in our own destiny!" So we came up with this idea of contacting people who would be in a position to spend money on public service announcements. And so obviously we thought of the American Cancer Society. We came up with this idea for this commercial that had this 2001 Star Child with a cigarette in its mouth; we thought it was really amusing and funny. This guy that my friend Chris knew—his name was Joe, he was a truck driver delivering text books—and he wanted to be, I mean he fancied himself a producer. He called the Society in some state and said, "Hey, we have these guys, they all work at ILM, they are bored, they have this idea for this non-smoking commercial."

We had done some storyboarding and he pitched the idea to them. They asked how much it was going to cost. I think we did it for like seventy-five hundred bucks or five grand. And they said great and gave us a check for the money and we did this thing at cost.

There was a facility in Richmond at the time. It was a low-rent motion control place. It was an ILM wannabe. We brought them this job, because ILM didn't want to let us use their facilities or stages. So we built the creature—I think it was built in the Monster Shop at ILM—and then we took it to Richmond, photographed it, and put the whole thing together. We used their optical printer and printed the whole thing. Then I had Ren Klyce—the guy who I worked with doing all the sound for all my movies. At the time he was in music school. He did this soundtrack so that we finished the thing and gave it to them. We thought they were going to laugh and think it was funny and amusing.

Of course, it got banned on all these networks, because they were so appalled by it. And that was sort of the beginning, as much of a sideways move it was, because we were not doing that interesting work or that profitable work. I think everybody worked for free. If you had the man-hours totaled up, it would have cost hundreds of thousands of dollars to make this thing, but we did it for seven grand. It kind of opened up the notion of being something like a director.

My second shot at directing was for a music video for Rick Springfield. That was a nightmare and I did that in San Francisco—and that's when I realized I had to leave that city.

SL: You had a full-blown professional crew for that?
DF: [*Laughs*] Well, there will be differing opinions about that. Yeah, the people that were working on it were paid to be there, but it was a very odd thing. Working in San Francisco, it was an odd time.

I had gotten that gig on the basis of our commercial. It had a budget of like $150,000, which at the time was a huge amount of money. Music videos were starting to happen, and locally people were doing Huey Lewis videos for $40,000—you know that was a pretty big band at the time.

Local people were kind of appalled by me, going, "Who is this guy?" "He is an assistant cameraman"—or at the time I was a "plate supervisor" at ILM. And all of the sudden I was there. It was a pretty big deal. You know, even commercials were costing only $200,000 at that time.

SL: How was it funded?
DF: I got on a plane with Joe the truck driver-slash-producer, and we

went to L.A. Somebody had seen our commercial and wanted to know if we wanted to do a music video. And so we had a meeting.

I never forget: it was one of the most hilarious experiences in my life, because it really pointed out that presentation is everything. They had given us the song that we had listened to, and we had these beautiful storyboards and these creature designs and the whole thing we were going to do. So we got into a plane with all these things, flew into Burbank, rented a car, and went to this music manager's office. We laid out all the stuff out for him, and he said, "Wow! That's amazing! How much is it gonna cost?" And we said, "Well, we think we can do it for $150,000." He said, "Really?!" To him it was not a lot of money, but to us it was an enormous amount.

So we stood up and the guy who posed as my producer had this giant kind of grim on his face and he said in this enthusiastic way that he had, "Thank you so much, we've never done anything like this before." And I remember watching these guys just going, "Wow, we just made the deal with these two chuckleheads," like, "What are we doing?" And I remember walking out of this office on Ventura Boulevard—it was about 110 degrees out—and I turned to him and said, "You're no longer . . . gonna speak at these meetings because you can't be trusted not to say something that's completely stupid."

So we went off and did this video and we kind of called together as many of our friends as we could. It was a four-day shoot and an enormous undertaking. Henry Selick was the art director, and Michael Owen shot it—you know it was good people. And then of course you have the local assisting cameramen.

And I remember the first day: We were shooting in an anodizing mill or something—it was horrible—and we had all these people in this horrible make-up and jumpsuits inside this place that was just a complete shit hole; an environmental disaster. And I walked in and there were all these people waiting and I said, "I gotta use the bathroom, I'll be right back." And I went in and threw up, thinking, "I can't do this, I don't know what to tell them to do." I had that stage fright.

SL: Did you feel like you were faking it?
DF: Well I thought, "Here are all those people that do this for a living and here there's me, and I don't do this for a living." Just to see their faces, and they were all sort of with their mouths open, "Where do we go, what do we do?" and it was just absolutely terrifying. And after having thrown

up, I walked out and said, "OK, here's what we are going to do," and "I wanna put the camera over here, and put the track over here." And I remember the first AC looked at me and said, "Really?" That's when I realized that I was not really going to be able to do what I wanted to do in San Francisco because it was just going to be too many people questioning me up there.

SL: So the reason you felt sick was—
DF: The enormous responsibility—well, you had to manage these expectations. And then of course, as soon as you assert yourself of what you want to do, everyone questions it. You see, I'm suddenly looking at a guy who does first AC for a living and whose job I was doing less than a year ago. And now he's looking at me and I'm like twenty-three, telling him what to do. "Really?" and you just kind of go, "Eh . . . yeah!" and they were all kind of shrugging and the attitude was like, "If that's what you want to do, do it, but we don't really approve."

So I realized I had to go to L.A. because I think in L.A., everybody's so unjaded and cynical; at least they'll do what I'll ask them to do, simply because they want to get on to their next job. The thing about L.A. that's so amazing is that people are extremely skilled, extremely experienced, and they have worked for enough chuckleheads; they are no longer judgmental. If you go to them and say, "Hey now, I've been doing some thinking: everything on the left side should go to the right side of the room and I think the camera should be upside down," they'll just say, "OK, give us five minutes and we'll do that," while in San Francisco or in New York, you tend to find that you have more, let's say, collaborators [*chuckling*]—probably more so in San Francisco, though I have had that in New York, too.

SL: Moving on with your journey to feature filmmaking; you were now inside the structure, I suppose?
DF: I did music videos and commercials for seven years when I was offered *Alien³*.

SL: Did you feel well prepared to direct a feature?
DF: Well, not prepared, but certainly enthusiastic. I certainly had an idea of what I thought a sequel should be or what I thought a movie should be. I felt that I had a body of work that people could look at and kind of go, "Well, here's what's to expect from this guy." It wasn't that

I felt ready or that the world was waiting for me to make a movie—but I was certainly waiting to make a movie.

You know that was the only reason why I put up with making that many music videos and especially the commercials: because the commercial business is, you know, quite a rat fuck. So the only reason to put up with that was to be able to get enough experience shooting, enough days that you felt sort of accomplished and at least able to run a set and tell a story—or string together five pictures. It was film school. In the end, it was *all* about being a film director.

It's interesting. Although I worked with some fabulously talented people, like Norman Reynold as production designer and Terry Rawlings as editor, in retrospect I probably should have made the film the way I made my commercials. The fact that I didn't was a mistake. Because then I would have had people that I had worked with before and that were invested in me—Alex McDowell or Marc Plummer—and invested in the notion of me succeeding.

And I had nothing but help from Norman, and nothing but help from Terry, but there were a lot of people on the production department, who were beholden to Twentieth Century Fox for their livelihood and that were just like, "God forbid we do something interesting, especially if the studio doesn't like it or feel they couldn't afford it."

And you know, I have not been on a set since that experience where I felt as hamstrung. It was probably one of the most expensive movies at the time and it seemed ludicrous to assume that some twenty-seven-year-old kid was given $56 million and that you're not gonna resent his neck. But it was an ill-conceived experiment and I think that it takes somebody who was tougher than I was and more accomplished and more concise and more able to express himself.

SL: So you feel you were not really in control of what was happening to you on that set?

DF: I was in control, but let's put it this way: a hurdler is in control, but he is not in control of the hurdles. You come out of the gate and you're in control of yourself—you can control whether you're going to hit the hurdle, if you're going to slow yourself down in order to be able to make all the hurdles, or if you're going to knock over a couple of the hurdles in order to go for speed. Those are the decisions you have, but you're not in control of the surroundings. My job is to put together a team and have an instinct about people and their behavior, and to have an instinct about what their faces look like and what they can bring to it and where they are going to be strong and where they are going to need help. And you put them into the situation and then you create this world around them, working with designers and photographers and costumers and set-dressers and you kind of try to create that thing where that person you've invested in—their face, their performance abilities, and the idea that you have about them—is going to be supported by the world around them. And then finally you try and sort of create a place where you can kind of give it over to them and just go, "Now it's for you; now this time is all about you playing and experimenting and trying this and trying that, and then we'll hone in on this thing together." And then finally the hope is, once we get there, it will serve the purpose of what I feel that moment in the movie is about!

Well, when you spend all of your time fighting about what are the themes and what is the content. What are ideas that you're trying to get across, and are those ideas too lofty or too pretentious and do they have any place in a sequel or do they have any place in science fiction, or in a penal colony . . . ? It's not good if you end up spending all your time arguing about what the contents should be in order for it to be the most successful movie—and by that I mean most profitable!

So I was too stupid—I didn't have somebody that could go fight for me on my behalf. I was the only person that could fight for me on my own behalf, and I was twenty-seven years old. And the problem with that is that of course you end up being total white noise. By the time two years are up, nobody wants to hear from you anymore. Every time you call, and there's somebody saying, "Here's the problem that I'm having," they're going, "Oh god, it's that guy on the phone again, uh?" So it started in a contentious way and it became more and more contentious. And I have just never been the kind of person who—you know I'm just not that over-contentious kind of guy.

SL: How involved were you in the editing process?
DF: I mostly participated in almost everything [*chuckling*]. You get to make certain decisions and then you second-guess on other things. A director is like a quarterback. You get way too much credit when it works and way too much blame when it doesn't. And the fact of the matter is that the situation was completely untenable, because the people that were paying for it had no confidence in the person that they had hired to execute it. So they were second-guessing it via remote. And they were

second-guessing it from six thousand miles away and we didn't have the same taste. I had a very different idea tonally of what I wanted. They thought it was going to be a drag, instead of confronting the problem and saying, "Look, here's the script that we love, and here's the star that we've already paid for, and here's the situation." It wasn't like you were working with David Selznick who says, "Here's what I'm presenting you with—say yes or say no." It was like, "Well we don't know what it should be." And you kind of come in and say, "Well I think it should be this," and they go, "It's fantastic—why don't you go over to England and start doing that?!" And you say, "That's great"—and go, "That's all gonna be great." And you go there and look at what they've already built because they had already gone through this dance once with somebody else before who was in your position. And you go, "Well I can't really use this stuff," and they go, "Oh, we would really like to see you use it as much as possible." And then you think because you're young and stupid you go, "I don't want to seem like I'm not a team player, blablabla." So waters get muddied. I don't know of any circumstances where the movie director's agenda is the same as the studio's agenda.

SL: Obviously this whole experience is still very much part of you. Looking at it now, do you know what you would do differently?

DF: I had the trust of the actors. I really felt like I was supported. And I had the trust of the production designer, the cinematographer, and the editor. But from the production standpoint . . . you know, today I run my productions in a very different way than most studios do. I look at the production manager and think, "That's *my* person, he's on *my* payroll." And people go, "No, no, he's on the studio's payroll."

*Alien*³ was a situation where a pipeline had to be filled, and a title had to be made—but you still sit there and go, "On a normal movie, the reason that a director has the authority that he has is that the studio has looked at him and seen the body of work and said this person's interpretation is what we want to see." And that was the initial thrust of *Alien*³. And that quickly faded. And I had that conversation with Roger Birnbaum, who said to me, "I can release a fifteen-minute black screen and call it *Alien*³ and do $15 million in the opening weekend."

And to a certain extend that's true: I think six months after we were shooting, they were still running a trailer for *Alien*³ that showed aliens coming to earth. It had nothing to do with the movie that we were making, and they were like, "It doesn't matter. That's what we do: we get the exhibitors all jacked up." And you just kind of go, "Aha, that's what the movie business is"—or rather, "That's what the sequel business is." And you know: I was just the wrong guy for a sequel.

SL: As you are luckily over that sequel business now, I am interested in the creative process you go through when deciding on a project that's your own. Let's discuss *Fight Club*: how did you get on that and what steps did you concretely go through during the preparation of the story?
DF: I read it as a book, and it started as a book. Josh Donen, who was a producer at the time and my agent now, sent it to me and said, "I am sending you a book and you have to read it tonight." And I sort of said, "I can't read a book tonight, I am cutting a movie and I won't have time." And he said, "Well this is a book you have to read tonight because Twentieth Century Fox is going to buy this book and you need to buy this book first," and so I agreed to read it that night, but asked him to give me a reason why I should read it. "Tell me something about it that will be inspiring to me as to why I should read it." And he told me about the scene between Tyler Durden and the Asian shop owner, where he holds the guy at gunpoint and says, "I want you to go out and I want you to be a dentist and that you go back to school, and if you don't, I'm gonna kill you."

And I just thought it was such an amazing idea for a scene and said, "Yeah, that's really great." And I called him the next day and he said, "You know what, Fox already bought it." And I had such a bad experience with Fox, I had no intention of going back there to go through that again. So I told him that that was probably it for me with *Fight Club*. And then he called a little later and said, "You know, Laura Ziskin in the studio likes the idea of you for this movie. You might want to go tell her your take on it." And I just said, "No, it doesn't seem like this is for me. I can't do the studio version of it." So he said, "Well, just tell her that, and what you think you *can* do."

So I went to Laura and told her, "Well, this is the movie I would make," and she said, "Well that sounds fantastic. How much you think you can do it for?" And I said, "Until I have a script, I can't tell you. But let's pick a writer that we all agree on, I'll go off with him and we'll come back with a script. We're not going to come back with a script and ask you, 'Here's the script, what do you think?' The process will be more like, 'This is the script that we want to make—that we're dying to make; that we're going to arm-wrestle and fight for. And if you want to do it, let's do it.' " So that's what we did: they agreed to that and so we went away for a year—fourteen months—and we came back with the promised script.

SL: How did you go about developing the story creatively?
DF: I never really thought about it. You know, it seemed kind of obvious to me—it wasn't much of a struggle. It seemed sort of like we needed to be able to gloss over an enormous amount of material quite quickly. We wanted to keep this density of information and we knew we wanted to cut back and forth in time, because that's kind of what the narrator is constantly talking about in the movie. It was complex, but I never looked up and said, "Oh my God, this is impossible. Nobody will be able to turn that into a movie."

I always feel I need to get the shape of the thing first. I admit I have a problem with the third act—I find myself most interested in the first and second acts. Unfortunately, by the time you get to the end of the movie, you're just exhausted, so it tends to be a little sloppier—and I'm a little bit that way about scripts. Initially, I find myself more interested in the world and where the characters came from, than I am interested in getting to the end in the most compelling way.

But, you know, the process differs. In *Alien³*, we were moving backward from the idea of sacrifice. In *Se7en*, we knew that we were kind of making this police procedural that would become this horror movie at the end. And then on *The Game*, again, we were working backward from this terrible ending that was going to write itself—and I guess we were sort of moving forward, too—moving forward with this sort of explainable *Twilight Zone*. In the end you can explain it pretty easily—explain it in movie terms. The only problem that we had on *Fight Club* was what we were going to throw out of the book, what are we going to kind of collapse in on itself from the book, and how are we going to end it? But other than that, it was fairly straightforward.

My process is different every time. You know, most of the time you're trying to identify the things that you love about the story and then bring the stuff that you don't like towards that.

And then there's only so much you can actually plan before you shoot it. Things actually never work out exactly the way you think they would and there is always chaos involved. It's actually quite important to have that and you need to be flexible enough to change things if they come up. You hopefully work with actors that are for example talented enough to take their lines into a direction that maybe I have never thought of.

Suddenly the whole thing makes sense, but from a different, richer perspective.

SL: Do you need a lot of feedback and communicate your ideas, or are you rather reclusive during the whole creative process?
DF: If a production designer says to me, "You know, I really hate that scene in the script," that is somebody I'm collaborating with, so I want to know. But when somebody who's doing costume says, "I wish you hadn't cast that person," you know, you kind of go, "I don't know what to do about it now." So it depends: If it's early enough in the process and it's somebody whose opinion I value, then I am more than curious what people think about it. Once you've decided to do something as your next movie, I don't really like to then sit down with people and go, "Tell me why I shouldn't do this." I don't really do that. If I'm enthusiastic about something, I just kind of go, "OK, let's get that out of my system."

SL: How would you describe the center of your creative enthusiasm that gives you direction during the storytelling process?
DF: Well, I mean I like to have done homework walking into something—the cynical or the half-joking side of me would say, "You know, by the time you start shooting the movie, it's pretty much made." And to a certain extent it is. 'Cause every moment is being weighed against this idea of what the thing should be that's in your head. So you are always sort of comparing it against the scene that you sort of previously put together.

Having said that, just comparing two things is not a very open or creative place to be in—and shooting does involve a lot of comparing of what you shoot with what you previously designed in your head.

In fact, you know I really dislike the process of shooting. I've always hated it. I really don't enjoy it. It's getting up early, it's a lot of stress and aggravation and compromise. I really enjoy designing films, I really enjoy working with writers, I really enjoy rehearsal.

SL: Not so much editing?
DF: No. I enjoy it more than shooting, but editing for me—I don't enjoy it as much as prep. I love prep. That for me is so much fun. You go on location, you look at stuff, you go, "Wow, what if we do this, what if we do that?" It's all this world of possibilities, and them all of a sudden it's like [*bitchy voice*], "Yeah, but you gotta be able to do it in two hours, and then you gotta be able to make a company move, and then you gotta

get everybody set, and then you gotta get that person into make-up, and than you gotta get a forced call-in because they were working late the night before." You know you have all that shit that you have to get through. And that's the stuff that I really don't like. If all it is was about sitting in this chair and waiting for all these wonderfully talented photographers, and actors, and costumers to kind of like show up and play dress up, that would be great, but that's like two percent of the job.

SL: So first AD is not on your list of dream jobs.

DF: The nice thing about being a first AD is that you're constantly brokering against reality. There is only so much you can do: It does take x amount of time to run thirteen hundred feet of cable, you know, whether you like it or not: six guys and one hour fifteen minutes. So there are certain givens: to me that job is almost preferable to the six months of trying to seduce a studio to paying what they always consider to be too much for a property. And then you go promising the moon because that's what you really want to do. You're promising what it is you want to do. And then it becomes this inevitable erosion of compromise. And so to me, I'd much rather be the guy who's being pragmatic than the guy who's standing next to the guy who's being pragmatic dreaming [*chuckles*].

SL: It seems to me that filmmaking is always coupled with a creative dilemma: how much subjectivity does it take in order to be unique and relevant, and how much objective convention is necessary so it can still be communicated successfully to a broad audience?

DF: It's all part and parcel of the same thing. The craft of filmmaking is the craft of storytelling and you're dealing with storytelling in a very specific environment and at a specific altar. And at the altar of cinema, there are the ways that things have been done and understood for 125 years. And that's a hard thing to break out of. If it's an idea that's meant to be understood quickly, then chances are—and it depends on how much time you had in the film to introduce that idea within your narrative—that in the first five minutes of any movie, you kind of have set up who the people are. You simply have to start somewhere. So there are certain conventions of it.

On the other hand, when it comes to, "Will it be understood by an audience?" I think you have to make movies for yourself. I don't know any other audience that you can make movies for. I think you have to sit down and think, "Would I understand that? Yeah, that would make sense to me," and then you go and you make that—and then if no one understands, that's the only way you can learn that you're being far too clever.

SL: Making movies for yourself, how would you describe your relationship to the audience: Is it identification or rather one of antagonism to their point of view?

DF: It can be both at the same time. The movie-going public never ceases to amaze me. There are very high-minded ideas that you have, that you put into very simple terms in a movie and gloss over it and throw it away—and you kick yourself for months and in editing while you sit there and say, "Oh my God, why did you throw that away, I should have really understood that. That was such a grand idea and needs to be part of this movie and now I have completely fucked up my opportunity to introduce it. What was I thinking? I'm such an asshole." And then you're walking down the street five years later and somebody goes, "Oh, you did that movie—I loved that thing about it." And then they tell you that they saw that which you believed was gone: it somehow must have survived as part of your storytelling.

And part of it is a bit like with acting: Acting is listening and thinking. And when you watch somebody who is thinking correctly, as an audience member you're walking lockstep with them as they're experiencing this thing. And you know it's not for real—it's a fake thing. The actors aren't really going through that, but they are learning a process of communicating an idea. And it's amazing how many of those ideas get through without ever a word being spoken about it.

The only fun of a first preview screening is watching the things that you never thought were that funny being really funny and all of the jokes that you thought would kill are falling flat; and all of the stuff that you thought was silly becomes scary, and all of the stuff that you thought was really scary is just making people uncomfortable.

SL: What do you make out of these audience reactions when you go back to the editing room?

DF: Well, you don't re-edit, you shape. Again, the experience of making a movie is—you know there are days, sometimes even months—between shooting two ideas. But when they are projecting, they are only seconds apart. So you have to adjust to the experimental nature of the chronology: I mean the chronology for you as a filmmaker. You know you may shoot the last scene of the movie on the first day—and you may not have a very good idea of who all these people are. Also, you are maybe forced to film out of context and in a way that destroys your initial concept of it—and it may not work. But then when you see something that you might have initially been struggling with for a long time, and you might discover that the thing that didn't seem right about it was because you hadn't seen the scene that precedes it. And if the scene just before had been shot chronologically, and you had the ability to move across town or time-travel or whatever in order to do these things back to back, then you could see that what you're doing is fine.

It's true that you always re-adjust things—because you experience things differently with a matinee crowd than you do with a late-evening crowd; you experience a movie differently on television or in a home theater than on a big screen. Movies have many lives. This whole obsession with the first weekend is just such bullshit, because it's not about the first weekend. If you really want to talk about whether the movie's going to make money, you talk about the third weekend. If it's still around then, then it's something. But then, everybody sits and goes, "Oh god, my movie just did $36 million domestically." But wait a minute: now it's going to be experienced in DVD form and now it's going to be experienced on network television. And now it's going to be passed by fans to other like-minded individuals that are going to become fans five to ten years from now. So now I have kids in my daughter's school who go: "Man, I love *Fight Club*," and you go: "Why are your parents letting you watch that? Don't come near my kid."

Forget the First Two Rules of *Fight Club*

Nev Pierce / 2006

From *Total Film*, April 2006, 120–127. Reprinted by permission of Nev Pierce.

You wake up in Hollywood, California. An unmarked building sandwiched between garages at the grubby end of the boulevard—where the Walk of Fame's stars dim with dust and butts. David Fincher's office. "The first article I ever read on *Fight Club* was Alexander Walker's," says Fincher (always Fincher; rarely David). "Yours will be the last."

Total Film and Fincher are in a Spartan, corpse-green conference room, adorned only with a wall-length notice board bearing a timeline of events relating to the "Zodiac" serial killer—the real-life basis for the "newspaper movie" the director hopes will be his next. The focus, however, is *Fight Club*, the 1999 box-office "disaster" Fincher is now "very proud and incredibly happy" to see hailed as an anarchic masterpiece and The Greatest Movie of *Total Film*'s Lifetime. "It's great. I'm flattered," he says, before showing the wry, self-deprecating wit he'll display frequently throughout our two meetings. "I mean, I don't think I can take the rest of the week off. . . ."

Fincher has become inured, at least on the surface, to critical praise or damnation. He's had to. Upon its release, Walker—the *London Evening Standard*'s late, infamously cantankerous critic—laid into *Fight Club* like a ten-pint drunk whose drink you've just spilled. "It is an inadmissible assault on personal decency. And on society itself. . . . It echoes propaganda that gave license to the brutal activities of the SA and the SS. It resurrects the Führer principle." On and on. Any *Total Film* reader won't need telling why he was wrong. And over the interviews with Fincher, Edward Norton, Helena Bonham Carter, Chuck Palahniuk, and Brad Pitt, Mr. Walker's coffin may as well be on a rotisserie; it's going to do a lot of spinning. "Forget the reviews," says Fincher, of the vitriol poured out by certain critics. "Nobody really gives a shit about that." More of an issue for the director was the audience reaction when the picture premiered at the Venice Film Festival. "It was a palpable disaster. It was like people couldn't wait to get out of the theatre, they were made so uncomfortable by the experience. I remember being a little bit, 'Uh-oh.' And Brad's drunk and Edward's drunk and Helena's drunk and they're all like, 'It's great and we love it' and I'm like, 'That's fantastic. You did notice that there were six hundred other people there who walked out ready to lynch us?'"

Then there was the box office. "I was in Bali and I got the fuckin' first weekend grosses and it was a disaster and everybody knew it was a disaster," he recalls. "And you're depressed for a couple of days, but then you go, 'If I knew then what I know now, would I not make it? No. I would have made it anyway.'"

Summer 1997. New York, New York. A baseball-capped figure sits outside a plush apartment, clutching a script. A security guard checks who he is. "David Fincher." A car pulls up and out steps Brad Pitt, worn out from a day shoot-ing Meet Joe Black. *"I'm tired, Finch," says Pitt, balking at the prospect of spending hours discussing* Fight Club. *"No, no, no, no. This is not a big, long conversation, it's a three-minute conversation," says Fincher. "All right," says the star. "Why should I do this movie?" "Because this will be one of the best movies you'll ever be in and probably one of the best movies I'll ever make." Pitt nods slowly. "Okay. Let's go get some pizza."*

I Am Jack's Inflamed Sense of Rejection

Sean Penn could have been Tyler Durden. "I just couldn't get the movie made at the scale I wanted to make it at," explains Fincher, of why *The Game*'s co-star didn't take up the fight. "And I love the irony of it being Pitt, ultimately." Sean Penn could have been the Narrator, too. "But he's too wise, too knowing. He's not guileless enough to be the Narrator." Sean Penn could have been Marla. . . . Okay, no. The studio wanted Winona Ryder. Fincher wanted Janeane Garofalo, but she was "uncomfortable with the idea of all this sex." Courtney Love was considered and rejected, for reasons unclear. (As Chuck Palahniuk tells it, "She was desperate to do it. Fincher said she was too obviously 'the type.'" According to Fincher, she was "romantically involved with Edward and that proved to be problematic.") Thanks to an agent's idiocy, Fincher even ended up pitching the role to *Seinfeld*'s Julia Louis-Dreyfus. "She had no idea who I was. I'm sitting there thinking of myself, 'My God, you are such a fucking loser.'"

Then there was Reese Witherspoon. "She's somebody else who the studio brought up," says Fincher. "I think she's amazingly talented, I just thought she was too young. When you realize Tyler doesn't exist and the Narrator's been abusing Marla himself, it needed to be somebody who, for lack of a better explanation, was there out of choice; not somebody who didn't know any better. I was at Brad's house and he goes, 'Look at this actress; don't think about it, just look at this actress' and he put on the sex scene at the end of *The Wings of the Dove*, when Helena's just so unbelievably sad. I thought she was emotionally exquisite in that movie."

A meeting was swiftly arranged, but Bonham Carter needed convincing. "I think her mother had read the script and just thought it was awful and I think that's partly why she was ambivalent about it. Actually, ambivalent may be giving the material the benefit of the doubt. She may have been repulsed by it."

You wake up in London, England. If you wake up in a different time, in a different place, could you wake up as a different person? Helena Bonham Carter, HBC, Hells, Judy (we'll explain later), what is your power animal? "Tim [Burton] thinks I'm a cat. He's a dog." Which historical figure would you fight? "I've never had the urge to hit anyone." Bonham Carter is at home. And she's laughing (she does this a lot): "Mum put the script outside her bedroom, because it was a pollutant! I didn't get it when I first read it, either. I thought, 'This is weird. Is this message particularly life-enhancing?' But once Fincher explained it to me, I just thought, 'I want to go with this; go with him.' He said he was making a comedy and I thought, 'I completely get your point-of-view now.' I wrote him a huge fax about my misgivings, you know? In it I just said, 'I've got to play it with a big heart.' Marla had to have a heart; otherwise she'd be just a nightmare. I was talking myself into it. By the end of the letter I'd convinced myself to do it."

Was she surprised to be offered the part? "I was, but I was also really pleased because I thought, 'At least somebody sees beyond the corset,' you know? That and at the same time it was just around the Oscar thing so in my cynical way I just thought, 'Oh, this is what happens when you're up for an Oscar.'"

Spring 1998. Beverly Hills, Los Angeles. Brad Pitt is a fidgety ball of energy, bouncing off the furniture in the rehearsal room. Fincher's laid-back in a baseball cap, shoeless feet stretched out on the script-strewn desk. He tosses a Nerf football to Norton, who pings it along to Pitt, back to Finch, onto Norton, back to Pitt, to Finch, to Norton, to Pitt . . . Who slams it home into the basket? "Score!" To one side, sitting in a cloud of smoke, sits Helena Bonham Carter, watching the boys "sizing each other up." Eventually, she stubs out a cigarette and calls, "Hey! Can I have a go?"

I Am Jack's Colon. I Get Cancer, I Kill Jack

"At the end of the shoot I gave Finch an x-ray of my lungs," laughs Bonham Carter. "I had to have an x-ray because I got bronchitis—surprise, surprise—during the six months of filming. And Fincher does so many takes and lots of smoke shots. He got obsessed with the smoke. It had to float in a particular way. So I was just always sitting there in a cemetery of cigarette butts."

"It was kinda funny," says Fincher. "Helena was surrounded by chintz at the Four Seasons, having this kinda civilized life, and then she would go to work at Fox and we'd give her black eyes and put lipstick on her teeth and make her hair all fucked up and make her chain-smoke and gargling old coffee and stuff. It was like she was visiting and she'd have to go down and do all these horrible sex scenes and then go back to the hotel and be polite."

The sex scenes were a particular challenge for the technical team, briefed by Fincher to make the actors look like "one of the statues at Mount Rushmore fucking the Statue of Liberty. It was as if you had these two giant monuments fucking each other and you can sort of fly around them with a helicopter, that was kind of the idea. It was kind of inspired by Francis Bacon. This idea of the twisted perversion of flesh."

Shooting them was resolutely unsexy, however. "It was really weird," says Bonham Carter. "Because me and Brad had to spend a whole day virtually naked, which wasn't bad I guess, with dots all over ourselves, like little stickers. He had white dots and I had black dots and we had to assume different positions in a very overlit studio and be surrounded by all of these still cameras. Fincher would just say, 'And . . . have sex! Okay. And orgasm!' It was just completely absurd, but Brad was very chivalrous."

And then there were the off-camera sound effects. "That was just HBC and I sitting in a room screaming our guts out," says Pitt. "The sad thing is we had no qualms about it, no politeness, no little hint of embarrassment—just go!"

"One of the studio's issues with the material was how we were going to handle the sex between Marla and Tyler," says Fincher, whose trade-off for the studio shelling out on Pitt's dentistry (they paid for the removable cap that ensured Tyler could have a chipped tooth) was that the star would sometimes take his shirt off. He did it twice. One of which was when he opens the door after sex with Marla—wearing a rubber glove. "We had that take starred and sent over to Fox under the guise of, 'Look! Look how good he looks, he has his shirt off!'" laughs Fincher. "I've learned that one way to control people is to give them other things to worry about. If you're worried that somebody is too fearful you can either try to empower them or you can give them so much to fear that they just don't want to be around you. Either way you've sort of neutralized them!"

The biggest concern of the studio, though, was not the sex, or the violence, but one line: when Marla lies back in bed with Tyler and says—and this makes even Tyler shudder—"I want to have your abortion."

"I always thought it was a good line and it made people uncomfortable," recalls Fincher. "But they didn't want to get into the whole Religious Right thing. I mean, this movie is the poster child for movies that should be picketed. And Laura [Ziskin, president of Fox 2000] begged me, 'Please come up with something else.'" Fincher agreed, but only on condition he wouldn't have to change it again. Then Ziskin heard the changed line ("I haven't been fucked like that since grade school"). "You know in *E.T.*," says Fincher, gleefully, "when his head extends up on his neck? Laura did the inverse. The first vertebrates in her neck just contracted wafer thin. She just cringed so hard."

You wake up in Manhattan, New York. Lose an hour, gain an hour. Edward Norton is taking two out from editing the modern western *Down in the Valley*, on which he is lead actor/cutter. His power animal? "It's pretty hard to top the penguin." His historical figure? "I'd be happy to go twelve rounds with any member of Bush's cabinet." He's recounting the grade school story and laughing hard. "They begged him to put the other one back and he wouldn't!" There's no doubt, Norton knows how significant *Fight Club* is. But for all his intellectual edge and perception—his demolition of the critics; name-checks from Nietzsche to Goya; spot-on analysis of how the film nailed the zeitgeist—the overwhelming sense from him is that *Fight Club* was, well, fun.

"We were looking at each other going, 'We can't believe a studio is going to give us this much money to make this movie. They're giving us $70 million to make a movie that they are going to fucking hate!'" he laughs. "From the beginning, when we got the book, we all had the same response, sort of half-laugh, half jaw-dropping that someone was saying those things. We felt that this is for us and our crowd. Not in an inside-joke sense, but very much this is about our times as we have experienced them. We definitely had the feeling that if a lot of people didn't understand it, then we'd probably done it right. Now and then I'll give a script that I'm working on to my dad. He's a very smart, very broad-minded guy. He loved *The Graduate*, and he gave me this look like, 'Why the hell would you want to do this?' In a way it was liberating because it confirmed that feeling that this was a generational statement to me."

And what is that statement? "In part, *Fight Club* turns on the Baby Boomer generation and says, 'Fuck you for the world you made.' Of course it's irritating, at the least, to some people." Little wonder *Fight Club* riled so many viewers, then—as Pitt acknowledges, "It attacks a way of life, it attacks the status quo that men have given forty years to. They can't roll over now."

But it did find an audience. With time, it connected. It was on the tip of everyone's tongue. Tyler just gave it a name. "We would have loved for it to be *The Matrix*, you know what I mean?" says Norton. "But it just couldn't be and it may have been the way it was supposed to be. The movie itself was like the experience of *Fight Club* is for the people in the movie. It was the kind of thing that you didn't want other people to understand, you didn't want other people to tell you it was okay, you wanted to find it yourself, talk about it with your friends and that's how it radiated out."

Norton discovered how much it had "radiated" when Dustin Hoffman phoned him up and asked him to read the Edward Albee play *Zoo Story* at his daughter's high school. "It's very much about the inability to connect with other people and the sense that maybe an act of violence is the only way to get someone to pay attention to you," says Norton. "And we did this Q&A after and these kids immediately started comparing it to *Fight Club*. This was six months after the movie came out. You could feel the parents and the teachers in the room looking around and whispering to each other, 'What is this?' It became the conversation in this entire school how this play is just the *Fight Club* of its time. I called Fincher up saying, 'There's a whole school of twelve-to-seventeen-year-olds in Santa Monica who are obsessed with the film and none of their parents even know what it is!' That was our experience of it, it kind of leaking in slowly. I went to some concert around that time and as I was walking out, these two young guys turned and looked at me and said, 'Nice to see you out and about, sir.' I was like, 'Aww, man, this is weird.'"

But the older generation still doesn't get it. "I really think that *Fight Club* is an expression of a lot of the same things that our parents' generation got out of *The Graduate*, but explored through a very different lens," observes Norton. "I think the Baby Boomer generation was a much more innocent generation than ours. *Fight Club* really, really got down into the textures of the world we grew up in and the psychological impact of those particular pop culture/marketing/advertising/materialist experiences. I'm not saying nobody over the age of forty-five understood the film—that's ludicrous, lots of people deeply appreciated it—but I think for the same reasons a lot of Baby Boomers didn't understand Nirvana, they didn't understand *Fight Club*. I think a lot of the Baby Boomers looked at their children and said, 'Why so negative?' I don't think they related to the ambivalence of our generation. We have grown up with so much broader a sense of global dynamics, of the impending catastrophes of the environment and the economy and world politics and nuclear war—all mainlined into us at a speed that they can't comprehend. I think that feeling of being overwhelmed at a very young age, being overwhelmed at the prospect of trying to engage in adult life, just didn't resonate for them the way it does for us. But I think at its core *Fight Club* springs out of a feeling of being overwhelmed and alienated, cut off from anything that feels like an authentic sense of being alive. If you choose to fully explore what are the roots of those negative feelings, on the way to maybe suggesting that there's a way out of that, you're going to lose a lot of people."

"My mom," chuckles Pitt, reflecting on the generation divide, "she actually justifies the movie because I play a character who's not really real. She can sleep at night, 'cause it's really Edward doing it!"

Autumn 2001. Manhattan, New York. The air is thick with smoke. People are screaming, crying, looking horrified at the sky. The second plane smashes into the second tower. The world has changed.

I Am Jack's Cold Sweat

"*Fight Club* was never meant to be, 'Watch out or this will happen!'" says Fincher, reflecting on the link between the film's skyscraper-smashing conclusion and the attack on the World Trade Center of two years later. "For me it goes back to the Monty Python routine where Graham Chapman says, 'Who can honestly say that at one time or another he hasn't set fire to some great public building?' For me it was more deeply rooted in Monty Python than it was in, you know, *Fail-Safe*. It was a very oblique look at where some of this could take us. Chuck Palahniuk is a prescient guy."

"Yeah," says Norton. "I think that you can carry it too far and yet I agree. I don't think that's what's being explored in *Fight Club* is deeply interrelated with, you know, those kinds of events, but on the other hand certainly there's something in there, when you're talking about the kind of furious compulsion to tear down, like, everything that's oppressive about modern consumer material society. You have to be careful, because there's nothing positive or valid in those real-world actions, but there may be something in the psychology of it that has echoes to the kind of frustrations that are being expressed in that film. . . ."

You wake up in Portland, Oregon. This is your life and it's ending one minute at a time. Chuck Palahniuk. Power animal: "Oh, the penguin." Historical figure? "Jesus would be good. It isn't fighting in the traditional sense. It's more consensual—exploring power through an organized kind of S&M. Jesus would understand that, because spiritually he was into endurance and asceticism." Palahniuk is where it all began. "I read scripts all the time," says Pitt. "And after a while you just start seeing the same thing. Then, out of nowhere, comes this voice: Chuck Palahniuk." Fincher seems genuinely awed by his talent; his "beautiful prose." "To me," says Fincher, "the movie is 60 to 70 percent of what the book is and that's as much as I think you could do in 1999 in Hollywood." Says Palahniuk, "I actually wish they'd taken more license with the book and surprised me a little bit more." Not that he doesn't love it. "It's raised the standards and made me disgusted with most movies!" And he has a line on why, perhaps, the likes of Walker and US critic Roger Ebert (who called the film "cheerfully fascist") were so down on *Fight Club*. "It strikes a chord with young men, but tends to frighten older men," he says. "They have the power, but they're not ready to give it up. They recognize the world they're moving into isn't their world, and that's gotta be scary." Palahniuk took a backseat with the adaptation. "My editor told me not to get excited when it was optioned because only 2 percent of books are ever optioned and only 2 percent of them ever get made into movies. I had some conversations with the screenwriter, Jim Uhls, but I thought I would just fuck it up if I tried to control it." He did, however, visit the set, taking along some of the real-life inspirations behind the book's unforgettable characters. "I briefly went down," he says. "I took a handful of friends who met the actors who were playing them. 'Tyler Durden' now lives in Bend, Oregon. He's a carpenter. He was a rebel who wasn't sure what he wanted but knew that he didn't want what he was getting. He was ready to fight everything just so he was fighting. Just a big bundle of anger and angst."

And Palahniuk helped the actors, whether he remembers it or not. "I spoke to Chuck," recalls Bonham Carter. "And I got a feel for the person who inspired Marla and I read the book in and out." The other touchstone was an idea from costume designer Michael Kaplan. Recalls Fincher, "He said, 'Here's who she is' and showed me a picture of Judy Garland. I was like, 'Run with it, it's a great idea.' We'd call her Judy, just out of fun. Or Liza. But mostly we called her Hells. 'Hells, daarrling!'" Kaplan wasn't the only unlikely voice, with Cameron Crowe having a somewhat surprising, but crucial, influence on the script. "I talked to Cameron," says Fincher, "because we had problems with Tyler. And he's like, 'It's easy! The real problem with Tyler is that Tyler knows the answer. You've got to take out that Tyler knows the answer, so that every time somebody says to him, "My life's fucked up, what should I do?," instead of him saying, "Well you do this" you have him say, "I don't know, I don't know your situation, I don't even know you, but if it was me, I'd try this, because at least you might learn something, even if it's painful." Screenwriter Andrew Kevin Walker (*Se7en*) was drafted in for the changes—about 20 percent of the script, by Fincher's reckoning ("Jim had done all the fuckin' heavy lifting")—but the Writers' Guild of America denied him a credit. Hence, the three detectives who try to castrate the Narrator are credited, "Detective Andrew, Detective Kevin, Detective Walker."

Autumn 1998. Beverly Hills, Los Angeles. Pitt's No smoke without ire: tossed Norton's stunt double down the stairs several times already. Eventually, Fincher will use take one. Now, he's heading for take twelve. Pitt grabs the guy and chucks him. . . . Out, out, out, missing the first flight of steps and—CRUNCH!—slamming like meat on a chopping block, down onto the first landing. Fincher gasps. There's a long, long silence. The crew is waiting. The director takes his hands from his mouth and says, voice questioning, "Um, cut?"

I Am Jack's Smirking Revenge

"Fincher does all these tough things and he's such a puss when it comes to blood and injuries," laughs Norton. "There's a shot in the movie where Brad throws me through the toll booth of a parking lot and I crawl under a car. It's an elaborate shot and Fincher wanted to do it all in one. So we did it a lot of times. Like a lot. Like twenty or twenty-five times. I remember going into a head state of like, 'Fuck it. I can do as many as he wants me to, because there's no going back now.' Eventually Brad started getting uncomfortable, around thirty-three or thirty-four, and he said, 'Look, seriously, no more. He's really getting beat up!' Fincher just goes,

'Last one, I swear! Last one!' So I went crawling under the car as hard as I could and I was too tired and I didn't duck enough and I really rang my head hard against the transmission and sort of screamed and he jumps up and goes, 'That was the one!'"

"Yeah, a lot of people got hurt," remembers Fincher. "We had people with dislocated fingers and broken ribs. We didn't want burly stunt guys, we wanted them to look like scrawny prep cooks and concierges and bellmen. The great news about actors is they all, ironically, look like waiters. . . ."

The oddest experience, though, was surely for the leads, whose injuries started mirroring each other. "It was weird," says Norton. "Like, I jammed my thumb really badly and then Brad jammed his thumb, and then he really took a bad shot to the ribs and he was hurt under his ribs and I remember thinking, 'Ooh, I hope I don't get that one!' And then like a week later I fell on it right on my ribs. I remember walking out of the soundstage holding my ribs and Brad was like, 'Noooo!'" It wasn't the only parallel. The pair did a lot of "fun things"—they learnt to make soap and, at the mischievous suggestion of Fincher, Norton hired the same truck as his co-star. He also chose to lose weight for the role of the Narrator, while Pitt bulked up for Tyler. "Fincher and I both thought a little bit of *Fight Club* as like a drug metaphor," says Norton. "The Narrator talks like a junkie. And the more the Narrator falls apart, the more in his mind Tyler is becoming more and more idealized. I don't remember if it was a conscious conversation between me and Brad and Fincher, but I know Brad got bigger and bigger the more the shoot went on and I got smaller and smaller and felt worse and worse and I think it just seemed right. It seemed like the right progression, because it takes him a long time to see that it's not empowering him anymore, he's turning into a bruised, scabbed skeleton and I think I tried to go as far as I could with that."

The differences weren't only physical, with the stars' acting styles contrasting, too. "Edward's strength is he always knows where he wants to be within the context of the story," says Pitt. "The drawback is sometimes his planning keeps it from being fresh, in theory anyways, but the guy is just so exquisitely good that he never gets in the way. I'm the opposite, I let the day dictate what's going to happen and so for me it's more of a hit-and-miss. The drawback for me is when I'm missing I'm really missing, I don't have that to fall back on."

"Brad's more anarchic," says Bonham Carter. "He's more instinctive and intuitive and playful and prepared to be extremely bad in order to release something interesting. I think people who are willing to go off the deep-end are going to be the most exciting and unpredictable. And Ed's got amazing facility but he's very intellectual. But they were both really impressive."

It was up to Fincher to juggle the different personalities and styles. "They aren't fuckin' puppets, you know?" he recalls. "No matter how far you stick your hand up their asses you can't make their lips move. A dance is two people and when you're dancing with a camera, a dance is five people. It can be tricky."

Everyone, though, is full of praise for the director, in a manner that he would no doubt find embarrassing face to face. "He's got the most encyclopedic knowledge technically of any filmmaker I've worked with," says Bonham Carter. Although, regarding the amount of takes he demands, she adds, "As long as the camera's moving, don't even start acting until take twelve!"

"I remember when Fincher sent me the book," recalls Norton. "I thought, just off having seen *Se7en*, 'This is such a great guy to make this movie because he is completely comfortable posing questions and refusing to give you the answer. That's the kind of courage needed to make *Fight Club*.' I mean, it's a high compliment to say, I think he just doesn't give a fuck, you know? He really doesn't. He's human, and more than he lets on he's as susceptible as any of us to that sort of reflexive disappointment when a movie doesn't catch a wave, but he never baulked at all. His leadership gave everybody the courage to say, 'We're going to go all the way.'"

I Am Jack's Broken Heart

You wake up in Hollywood, California. It's the second meeting with Fincher, after a weekend spent discussing *Fight Club* with half its cast. His power animal? "A scorpion." Historical figure? "I don't know . . . Irving Thalberg." He chuckles, "If I had a dime for every person that was offended by that movie, I'd buy the negative from Rupert Murdoch. I was born to make this movie." You wake up in Beverly Hills, California. "It's an amazing movie," says Pitt. "It's provocative, but thank God it's provocative. People are hungry for films like this, films that make them think." You wake up in London, England. Bonham Carter says, "Fincher's got a big streak of a girlie. He's a huge softie. He's deliciously soft and vulnerable and a really nice person. He bullies everyone but he's not a proper bully, it's 'Come on, cry babies! And again and again and again!'"

You wake up in Manhattan, New York. "Fincher can be a pretty hard-ass in his talk and sarcastic," says Norton. "But I think it's not insignificant that he decided to put the ending in a different place than the book. You know, even though the Narrator's shot through the cheek and the world is falling down, when he turns to her and says, "I'm okay," I actually believe him. Like it doesn't matter, you still have to ultimately link up with other people and care about other people if not all the bullshit around you. I thought it was kind of hopeful." You wake up in Hollywood. Again. "It's less of a love story than it is an apology," says Fincher. "It's an apology for bad behavior."

Autumn 1999. Venice, Italy. The premiere audience hates the picture. It doesn't matter. The credits roll, the house lights flicker on. Pitt turns to Norton and smiles, "That's the best movie I'm ever going to be in." The crowds are dispersing. Some people storm out shouting, "Fascists, fascists!" Norton nods, "Me, too."

Nev Pierce is a journalist and screenwriter. You can read more of his work at nevpierce.com.

David Fincher of *Zodiac*

Shawn Levy / 2007

From the *Oregonian*, March 2, 2007. Reprinted by permission of Shawn Levy.

"What do you think? What are our chances? Do you think anyone will go to a movie that lasts this long and requires this much of its audience?"

Usually it's the journalist who asks the questions during an interview. But these queries come from David Fincher, director of *Se7en*, *Fight Club*, *Panic Room*, and, now, *Zodiac*. It's a fine new film about the crimes of and hunt for the infamous Bay Area serial killer of the 1970s who called himself by that astrological name in taunting letters to the press and police.

Like other Fincher films, *Zodiac* is full of violence and drama and movie stars (Jake Gyllenhaal, Robert Downey Jr., Mark Ruffalo) and exquisite craft. But, also like other Fincher films, it's long and dark and complex and demanding. Although it's likely to satisfy anyone who enjoys Fincher's other films or such dense entertainments as *The Departed* and *The Usual Suspects*, an estimated $85 million of studio money is at stake. No wonder Fincher is seeking a little affirmation.

Now in his mid-forties, Fincher spent his childhood in the Bay Area—where he witnessed the Zodiac era in real time and had George Lucas as a neighbor—and his high school years in Ashland. He spoke to the *Oregonian* recently from his Los Angeles office.

Shawn Levy: *Zodiac* is a story about real people who were brutally murdered or wounded and who are either still around or still have families alive. Do you feel an obligation to the survivors and relatives?

David Fincher: Yes. You know, we could've made this movie without ever having interviewed anybody, and we didn't want to do that. We wanted to get the real story, and we wanted them to know that we didn't just want to depict their anonymous suffering as "Victim No. 4." We wanted to know what really happened and the fallout from it. I feel a responsibility to that. When you're portraying people's real lives, you owe them the responsibility and dignity of telling them what you're gonna do and then sticking to that. My reputation aside, I really don't set out to offend anybody. And especially not people who've suffered.

SL: The film is built around this trio of people trying to solve the crime (reporter Paul Avery, detective David Toschi, and cartoonist and independent investigator Robert Graysmith). Do you feel particularly close to any one of them in personality or attitude?

DF: I feel about the same for all of them. They're sort of all pieces of who I am. Avery, the pro, says things like, "This guy killed only five people; more people die every year in the East Bay commute." He's the tortured realist; he'd love to get involved and get broken up about stuff, but he doesn't. And then Toschi, who thinks you have to let things go. Graysmith is the compulsive part of my personality.

SL: Internet sites that follow film production have suggested that this film might have been out sooner, maybe in time for Oscar consideration. Was there a lot of delay in finishing?

DF: Well, making movies is hard. It takes a long time. And we reshot a lot of stuff, and some of it's better and some of it's not. We had to play around with it and do some test screenings, with the intent of assuaging everyone's fears. And we didn't. So then you go through that whole rigmarole of, "Let's all see what the movie actually is." And we did that for six months, and it got to the shape that it has now. We reached a concession point. I wasn't gonna make it any shorter, and they weren't going to let me make it any longer. So it's where it should be.

SL: What sort of things did you lose that you wish you had saved?

DF: There was some stuff in the original cut that I would have loved to have seen in the final cut, but they just wouldn't sit still for it. There was an entire scene where the cops run down some district attorney with their case against Arthur Leigh Allen (a suspect). And I just love it because it's so *Charlie's Angels*: just three guys talking into a speakerphone. But the audience was, "You're kidding, right? Five minutes of guys talking into a speakerphone?" Well, the audience spoke, and the audience said no.

SL: You took great pains to achieve a period look for the film, it seems to me. What portion of your attention do you reckon you put into things like decor and props and wardrobe?

DF: Probably far too much! I hope it's the right amount. It starts early on. We would always try to find anything that was real. Reality is good enough for me, and that's what we did. "What would the outside of this character's house look like?" Well, we got some pictures and we knew. Between the truth and something that was beautiful, we opted to go with the truth.

Our other mantra was, "Let's make sure that we don't do pastiche." It's one thing to do an homage, but I didn't want to make a movie about sideburns. I wanted it to be a movie about people, and I wanted it to be about the seventies in San Francisco that I knew growing up. So when in doubt, I would reference old photos and go, like, "Yeah, that's about how many Volkswagen Bugs you'd see on the street, so that's what we'll do."

SL: When you did that visual research, did you find that the period differed from your impressions from your childhood?

DF: It was pretty much as I remembered it. The one thing that changed was my understanding of the Zodiac case, which was based on a seven-year-old's memory. As a kid, I always thought Zodiac's body count was much higher and that there was this huge manhunt to find this guy. It turns out it was two guys with these rotary phones and Bic pens. Even when they were telling us on television that they were going through computer files comparing fingerprints, the reality was that the technology didn't exist in any truly useful format until later. The seventies was a little bit of a technological backwater. They didn't have fax machines. And we wanted to talk about that—not to harp on it but to remind people that those times were more primitive.

The Devil Is in the Detail

Nev Pierce / 2007

From *Total Film*, March 26, 2007, 62–67. Reprinted by permission of Nev Pierce.

"The guy gets two takes. If he doesn't get it, cut his fucking arms off and leave him in the alley."

It's January 6, 2006.

Day 77 of the *Zodiac* shoot.

David Fincher is a little tetchy.

A monitor plays back the latest take of Robert Downey Jr. and Jake Gyllenhaal trading information in a smoky Los Angeles-standing-in-for-San Francisco bar. "This guy . . ." says Fincher, showing an assistant director the extra offending his eye, ". . . staple his feet to the floor."

Across the floor, the actors wait for the next take. "He's pissed," Gyllenhaal mutters to Downey. "Can you hear him?"

Fincher tosses his headphones onto a hook and turns to face *Total Film*. "Hopefully one day. . . ." He sighs. ". . . This will all be worth it."

March 2, 2007. *Zodiac* opens in America. The poster declares "From the director of *Se7en* and *Panic Room*," but audiences shouldn't expect head-in-a-box shocks or a whiplash thriller. The reality is an engrossing, seventies-set account of how a naively tenacious cartoonist (Gyllenhaal),a drunken reporter (Downey), and two polyester-clad cops (Mark Ruffalo and Anthony Edwards) tried to find a publicity-craving serial killer. The drama isn't in the poster's fog-shrouded image of the Golden Gate Bridge, but the pain-clouded eyes of the story's desperate investigators. Steven Soderbergh thinks *Zodiac* is Fincher's best film. James Ellroy claims it's "one of the greatest crime movies ever made." John Travolta's "feeble farce" *Wild Hogs* beats it to number one at the US box office. So it goes.

David Fincher was seven when he first encountered the Zodiac Killer. One day, he noticed the Highway Patrol was escorting his bus home from school. He asked his dad about it. "Oh, that's right," said Jack Fincher, a *Life* magazine journalist and author. "There's a guy who's murdered four people and he's sent a letter to the newspaper threatening to shoot out the tires of a school bus and kill the children on it." Fincher laughs about this now—"I remember for the first time really wondering whether my parents were competent to take care of children . . ."—but the incident stayed with him. It persuaded him to read James Vanderbilt's adaptation of Robert Graysmith's bestselling books on the killings (*Zodiac* and *Zodiac Unmasked*), when his natural instinct had long been to avoid serial killer material, having made the most notorious serial killer thriller ever: *Se7en.*

"When he said he was interested, I was floored," says Vanderbilt. "But he said, 'I've done a serial killer movie. I'm not interested in repeating myself. I see something closer to *All the President's Men.* It's a newspaper story.' I was like, 'He gets it!'"

"Oh, I like that one a lot!"

David Fincher is in a good mood. He watches a scene play back with Downey Jr., who's stood in sweaty safari jacket and sandals as hard-drinking and drug-shoveling San Francisco Chronicle *reporter Paul Avery. The atmosphere is light, chit-chatty.*

"What does your tattoo say?" asks Céan Chaffin—Fincher's whip-smart regular producer and his long-time girlfriend—indicating Downey's ankle.

"Elias. It's my actual last name."

A crewmember leans into the room. "Do you need a rehearsal?"

Fincher points at Downey in disbelief. "For him to look like a drunken reveler?"

Zodiac is not a serial killer movie—it just happens to have a serial killer in it: a man who terrorized San Francisco and Northern California in the late sixties and early seventies and who became the most notorious multiple murderer since Jack the Ripper. Rarely have so few bodies generated so much ink. In a series of taunting, boastful letters to the *San Francisco Chronicle*, Zodiac claimed to have killed at least thirty-seven people, but history records only five confirmed kills. He just had a knack for marketing. "He branded himself before he gave a name," says Vanderbilt. "He put out his version of the Nike swoosh: the first letter was signed with just the crosshair symbol. . . ."

The symbol would haunt San Francisco for years. But Fincher wanted to get beyond the horror and the hype to the reality of the killings—and the effect they had on those who investigated them. *Zodiac* producer

Brad Fischer, who developed the material with Vanderbilt, recalls his first meeting with Fincher, "He said, 'My hat's off to you guys for taking this massive amount of information and putting it all into this 158-page document. Now let's put the script in a drawer and go up to the Bay area and meet every single person who was involved in this investigation.'" So they did, spending eighteen months interviewing witnesses, detectives and surviving victims. Fischer hired a private investigator to track down Mike Mageau, who survived being shot by the Zodiac—as recounted in the film's chilling opening—but has since led a dislocated life, largely on the streets. When Fischer interviewed him, he was in jail in Las Vegas.

"We also met the two informants who went to the police about [prime suspect] Arthur Leigh Allen," says Fischer. "When you sit there and look somebody in the eye and they're telling you about this person who said he was going to write letters to the press and call himself the Zodiac Killer and shoot out the tires of a school bus and pick off the kiddies as they came bouncing out . . . you get a clearer sense for yourself of whether you feel he's full of shit. And we didn't get a feeling he was full of shit. That's why it was important."

Everything in the script needed to be verified. Police reports were studied, urban legends were cut. The Zodiac killings crossed jurisdictions and proved a bureaucratic nightmare for the investigators. Researching the film actually highlighted evidence that had previously been ignored or forgotten, while interviewees were more receptive to Hollywood than to the law. As Fincher has it: "Making a movie is a lot friendlier than being the Department of Justice's eighth investigator in thirty-five years."

Still, sitting in the edit suite, halfway through the shoot, Fincher is musing: "I don't know how many people are going to believe that what we're telling them is true. . . ."

On screen, a pretty girl is lying by the picturesque Lake Berryessa, being stabbed to death. She sobs. She screams. A hooded man knifes her repeatedly. "She was good, man," reflects Fincher, of Pell James, who played Cecelia Shepard, Zodiac's fourth murder victim. "She was so game. My God. We did thirty-five takes of that stabbing because we just couldn't get the piece to look like he was actually stabbing her. So we shot thirty-five takes and then we went back the next week and shot thirty more. She was black and blue. She got it, though."

Fincher talks about *Funny Games*, Michael Haneke's ruthless anti-thriller. An upsetting exploration of everyday violence, it's clearly a reference point for the eerily straightforward murders in *Zodiac*. "I want it to be simple," says Fincher. "Here it is: it's right here. A guy comes in and goes, 'I'm going to tie you up. Get on your stomach.' And all of a sudden, you're just fucked."

Bryan Hartnell, who survived the Berryessa attack, was consulted for the scene. Fincher is a little concerned about how he'll react to a joke—about his studies—which they've put into the dialogue. There's clearly a tension between dotting every "i" and entertaining an audience (as it turns out, Hartnell will be more than satisfied with the finished picture). "It's walking the line," says Fincher. "Ken Narlow [a detective involved in the Zodiac case] was there on the day we shot the stabbings. As soon as they walked out the trailer, he burst into tears and couldn't watch. He just said, 'They look so much like them and I forgot how young they were—oh my God.'"

Fincher feels a sense of responsibility to that. It's one Hollywood has not always felt. Back in 1971, *Dirty Harry* riffed on the real-life killings (with Zodiac cunningly renamed "Scorpio"), even as the killer was still sending teasing letters to the *Chronicle*. "People were in fear. It was upsetting, the letters and the taunting," says Fincher. "Then *Dirty Harry* sort of used Zodiac as a jumping off point. . . . There's a big moment in *Zodiac* where the police department watch it and kind of go, 'Wow.' And all those guys cooperated with that movie. I'm sure Dave Toschi [the detective played by Ruffalo] met with Clint Eastwood. He certainly met with Steve McQueen [for *Bullitt*]." Nonetheless, Eastwood—a revered figure at Warner Bros., who co-financed *Zodiac* with Paramount—is notable by his absence from the *Dirty Harry* footage shown in Fincher's film. "He didn't want to be in a serial killer movie," says the director, with weariness but no recrimination. "I guess he's done enough of them."

Harris Savides, the cinematographer, has made final adjustments to the scene lighting.

"I like it," says Fincher. "It feels real."

Gyllenhaal wanders over and puts his arm around Savides. "Watch out," says Fincher. "You'll get a hug."

A Starbucks run arrives. The production assistant makes sure Fincher has decaf. "They don't want to get me hopped up!"

Downey and Gyllenhaal sit on the bar stools, ready for action. Take one. . . .

Downey: "What's that drink you're drinking? That's my real question to you."

The script supervisor turns to Fincher: "Did you like that line he added?"

"No. I hate it when he does that."
Take two, take three, take four. . . .
Gyllenhaal: "It's called a Blue Alga. It's redundant, but it's good."
Fincher calls across: "Speaking of redundancy. . . ."
Take five, take six, take seven, take eight, take nine, take ten. . . .
"Last one," promises Fincher.
"What does that mean?" Savides asks the script supervisor.
"It means there's five more," she says.
There are actually two more takes.

In the edit suite, the Berryessa sequence ends and another scene flickers across the wall-mounted monitor: Gyllenhaal as *Chronicle* cartoonist Robert Graysmith, walking across the newspaper offices to where the staff has gathered to read another letter from the killer. Fincher wants to know if it looks "period." He's concerned to avoid kitsch. "I didn't want to make a movie about sideburns; I didn't want to make a movie about plaid and flared pants, bell bottoms and platform shoes."

He hasn't. Stylistically the film will be considered a departure for Fincher: the MTV auteur, famous/notorious for his envelope-pushing camerawork and supposedly in-your-face aesthetic. Visually, it's relatively simple: two-shots, few cuts, stable camera. Some reviewers will say this is the director maturing. They'll be wrong. He's just using the right tools for the job. The frame-rattling visual virtuosity of *Fight Club* matched the anarchy and aggression of Tyler Durden. The elaborate, digitally enhanced track through *Panic Room*'s house established the geography of the claustrophobic thriller (and, alright, maybe there was a little bit of showing off). And in *Zodiac*, the camera's steady, matter-of-fact focus on people is because that is where the story lies. As ever, Fincher uses CGI and whizz-bang visuals only when it's necessary—as in a key scene when dogged detectives Toschi and Bill Armstrong (Edwards) walk through the *Chronicle* offices and digitally generated symbols— from the killer's coded messages—hang in the air. A passing of time, growing obsession and a sense of panic are all deftly conveyed in a few seconds. It's superbly economical storytelling (though it cost thousands of dollars). "He could have shot the shit out of this thing," says Vanderbilt. "And I think the reason he didn't is not because he's 'matured,' but because he's a great storyteller and he just wants to serve the story. And that's why he's such a joy to work for." A joy for the screenwriter, then, and the producers—but a Fincher gig is never easy on the actors. . . .

"My first day was sixty-eight takes with Jake and I was like, 'Please kill me,'" says Mark Ruffalo, whose nuanced, subtle turn as worn-down cop Toschi is the stand-out in an impressive ensemble. "When Fincher came walking over at one point I was like, 'I hope he's coming here to fire me.' Then I realized it had nothing to do with Jake and I. . . . Well, maybe the last thirty takes were us, but it was a huge dolly crane shot with thirty extras, five pages of dialogue, and a really intense scene. . . . So there were a lot of things in play. It doesn't mean he doesn't respect the actors and their processes, but he does want people to be the best he believes they can be. Sometimes with 'movie stars,' we want to come in and be a little lazy and do our 'good enough' and go home . . . [but] I know what David's set up is. He's taking a stab at immortality—he knows that. Somewhere along the way I think Fincher said to himself, 'Good enough is not fucking good enough.'"

"He's kind of a sweet guy," says Downey Jr. "But then you're on the set and he knows more than most directors and more than is probably appropriate. So he's just . . . I hate to say 'right.' . . ."

Robert Downey Jr. is on fire. The resurgent actor has been smoking nicotine-free cigarettes throughout his latest scene. But, for reasons best known to himself, he's been stubbing the butts out in tissue paper—which has finally ignited, underneath Gyllenhaal's seat. There's much laughter.

Fincher walks past and Downey offers an exaggerated flinch. . . .

The scene resets. Fincher disappears to the monitor and calls across: "Last one."

"Yeah, right," says Gyllenhaal.

"Have a little faith," says a crewmember.

"Come on!" says Gyllenhaal. "We're going to fuck all night!" At lunch, he looks tired.

"I don't want to satisfy that part of David that enjoys having people hear that it's not easy," he says, of the repeated takes. "But it gets tedious. It really does. . . . It can be pretty intense."

October 17, 2006. Fincher is considering his actors, the difficulty of managing performances and personalities. "The alchemy of it is so complex," he muses. "You know, it's easy to like people for two hours. . . . It's hard to like people for 120 days. They do kind of get on your nerves."

He isn't referring to anyone specific. But it's obvious from being on set that some actors find it frustrating: the marathon of capturing the mini moments that correspond to the movie in Fincher's head. "You know, Downey likes to play, but he likes to know there's light at the end of the tunnel." And how did Gyllenhaal cope? "I can tell you I don't think he had a real good time," says Fincher, who cast him on the basis of *Donnie Darko*. "But I can also tell you that I still sleep at night. . . ."

He leans back at his desk. Face deadpan.

On the wall there's a painting of waves crashing against a beach, with a motto of sorts inscribed across it: "PITILESS PURITY DUDE."

His office is clean; hard-edged and functional.

There's a couch, but it doesn't look slept on.

There are books of photography on the coffee table, but they don't look read.

Work goes on here.

On the desk are notes from Fischer, Vanderbilt, and Warner Bros. about the latest cut of *Zodiac*.

The final version is yet to be locked down and Fincher will continue to tweak and trim for a few weeks, even as he starts shooting his next collaboration with Brad Pitt, an ambitious F. Scott Fitzgerald adaptation *The Curious Case of Benjamin Button*. (The leaner cut will prove less artful in places, but arguably more arresting.)

For now, he's considering how to market the movie. Ironically, given Zodiac was a master of self-publicity, it's proving difficult. He glances briefly at the poster, propped against the wall. "Obviously there's no way they're going to put a poster up which doesn't talk about *Se7en*," he says. "But my point is, 'If you want bad word of mouth, you'll make people think this is *Se7en*. . . .'"

Fincher is fascinated by the idea that the Zodiac's compulsion, ultimately, wasn't killing, but communicating with the *Chronicle*. "That became far more gratifying and seductive than what he started out doing. . . ." So, he was an attention seeker: surely a trait a director can identify with. It may be the basest reason—behind the exploration of ideas, the interest in human behavior—Fincher directs. "Look," he says. "There are times when you're [in a screening] ready to throw up and fifteen hundred people all laugh at a joke you worked so hard to get right or they all gasp. It's pretty great you can make that happen. It's the trained dog in every director that, you know, has that need and wants to do a back-flip and see everybody clap."

A sort of pathological need to be liked?

"I'm not that hooked on being liked!" He laughs. "But I enjoy being able to manipulate, being able to elicit. . . . I think that's fun."

Marketing, it's fair to say, is less so. *Zodiac*'s imposing-but-chilly one-sheet campaign doesn't present it as an intriguing cold case or give it a human face and Fincher is going back and forth with the studio to ensure the trailer "doesn't insinuate it's *The Grudge* or something. . . ."

He speaks with a mix of incredulity and faint amusement. For the director who survived *Alien³* and the marketing battles of *Fight Club*, this is a mere skirmish. The important thing is finishing the movie. "Films aren't finished," he notes. "They're abandoned." So, was it worth it? "I won't know," he says. "I won't know for ten years."

Nev Pierce is a journalist and screenwriter. You can read more of his work at nevpierce.com.

A Curious Case of Friendship

Scott Bowles / 2008

From *USA Today*, November 28, 2008. Reprinted by permission of Guy Scott Bowles, staff writer, *USA Today*.

Brad Pitt is about to crush a dog.

"Hey, that's a living creature," David Fincher calls out to Pitt, who is zipping around the director's cavernous Hollywood office on a Segway, a stand-up, motorized scooter. "Try not to kill the living things in here."

Pitt has peeled into the converted bank building with Lenny, a playful bull terrier that serves as office mascot, chasing the star. Pitt corners Lenny in a dead-end hall. The dog freezes, startled to go from predator to prey.

"I got it, I got it," Pitt says, reversing the scooter a few inches from Lenny's snout and whizzing past Fincher to terrorize human employees. "You worry too much."

Fincher shakes his head. Three movies together, scores of stunts, years of ducking paparazzi, "and this is how he's going to kill himself."

Fincher had better hope not. Since Pitt and the director met fifteen years ago, they have become close friends—and crucial components in each other's professional lives.

Fincher provides Pitt gravitas. He may have received an Oscar nomination for his role in *Twelve Monkeys*, but Pitt is the first to acknowledge that his dramatic chops are more recognized in Fincher's *Se7en* and *Fight Club*.

Pitt, in return, bestows Fincher inordinate clout. For a guy who has never made a blockbuster, Fincher is able to make the movies he wants, glum endings and all, thanks in part to his friendship with the most famous actor on the planet.

Soon, they could be introducing a new dynamic to their relationship:

Oscar consideration. Their latest venture, *The Curious Case of Benjamin Button*, which opens Christmas Day, has topped many prognosticators' Academy Awards lists, including for acting and directing.

Not that either walks with Oscar swagger, particularly when you put them in a room together. They may be all business on screen, but talking with them in private is a little like trying to study at a frat party.

Straight answers are out the window. They can be crude and cutting and speak in shorthand that puzzles even colleagues.

"Sometimes you have to interrupt them just to get them to speak English," says Taraji Henson, who co-stars as Pitt's mother in *Button*. "They're like brothers—opposite in the way they act, but they understand each other the way families do."

If that's the case, Pitt, forty-four, is the goofball younger sibling, the Costello to Fincher's Abbott.

"Why's he called Lenny?" Fincher, forty-five, asks Pitt as the dog follows the two men into Fincher's office, where a breakfast of bagels and cream cheese awaits. "What's he named for?"

"He's named because it's easier for dogs if they have names," Pitt says. "And I believe Lenny comes from his owners, who named him."

Fincher drops heavily in an office chair, amused that the cracks will begin this early in the day.

"It's amazing," he says, "that we've ever gotten a movie made."

Not the Dashing, Slick Pitt

Button almost wasn't made. Based on a 1922 story by F. Scott Fitzgerald, the idea bounced around Hollywood for nearly two decades. The tale of a child born with an old man's body who gets younger as he ages stymied studios uncertain how to flesh out the short story. And creating a decrepit infant who becomes more vibrant over time was a special-effects nightmare.

When screenwriter Eric Roth got hold of the script, it turned into a Forrest Gump-meets-Tim Burton saga, and Fincher was sold. "We had the story," Fincher says. "I figured the special effects would come."

Still, both director and star would have to wade into unfamiliar waters. Pitt would have to get ugly, Fincher happy.

Pitt has played unsavory before, a remorseless serial killer in *Kalifornia* and a deadly gunslinger in *The Assassination of Jesse James by the Coward Robert Ford*.

But Pitt's fame has always stemmed from playing versions of himself:

dashing, grinning, quick with a quip. There's a reason his biggest films—
Mr. & Mrs. Smith, the *Oceans Eleven* franchise—showcase the slick Pitt.

To play Button as a senior citizen, he had to be caked in makeup and
wear prosthetic noses and scalps. For much of the movie, he abandons
his own body entirely, providing a face and voice that are digitally imposed on other actors including a dwarf, a disabled man, and children of
all ages.

Fincher had to abandon the brutality that has marked films such as
Zodiac and *Panic Room*.

"I think he had to display the side he's shy about showing," Pitt says.
"The side that's a father, that's really very sweet. He doesn't like to let it
show, but it's there."

Perhaps, but Fincher also is known for being a tortured filmmaker. "If
he doesn't get the shot he wants, he's physically pained," Henson says.
"His shoulders hunch. He gets sweaty and flushed. He'll say things like,
'I'd have the perfect shot if that (expletive) extra would stop looking in
the camera.'"

About the only thing that relaxes him, she says, is Pitt.

"He's David's muse, partly because he's so easygoing," she says. "He'll
crack a joke, or they'll start ripping on each other, and everything is re-
laxed again."

Still, there are hurdles to filming a Brad Pitt movie. Namely, Brad Pitt.

Up to two dozen photographers shadow him wherever he goes. (For
this interview, he arrived on his nondescript Ducati; the helmet allows
him anonymity on the street to elude the "razi," as he calls them.)

The set was placed on "Pitt Patrol." There were body doubles and de-
coy cars. Pitt's driver never crossed an intersection when it turned green.
He waited for it to turn yellow to leave law-abiding photographers at the
red light, though few obeyed the signal.

The swarm of attention made the decision to film in New Orleans
an easy one. *Button* became the second Hollywood feature film, behind
Denzel Washington's *Deja Vu*, to film in the city after Hurricane Katrina.

The locale provided Fincher peace to shoot in relative quiet.

"After the storm, it was like someone had taken a squeegee," he says.
"I mean, there was no one around, not even birds. But there was still
this spirit there that people weren't going to be defeated. I consider this
movie a love poem to New Orleans."

Pitt, too, fell in love with the area. He bought a house where he, An-
gelina Jolie, and their six children still escape to "a sense of normalcy, if
there's such a thing."

"It's the only place where my family can have a sense of privacy," he says. "People there have other things to worry about than all this silliness."

On the Same Ending Page

Not that Pitt is opposed to a little silliness. After all, he discovered Fincher after a drunken night in Tijuana.

The actor says he felt like seeing a movie "after a night of utter debauchery" in Mexico in 1992. He settled on *Alien³*, Fincher's feature-film debut. The movie's malevolent tone and (spoiler alert) stunner conclusion—the young director killed off Sigourney Weaver's character, Ripley—earned the movie abhorrent reviews. It grossed $53 million, the worst in the franchise.

Pitt loved it.

"I remember walking out of the theater thinking, 'OK, that was not what I expected,'" Pitt says. "That wasn't a Hollywood ending. It really stuck with me."

"Maybe it was the hangover," Fincher jokes.

Soon after, Pitt got hold of the screenplay for *Se7en*, Fincher's cop drama about a serial killer who murders based on the Seven Deadly Sins.

Pitt immediately signed on, with one caveat: The studio could not change the film's final scene (spoiler alert 2): Pitt's character executes the killer.

Pitt and Fincher found they clicked on set, despite stark differences in style.

Fincher loathes being in front of the camera. He rarely grants interviews. He tends to dress like he's settling in for a Sunday afternoon of football. The divorced father of one lives only a few blocks from Pitt in the Hollywood Hills, but Fincher often drives separately when they socialize to avoid shutterbugs.

Pitt, by contrast, seems at ease with any lens. Considered one of the most patient stars with paparazzi, he's perpetually braced for an unexpected photo op. Even when carousing with Lenny outside in eighty-five-degree temperatures, he never removes his red felt fedora.

But for all their differences, they discovered they shared a similar sense of humor and irreverence.

After *Se7en* wrapped, Fincher wondered what should be done with the bloated mannequin used to re-create the murder of a four-hundred-pound man.

"Let's save it for the party at the premiere," Pitt told him. "And fill it with bean dip." Studio executives nixed the idea.

But when they tried one last time to change the movie's ending, Pitt and Fincher's friendship was permanently bonded.

"They tried all kinds of things to change our minds," Pitt says. "We wouldn't budge. David isn't afraid to use an ending that works, even if it isn't the one you want. That's why I trust him. If he wants me to do a movie, I say yes first, then find out what it is."

Fincher is getting uncomfortable with the public praise. As the morning wraps up, he heads back to his desk. There are still finishing touches left to make on the film.

Pitt is ready to play again. He hops out of the chair and heads for the scooter, looking for Lenny for round two.

"I'm trying to get David to be in a gang with me on these things," he says. "He thinks we'd look like a couple (jerks)."

He turns on the scooter.

"But I can change his mind."

In Conversation with David Fincher

Nev Pierce / 2009

From *Empire* 235 (January 2009): 163–68. Reprinted by permission from Nev Pierce.

Doom, gloom, destruction, angst, rage, suffering, torture, alienation, paranoia, loneliness . . . David Fincher is nicer than you think. He does not wear a cowl, write script notes in blood or—to the best of Empire's knowledge—sleep in a coffin. He is a well-adjusted human being. Warm. Funny. Smart. He just happens to make movies about death.

Alien³ is an AIDS metaphor; *Se7en* about damnation. *The Game* is discovering the worth of life, *Fight Club* wishing it away, *Panic Room* fearing for it, *Zodiac* losing it to the drip, drip, drip of professional obsession.

Now comes *The Curious Case of Benjamin Button*, Fincher's seventh feature in sixteen years. A loose adaptation of an F. Scott Fitzgerald story, it's about a baby born with the physicality of a pensioner. As time passes, Benjamin (Brad Pitt) gets younger. He experiences life—and love (with Tilda Swinton and Cate Blanchett)—in reverse. Around the release of *Zodiac*, with its steady camera and true story, some critics suggested Fincher was growing up, as if his previous work—particularly the affront of *Fight Club*—was somehow immature; as if growing up is always a good thing. The same commentators will likely see *The Curious Case . . .* as another departure, or just the continuing maturation of the erstwhile MTV auteur.

But this is rather patronizing. Isn't Fincher just using the right tools to tell a story, a story that fascinates him? And while, yes, you can say *The Curious Case of Benjamin Button* is a grand Hollywood romance, you can also say it's an epic about the inevitability of destruction. Dust to dust, ashes to ashes. . . . As *Fight Club*'s Narrator has it, "On a long enough timeline, the survival rate for everyone drops to zero."

Or you can just say it's a good yarn. These things can be overthought. For though Fincher is often compared with Kubrick—for his visual vigor, meticulous preparation and exacting on-set standards, no doubt—his favorite film, on most days, is *Butch Cassidy and the Sundance Kid* (a love he shares with Pitt). Sure, he likes to provoke, poke, get a reaction. But he also likes to entertain. He saw George Roy Hill's western when he was eight and knew immediately he wanted to be a filmmaker. And, with George Lucas living down the block, it didn't seem an impossible aim. He went to work with Industrial Light & Magic, moved to Los Angeles and shot commercials and music videos, before realizing the dream that became a nightmare in *Alien³*. The lesson of that picture was to become belligerent: fight for what you want, because it's your name on the credits. He let too much go. He wouldn't do so again.

Empire sent editor-at-large Nev Pierce to Fincher's Hollywood office for two lengthy conversations with the director. "Fincher has a reputation for not suffering fools lightly, which is not good if you're a journalist," says Pierce. "When we met he was also still in a really intense period of post-production, working on the special effects needed to 'age' Pitt. And there was a lot of online chatter saying he was rowing with the studio, because they thought the film was too long. . . . In short: he had every reason to be bad-tempered. Instead, he was a laugh."

Empire: So, we hear the big issue with the movie is it's too short . . .
Fincher: That is the big problem with most movies! [Laughs] Studios always want movies to be as short as they can be. And, you know, you want to be there, make the most impact you can, then get the fuck outta town. I'm down with that. You know, if you asked every person who's ever seen a version of this movie what their least favorite scenes are, you could get the movie down to an hour. But if you ask those same people what their favorite scenes are, it would be four hours. Somewhere in the middle lies the truth.

Empire: You've been interested in *Benjamin Button* since 1992: what's so compelling about it?
Fincher: I think that everybody believes, in some way, shape, or form: "If I only knew then what I know now." It would be great to take these kinds of short cuts through life, knowing what we know now, but isn't that kind of what life's about? It's not just an accumulation of those tidbits of knowledge: it's the maturity to be able to use that. 'Cause certainly we all sit down and tell our kids, "This is not important; this is important," and they look at you and go, "You're so stupid! You don't know

anything. You don't understand!" So I think it was that. And I liked the idea of a love story where two people were born and the sweet spot for when they were going to be together was later in their lives, when they were more alike.

Empire: Were you familiar with the story or any of Fitzgerald's work?
Fincher: You know what? I'm not familiar with Fitzgerald's work at all. I read the short story, ironically, after I read Eric Roth's draft of the script and I sort of realized, "Huh, these two things aren't related in any way!" In a weird way I respect that more. I can imagine that his brief was, "We love the basic notion, the drama of somebody aging backwards . . ."—because, of course, we all believe youth is wasted on the young—" . . . so what would you do with this?" And then he went off and did something with it. And the beauty of it, I think, and the thing that I really responded to—and didn't respond to as much the first time I read it—was he had written two characters who were not doomed without the other. So much of romance is Romeo and Juliet; it's codependent love: "I'm nothing without you, I'm half." And I love the fact that he had characters who just went about their lives and lived with other people and did their thing, and then finally they had enough experience, so when they get together, when they have that honeymoon period, you kind of go, "Aaahh . . ." [breathes sigh of relief]. And then, of course . . .

Empire: It all goes pear-shaped.
Fincher: Yeah. It all goes horribly wrong.

Empire: The idea of youth being wasted on the young. . . . It's accepted, but it's great when you're young: you don't have the same doubts and fears you have later. . . .
Fincher: Yeah, exactly. You're bulletproof. I agree. I think the interesting thing in the movie is to take a guy who is young, make him look old, put him among old people, have him raised by old people and then he has this sort of . . . I think in different circles people describe it as a stoicism, but it's not: it's just that he lives in a world where people are there one week and then they're taken out on a stretcher and put in the ground. Life is a very transitive thing in his eyes, so what does that make you like? I think that's interesting. I think Brad Pitt is really good in this. He makes it really. . . . It's a funny thing, 'cause it's such a. . . . I mean, classically you think that the character is sort of a wallflower. But as a vessel through which to experience life—or a life—it's kind of amazing.

Empire: What, the concept?

Fincher: The character as a vessel through which you can experience life, or experience this life, this movie life, is an interesting one, because he does see so much and does comment on so little and he doesn't try to change the way things are.

Empire: And you like the fact the characters aren't doomed by love?

Fincher: They aren't committed to one another out of desperation. They're not needy. It's not that the presence of the other fulfils a need: it's a choice. I'm just tired of the ballad of codependency, you know what I mean? I like to see two adults in a movie deciding to be together, instead of teenagers caving in.

Empire: Do you think your attitude to love has become more pragmatic and changed since you were twenty-two?

Fincher: Yeah, I would think. I would hope. Not pragmatic, but more realistic. I think that you, you know . . . I think everybody realizes that that kind of fulfillment is . . .

Empire: There's a time when love is needy and a time when it's like, "You know, we could cope without each other, but we don't want to. . . ."

Fincher: We're making a choice to be here. Because quite honestly it's difficult to live with somebody else! And I don't just mean Ceán [Chaffin, Fincher's long-time partner and producer]! My sister called when she was twenty-one, twenty-two and said, "Are you coming to my wedding?" I said, "Oh, God. How old are you?" "Twenty-two." I said, "I'll come to the next one. . . ." [Laughs]

Empire: Did that prove prophetic?

Fincher: Yes, as it turns out.

Empire: You're the middle child of three. What was your upbringing like? Was it a happy house?

Fincher: I think so, yeah. We were left alone for the most part. I mean, I saw my parents every night at dinner and every morning for breakfast, but between breakfast and dinner you were pretty much on your own. From the time I was ten, nine . . . let's see, probably from third grade on, we weren't really expected to check in, unless we were going to be late home for dinner. It was just a different time. They didn't know what serial killers were then.

Empire: Your dad was a journalist and a writer. He wrote a script called *Mank*, about the *Citizen Kane* screenwriter Herman J. Mankiewicz. Did you consider making that?

Fincher: We tried. It was too expensive. Because if you're going to make a Hollywood insider movie—it's nothing to do with Hollywood really, it's Hollywood in the late thirties, early forties—you've got to make it really cheaply. We had a chance to make the movie for, like, $13 million, back in 1998 and, um, [guiltily] I wanted to make it in black and white. [Laughs] And that fucked up all those home video and video sell-through and cable deals. I haven't read it in a while. I probably should.

Empire: Did your dad write a few screenplays?

Fincher: Yeah, he wrote a couple. That was the best of them, I think. He wrote a screenplay once about a divorce case. It was kind of based on the Keanes. Remember in the sixties, the guy who painted those pictures of the children with the giant eyes? They were in this bitter divorce. It was a very, very sardonic screenplay about two parents trying to prove what bad parents they are, so the other will get stuck with the kids! It was pretty funny! [Laughs] But it had an awful sentiment! But it was funny. It was a good script.

Empire: There's an element of your work—in *Se7en*, *The Game*, *Zodiac*—that is about professionalism and obsession. Is that something you think you got from your dad?

Fincher: My dad wasn't very obsessive. Slightly compulsive, but not obsessive. You know, my dad did used to say, "Learn your craft; it will never stop you from being a genius." It's like, "Do the hard work, figure out how it works. . . ." My dad worked a lot, but he paced himself. He paced himself a lot more than I think I probably do.

Empire: You've talked before of fight clubs being a metaphor for drug use. . . .

Fincher: Yeah, or the need for . . . the secret society, certainly.

Empire: And your mum worked in a methadone clinic. Did you have any experience of her life in that regard?

Fincher: My mom was a medical heath practitioner, so certainly [whispers] nothing I can talk about. We definitely, you know . . . the dangers and ugliness of heroin addiction was not something that . . . I mean, I didn't get it from movies of the week. I got a pretty straight scoop, you know, from running into those people and having them throw up on your shoes. I think she stopped doing it when I was twelve, thirteen, or fourteen. She went to work in mental health. Got out of addiction. . . . It was just something we knew about. Again, Marin County in the sevnties, there was a lot of drugs. Not a lot of people were shooting up, but certainly a lot of people were doing Quaaludes and smoking a lot of weed. That was a big part of it.

Empire: So your mum went on to work in mental health, while your dad wrote a book about the brain, *Human Intelligence*. The two of them had quite an interest in the human psyche. . . .
Fincher: Yeah. It played well together. My dad . . . he was an intellect and sort of a Monday-morning quarterback. My mom was—and still is—very much of a humanist and very interested in social causes, and both were extremely liberal, good people.

Empire: Has your mum seen *Se7en*?
Fincher: She has. I think she saw it at the premiere. I don't think she was that impressed with it. I think my mum liked *The Game* a lot. It's weird: you never know the subsets of people who like different things about your work. You know, it's like accountants and lawyers all love *The Game*, and college students and perverts all like *Se7en*.

Empire: When you and Brad got involved with *Se7en*, was this independently or was one of you kind of auditioning the other?
Fincher: [Long pause] I don't know if we were auditioning. You know, it's funny: I had my own ideas about what I thought he was. . . . There was no doubt that he was the spark in *Thelma & Louise*. Even now it's easy to see that's part of one of the reasons that movie is so memorable. And I had known Dominic Sena very well, we were partners, and he told me about working with Brad on *Kalifornia*, in glowing terms. I don't think it was mandated. I don't think the studio said, "You have to meet with Brad Pitt," but I think they had an inkling this was the kind of thing he might be looking for. So we just sort of met each other as, you know, "We may be working together. . . ." I certainly wasn't auditioning and I don't think I was auditioning him. I just wanted to see what he was about. I'd gotten in Gene Hackman at one point, early, early on. . . . Never dreamed, quite honestly, that we could get Morgan Freeman. You know, just, it never occurred to me, because I was like, "I can't show this to Morgan Freeman!" [Laughs] And I didn't think of Brad Pitt because, I

think, he was just out of sight. He was so busy. He had *Legends of the Fall* and *Interview with the Vampire* back-to-back, and I met him after that. So the fact he was interested was interesting to me. I didn't really know what to do with Mills until I met Brad and then I was like, "Oh wow! We can have him say anything!" So, no, I don't think it was an audition as much as it was just I had heard so many good things that I knew it couldn't be true, so I wanted to see for myself and pass judgment.

Empire: Maybe it's thanks to *Johnny Suede*, but some people still think of Pitt as just a beefcake. There's obviously more going on there. . . .

Fincher: I think if people underestimate him it's probably because he's engineering it. He's a crafty guy. I think he's smart enough that he'll have a career like Paul Newman and he'll let people's appreciation of him catch up. But the fact of the matter is, I don't know that he needs the encouragement! [Laughs] I think this is somebody who's pretty comfortable with what he's doing and very successful at it. If history treats Brad any better than the present day, then it's just not fair!

Empire: You've talked about various projects together, like *Fertig* [aka *They Fought Alone*, based on the biography of American civil engineer-turned-World War II guerrilla fighter Wendell Fertig]. Could that happen?

Fincher: [Deadpan] I'm not at liberty to comment. That's ongoing litigation and I'm not at liberty to comment. . . . Yeah, we've talked about a lot of stuff. I'm working on this thing right now, *Black Hole* [an adaptation of Charles Burns' brilliant, bizarre graphic novel about an STD that causes mutations], which is Plan B, his company. We've talked about a lot of things, *Fertig* being one of them. I still have to talk him into *Fertig*. He doesn't . . .

Empire: . . . fancy the idea of eighteen months in the jungle?

Fincher: I don't think anybody fancies the idea of that, unless we can shoot in, I don't know, a resort! No, I think all of the criticisms levelled at the script, up until this point, have been valid ones, but I also think it's just one of the great fucking stories. I talk with [*Chinatown* screenwriter] Robert Towne twice a week and he's working. . . . It could be one of the five greatest movies ever made. It's that huge. So hopefully we'll get a script and we'll put it in front of him and he'll die to be involved.

Empire: *Fight Club* is now regarded as one of those great movies, but at the time it got a bit of a kicking. Were you surprised by the virulent reaction it got from some critics?

Fincher: Yeah. I'm always surprised at how seriously people take movies. You know, it always surprises me what people get their bowels in an uproar about. It's a movie. It was interesting to me, the critics who felt they had a moral obligation to "the broader audience" to warn them. But it didn't surprise me that some people didn't think it was funny. It didn't surprise me that some people thought it was morbid. It surprised me, the people who went out of their way to save other people from this experience. I thought that was kind of silly.

Empire: When you make a movie that cost $60-odd million and then it makes $37 million. . . .

Fincher: Did it make that much?

Empire: Did it break even?

Fincher: I happen to know that the movie's in the black, but there's receipts and there's worth. They are two different things. Because there are movies that make money and there are movies that are worth money, and sometimes the movies that are worth money make money later on. I honestly believe *Fight Club* is a title Twentieth Century Fox knows is going to make money for them in perpetuity.

Empire: You made your first feature, *Alien³*, with Fox. Referring to your background in ad-directing, David Giler, the producer, called you a "shoe salesman." . . .

Fincher: I think that would probably be one of the most polite things Giler ever said about me.

Empire: When the film got criticized, were you attacked for stuff you'd been forced into doing?

Fincher: No, you're not forced. . . . There were a lot of enormously talented people working on that movie. It's just a movie starts from a unified concept, and once you've unified the concept it becomes very easy to see the things you're not going to spend money on. And if a movie is constantly in flux because you're having to please this vice-president or that vice-president of production. . . . I think a movie set's a fascist dictatorship—you have to go in and know what it is you want to do, 'cause you have to tell ninety people what it is you want to do and it has to be convincing. Otherwise, you know, when they start to question it, the horse can easily run away with you and it's bigger than you are. . . . So that was a movie where the time was not taken upfront to say, "This is what we're doing, and all of this is what we're not doing." So as we were shooting, a lot of people—I suppose in an effort to make it "better" or "more commercial" or more like the other ones they liked as opposed to the one that you liked—took to being extremely helpful, so that this could be more James Cameron than James Cameron. And of course, you're sitting there going, "Guys, remember I don't have any guns. I don't have any tripod guns or flamethrowers or any of that shit!" If a movie gets off on a wrong foot, when you've never done it before you assume everyone is going to be there to help you right the ship, but really you're beholden to a lot of banana republics.

Empire: As each film goes by, have you found any more enjoyment in the process?

Fincher: No. I still love the same things I've always loved about moviemaking, which is I love the enormous potential of the moment and I love, you know, what it could look like: it could be in this house, and it could be with the light streaming through the windows there, and it could be with dust floating in the air and it could be wonderful. . . . And then when you get down to it, it's like [shouts], "We have twelve minutes to get this shot before lunch!" It's like, "The guy's make-up is peeling off! You can see his sideburns. We have twelve minutes before lunch. . . . Alright, fuck it. . . ." It's that whole, horrible reality of making movies which is: you have to stay on schedule and they have to cost a reasonable amount of money. It's the "you have tos . . ." that I hate. I love the "what could be . . ." I hate what it has to be.

Empire: You're known for doing a lot of takes. Like when that stunt guy got thrown down the stairs in *Fight Club* twelve times and you used . . .

Fincher: . . . take one! Poor fucker.

Empire: Does anyone go, "I'm not doing take thirty-seven. That's enough"?

Fincher: Yeah, I had Michael Douglas say that to me a couple of times [on *The Game*]. But a lot of times when the actor's exhausted and has over-concentrated on something, they're usually right. But you've got a lot of people you're trying to turn into a ballet, and it can be tricky. I remember on *Panic Room* there were a couple of times when I'd say to an actor, "What did you want to do with this?" and they'd say, "What difference does it make? You already got it all worked out." And you don't want to be that guy. I'm not making movies with wooden Indians: you want people to push back; you want to find a meeting. If you're going to cast somebody, then obviously they've got something which is special.

Empire: So actors *aren't* cattle?
Fincher: I don't believe actors are cattle and I don't believe Hitchcock said that. He said they should be "treated as cattle." And in some cases I think that's true. You know, look: there are a lot of people who choose that line of work because they simply like the attention and it's your civic duty to make sure they're punished for that. But I also think there are people who are truly skillful and truly magic. . . . When something's great and there's a little bump in the track, you're going to go with the thing that's great. I always do. Look, actors are doing the same thing with me that I'm doing with them, which is if you've worked it out too much in the mirror then we're just checking off a list. One of my problems with Hitchcock, who I think was . . . I think Hitchcock was an amazing voice, he was an applied scientist, he was an engineer, he engineered images and he understood images much better than he understood people. But you know, the crappy dialogue he gave to those people to move the fucking narrative along, I couldn't ask somebody to say some of that stuff! And I've asked people to say some ridiculous things before; there are times when you're stitched into a corner. You know, there's stuff in a Hitchcock movie that you look at and you're just like, "Oh my goodness!" The confidence you must have in order to insist on someone saying that, I don't know that I could ever muster that.

Empire: *Panic Room* sounded like a nightmare.
Fincher: It was. But again, it was a nightmare of my own construction so I can't complain too vociferously. The thing is, it's truly a Hitchcock film in that Hitchcock said by the time he started shooting he'd already finished the movie. I'd already made the movie three times by the time I was shooting it. You know, the thing I learned is you want to be prepared but you don't want to be that prepared, because you're just going to be terrible because . . . I was bored, I was just bored. And I really liked the people. I loved Forest Whitaker and I loved Jodie Foster and I loved Jared Leto and I loved Dwight Yoakam and I loved Kristen Stewart, but I sort of did them a disservice. I was just like, "Come on! We're done with this!" I tried everyone's patience I think, to the detriment of the film. There were times when I'd look over at Forest and we're shooting take

seventeen and he's just rolling his eyes going, "My God. I don't have it in me anymore to be real about this."

Empire: "Can I go home now?"
Fincher: Yeah, please! And you have a ten-year-old in every frame. It's tough and she was great, but we made this rule upfront: we're never going to cut to the kid. She had to be in every frame with the multi-Academy-Award-winning actress. Poor fucking Jodie, because the room was so small I had to be at a monitor twenty-five feet away, so she did half of the directing.

Empire: Talking of Academy Awards, as soon as *Benjamin Button* was greenlit people started saying, "Oscar. . . ." How do you feel about that?
Fincher: If you look at what the shorthand of that means, in the grasp of those who don't have a grasp of much, I guess it's a nice thing. But it's also. . . . I think that too often becomes, you know, "Well, it's not a Robot Movie, so it must be one of those End of the Year Movies!" It's like, well, there are two seasons: the End of the Year season and the Robot season. So it has to fall into one of those categories! I don't know.

Empire: Was the issue with *Zodiac* that certain people couldn't decide if it was a Robot Movie or an End of the Year Movie? Because they saw the words "David Fincher" and the words "serial killer." . . .
Fincher: Yeah. "It's a Fall movie!" "It's a Back to School movie!" Um, I don't know. . . . I think you may have already given it more thought than the people whose job it was to market it.

Empire: You've been developing *Heavy Metal* and *Torso*, among other projects. Any idea what you're doing next?
Fincher: I'm sleeping for six months! I think I'm whoring myself out to come to fly around Europe and defend my honor, but I don't honestly know.

Empire: You still shoot commercials from time to time. Is that a chance to explore new techniques?
Fincher: Recently I did a commercial for the new iPhone, which was fun to do. It was a little, tiny story. I got to work with people I don't normally get to: cameramen, electric departments, working with different visual effects companies. You get to kind of like play around. I guess, maybe, I shouldn't be saying that . . . but I do. I look at it as, "It's time to recharge.

It's not your story: it's the story of this pair of shoes or the story of this product. . . ." So you get to kind of, like, apply your craft. . . . I don't look at it as slumming. A lot of people do, I think, but I guess 'cause I came from the slum I don't look at it that way. I look at it as a chance to play. I mean, it's gotten sillier, it's certainly gotten sillier over the years. I did a cell phone commercial with Pitt and we must have had thirty people from the agency. I mean, granted, I'm sure it was not to witness the cinematic flourishes of David Fincher, I'm sure it was to be able to hang out with Brad Pitt and get a picture, but we had more agency than we had extras. I was like, "Okay, here's the holding tent for the agency and here's the holding tent for the extras."

Empire: You made such a scathingly anti-consumerist picture in *Fight Club*. Has your commercials work ever struck you as ironic?
Fincher: I think *Fight Club*'s selling something too. It's just not necessarily selling the same thing that Procter & Gamble is selling. You know, look, when you're doing a commercial for Coca-Cola you're positing an alternative world where Pepsi doesn't exist. And when you're making *Fight Club* you're positing a world where people's priorities are not as fucked up as they are normally . . . certainly not as fucked up as they are in commercials. I don't know. I think my own personal beliefs run more parallel to *Fight Club*. But I don't do commercials, like, waterbed store commercials or Toyota dealership commercials. I'd never do a commercial where people hold the product by their face and tell you how great it is. It's always like . . . I'm making film. Yeah, maybe someone pops a beer and does a pour, but I'm selling something else. I'm not selling necessarily the product or the good times. You know, when you do a shoe commercial you're really selling physical ability. Everybody really knows there's not that much difference between Adidas and Nike, and if they don't, then they're ripe for the picking!

Empire: *Fight Club* is rare, in that you don't often see movies that point something out as opposed to being part of the whole consumer culture. . . .
Fincher: Movies are fashion. They are seasons. They are designed to take your money. I mean, let's not kid ourselves: they have way more to do with shoes and coats than they do with art. But you're entering into a bargain with a willing participant who is saying, "Show me! Have control over everything I see and hear for the next two hours!" That's a really powerful place to put yourself in and you can either accept the

responsibility of that or you can play to it. And either way is fine, which-ever you choose to do. I've just always preferred the kinds of movies where I walk out of the theatre going, "Hmmm. I don't know about that. That's sort of true. Goddamn it, that is true!" I like thinking about stuff, but I like my television like that too, I like my music like that. I like some-thing with a little riptide to it. But there are people who want to be made to feel better about themselves.

Empire: I left *Se7en* wanting to shoot someone. . . . I was shell-shocked.
Fincher: Some people find that an affront. They're like, "Why do you want to do that? Why do you want to ruin my Friday night? I just want to go to a pub and have a good time!" And those are the people who, predominantly, look at a movie like *The Game* and go, "Yeah, it's kinda cute." You say you went to the pub and were sort of shell-shocked, I look at that and I go, "Great!" And I think you look at that and go, "I'm looking for those kinds of experiences when I go to the movies." There are other people, I remember standing outside a theatre when *The Game* came out, and this guy came out and was like, "Fuck that movie." [Laughs] And I remember going, "Well, that's a perfectly valid response . . ." because it is a movie that kind of nee-nah, nee-nahs you.

Empire: There have been a few films this last year where it's been like, "That was fun. I will never think about it again. . . ."
Fincher: Made a couple of those movies. Know exactly what they're intended to do. I mean, I'm all for . . . Look, you know, *The Terminator* for me was that, a popcorn movie, but it was just so unbelievably mus-cular. . . . If it can do more, great, more power to it. [Film is] . . . sort of an amazingly powerful medium to just stroke people, but there's a lot of that and there's room for it, I like it. I loved *Terminator*, I had a ball, I loved *The Road Warrior* (*Mad Max 2*), but I also liked *All That Jazz* and *8½*. You know, not every night is Friday.

Empire: There are few films you see that actually stay with you.
Fincher: Yeah. Even through dinner.

David Fincher British Film Institute Interview

Mark Salisbury / 2009

From the *Guardian*, January 18, 2009. Reprinted by permission from Mark Salisbury.

Mark Salisbury: David Fincher, let's start at the end, as Button does, and talk about *The Curious Case of Benjamin Button*. It's kind of a departure for you, in that it's a love story, but with an unhappy ending.
David Fincher: Yes, everybody dies.

MS: This project has been around for a long time. You read it sixteen years ago?
DF: Yeah, I read the first draft that was deemed unfilmable. And over the years, I heard about who had it and who was going to try next. I read Eric Roth's draft in 2001/2002.

MS: So what was it about this draft that sucked you in?
DF: I just thought the final image of a seventy-four-year-old woman holding a seven-month-old baby and helping him through death, I just thought it was a beautiful way to end a love story.

MS: We have to talk about how you created this amazing character, Benjamin Button, with CGI and Brad [Pitt]'s head on other people's bodies. Let's not forget that it wouldn't have worked if Brad wasn't fantastic, and he is fantastic in this film. But technically, it's astonishing. So can you talk a little bit about that process, please?
DF: Well, the technique of using someone else's head has been around for many years—they use it in stunts, to have people jumping over burning buildings on motorcycles and stuff. So they'd lop off the heads and put the actor's head on the body. Initially, in discussions with Brad, he

said that he didn't want to play seven or fifteen years in somebody's life, that he wasn't interested in organizing that kind of a hand-off. But if we wanted him to play the whole of somebody's life, that was something that would interest him. Now, we knew that Benjamin needed to be four feet tall and eighty-five years old. There was also the question, not just of the character's stature as he's learning to stand and get out of a wheelchair and walk on two crutches and then with a cane; but there was also the makeup issue. Silicone appliances—probably 80 percent of ageing in the movies are silicone appliances—but they can only do certain kinds of things to their faces. For instance, one classic example of old-age makeup is that they build out the cheekbones and build out the brow in order to make the eyes look sunken, because as you get older you lose fat tissue in your face and so your eyes recede. It's called "skulling." And people get gaunter as they get older, and we couldn't do that with traditional makeup techniques. And we certainly couldn't do that on a four-foot-tall body. So what we decided to do was cast actors to play Benjamin at different heights, and got them to wear blue socks on their heads and lopped their heads off and put Brad's head on them, which is easier than it sounds. We needed to have a workflow or factory assembly-line way to do that, because we had 350 shots that we had to do. So by using a lot of different techniques available from videogames and animation, we were able to figure out a way that Brad could perform the face, and we could capture his eyes and how his mouth moved, expressly frame for frame, and then puppeteer a sculpture that we could scan into a computer, a virtual version of his head, so that we could take masks away from his face and he could "puppet" himself. And that's what we ended up doing.

MS: And you got all the Brad stuff done after you shot all the other actors?
DF: Yeah. The actors in New Orleans—we called them the Smurfs because they had blue socks on their heads—they could act out the scene and people could touch them and they could interact and move around. Then later, when we decided which pieces we wanted to use, Brad came in to perform. It's like the looping stage, but instead of just the voice, he would do all the expressions, and we'd take those bits of digital information of his face and use that imagery to push the pixels of him as an eighty-five-year-old.

MS: Let's talk a little bit about how you came to be a filmmaker. You were born in Denver, Colorado, but moved to Marin County when you were two, and you lived down the street from George Lucas. As a kid you were quite artistic: you took photographs, you drew, you conned your parents into giving you a movie camera rather than a gun, so was there a eureka moment, when you realized that you wanted to direct?

DF: It was pretty clear. The eureka moment was when I saw a behind-the-scenes making-of about *Butch Cassidy and the Sundance Kid*. It was kind of a shabby EPK that had been cobbled together, but it was narrated by the director, George Roy Hill. And it was the first time I'd ever conceived that films didn't happen in real time. I was about seven years old, and I thought, "What a cool job." You get to go on location, have trained horses and blow up trains and hang out with Katharine Ross. [audience laughs] That seemed like a pretty good gig. So that was pretty much it for me. And the guy down the street was making *American Graffiti* and then *Star Wars*. I lived in Marin County at a time when they made *The Godfather* at the Marin Art & Garden Centre, and *THX 1138* was shot at the Marin Civic Centre, and *The Candidate*. Michael Ritchie was making films, Phil Kaufman made *Invasion of the Body Snatchers*. There were a lot of people doing this; it was just everywhere. Everybody on my block wanted to be a moviemaker.

MS: And how many did? Just you?

DF: A lot of friends of mine work in animation and design websites and, for the most part, they're all kind of in the movie business, tangentially.

MS: But you didn't go to film school like a lot of your contemporaries. You chose to work in the business: you worked at ILM [Industrial Light & Magic] for three years, for example. Why did you choose to work inside rather than be a student?

DF: It was a great gig, and it was a great time to get a job working in special effects, because you could make a real living and it seemed like a better thing than spending $35,000 a year going to film school. And the other thing was, the only film school that I was interested in, because I wasn't very bright, was USC, and every film that you make, they own. So I thought, "I don't know if I want to pay them to own my movies." [audience laughs] That doesn't make sense to me.

MS: So you worked on *Return of the Jedi*, but nothing to do with the Ewoks, I hope.

DF: I did, but I actually worked on the tanks that tried to kill the Ewoks. That was my personal contribution. [audience laughs]

MS: For that we applaud you. And then you started to make pop videos, just when pop videos were being taken seriously.
DF: Were pop videos ever taken seriously?

MS: Well, more than they are now. People don't watch them now.
DF: OK, yeah, for good reason. It's interesting, I just grew up in a really interesting and bizarre place in a bizarre time. There was a real nexus of things. From third grade, I was making movies in 16mm, and every year, in film class—and everybody took film—they'd give you a song, a 45 and they'd say, "Make a film to this song," because there was no sync sound. So you'd go out and shoot stuff with your friends, and you'd cut it and it was made to that song. So when MTV came along, people went, "We want you to make a film to this song," and I thought, "I actually know how to do that. That may actually be the only thing I do know how to do." That was a good gig for me.

MS: So did you treat them as a film school?
DF: Yeah. I hate to say this because I took millions of dollars from people to do these things. But the day that they started to put your name on it was a horrible day for me. I just thought it was so cool that you could try out this stuff and no one would ever . . . you know, they'd blame it on Michael Jackson. [audience laughs]

MS: But movies were always the goal, when you were making videos like "Express Yourself," that *Metropolis* thing.
DF: Yeah, we thought that was good fun. I don't know, she came up with that idea. She was like, "I wanna do *Metropolis*," and I thought, it's her million bucks.

MS: At what point did Hollywood notice you? Was there one video that put you on their radar?
DF: No. You know, Hollywood always pretends not to notice you. I don't know. In a weird way, you have to be in LA long enough before anybody will realize that you're serious about it. The last thing they want to do is enable people who aren't going to be dedicated to their cause. I'd been making videos for ten years, and this sounds stupid but I'd been there for six or seven years and felt like I had been there forever. I mean, I moved there in 1984 and started Propaganda Films in 1987, so I'd been doing commercials and videos for eight or ten years before anybody gave me a shot at making a movie. And I wish they hadn't.

MS: The film we can't mention.
DF: Yeah, let's not.

MS: But there's this fantastic quote that I found, where you said of *Alien³* that "a lot of people hated *Alien³*, but no one hated it more than I did."
DF: I had to work on it for two years, got fired off it three times, and I had to fight for every single thing. No one hated it more than me; to this day, no one hates it more than me.

MS: At the risk of opening old wounds, what did you take from that experience that has subsequently helped you in your Hollywood career?
DF: It was a baptism by fire. I was very naive. For a number of years, I'd been around the kind of people who financed movies and the kind of people who are there to make the deals for movies. But I'd always had this naive idea that everybody wants to make movies as good as they can be, which is stupid. [audience laughs] So I learned on this movie that nobody really knows, so therefore no one has to care, so it's always going to be your fault. I'd always thought, "Well, surely you don't want to have the Twentieth Century Fox logo over a shitty movie." And they were like, "Well, as long as it opens." So I learned then just to be a belligerent asshole, which was really: "You have to get what you need to get out of it." You have to fight for things you believe in, and you have to be smart about how you position it so that you don't just become white noise. On that movie, I was the guy who was constantly the voice of "We need to do this better, we need to do this, this doesn't make sense." And pretty soon, it was like in *Peanuts*: WOP WOP WOP WOP WOP! They'd go, "He's doing that again, he's frothing at the mouth, he seems so passionate." They didn't care.

MS: Have you grown to like it since then, *Alien³*?
DF: God, no! [audience laughs] But I don't look at anything after it's done.

MS: So that alternate cut on the DVD special edition whatever it is—that's not yours?
DF: I don't know who did it, I've never seen it, I can't comment on it.

MS: So after that experience, you went back to making videos. Did you think that was it as far as features were concerned?
DF: No. The great news about Hollywood is that there is no better place

to fail upward. I figured that there were people who had made worse films than I had and they were still working, so I figured I'd get one more shot. So finally, I got a script by a guy who was kind of in my world, and thinking about films the same way I was, and revered the same kinds of movie that I revered—Andy Walker, who had written a script called *Se7en*. He couldn't get it made and had rewritten it thirteen times in order to make it more "likeable." [audience laughs] So this script was floating around and my agent, who's very sweet and always very hopeful, said, "You know, New Line is interested in this. You might like this, and they might want to make it with you, so maybe you should read it." So I read it, and got to the end, with the head in the box, and I called him and said, "This is fantastic, this is so great because I had thought it was a police procedural; now it's this meditation on evil and how evil gets on you and you can't get it off." And he said, "What are you talking about?" And I talked about the whole head-in-the-box thing, she's been dead for hours and there's no bullshit chase across town and the guy driving on sidewalks to get to the woman, who's drawing a bath while the serial killer sneaks in the back window. And he goes, "Oh, they sent you the wrong draft." [audience laughs] And he sent me the right draft, and there was a guy driving across town on sidewalks, serial killer sneaking in the back window. And I said that I wasn't interested in doing that. So I went and met with Mike De Luca, who was ostensibly at the time running New Line, and I said that I really liked the first draft, not the thirteenth draft. And he said, "Me too." So I asked what he was going to do, and I was laying out what I wanted to do on it. And he said, "Close the door." And then he said, "If we develop this and get into a dialogue about changes that could possibly be made to this material, there's no way that we could make this version of it, because I'll have fifteen people looking over my shoulder who are going to be reading these pages as they come in. But if you say that you'll make this movie, starting in six weeks, we can make this version of the movie." So I said, "OK, let's go do it. Put the head in a box." And that's how the movie got made.

MS: And the look of the film is one of many things that's so fantastic about it—the decaying dark. Apparently, New Line wasn't happy with how dark it was, initially.

DF: I liked it, I thought it worked well; it could have been a little darker for me. But I just don't like it in movies, when people are wandering around with flashlights, that you can see everything behind them, when they're saying, "Oh my God, I can't see two feet in front of my face without this." With that stuff, I just want to shoot myself. So, for instance, I like this sequence in *Klute* where Donald Sutherland goes after a sound and he's chasing somebody who may or may not be on the roof, and he runs upstairs, and the whole thing's lit with a flashlight. And you look at that and you know that's what it's like to be running around with just a flashlight, because there are times when you just can't see anything. I like that kind of movie.

MS: Did the *Saw* guys give you any money for completely ripping that film off?

DF: Haven't seen it. Look, people come up to me and say, "You started torture porn." And I say, "Fuck you." I actually think we were fairly responsible about the notions of the violence. I thought what was amazing about what Andy prescribed in his script and what he was so adamant about was that you don't need to see stuff. He unlocks the Pandora's box of your imagination, in a really gripping way. Now, you watch *Law & Order SVU*, and they're walking in the hallways and they say, "We found semen in the eye socket." [audience laughs] I would never do that. But we had a lot of people insisting they'd seen more than they did. I almost had a fist-fight with a woman at a Beverly Hills cocktail party because she said, "There is no need to make a stand in of Gwyneth Paltrow's head to find in the box. You don't need to see that." And I said, "Well, we didn't." And she said, "Oh yes, you did." [audience laughs] So, the imagination, if properly primed, can do more than any army of makeup artists. That was always my thing: get people to fear it, get them to see it in their heads.

MS: Talking of fist-fights, we're going to skip *The Game*, which I think is a fantastic film, and talk about *Fight Club*. Clearly you were reticent to go back to Fox after your *Alien³* experience, but they supported your thing.

DF: But they were all fired, that's the beauty of it. [audience laughs] Every time somebody comes and says, "You've gotta scratch our backs," I say, "Why? You're not going to have this job in eleven months. I wanna talk to your assistant." [audience laughs]

MS: So all the assistants helped you make one of the most amazing, daring studio films of all time.

DF: No, they knew what they were doing. Look, I'm not sure Rupert Murdoch read the script or the book that the film was based on, but Bill Mechanic and Laura Ziskin, when we started talking about it, we were talking about this naughty little poke-in-the-eye cult book. I'd tried to buy the book when it was out before Fox bought it. And really, it's not Fox, it's Fox 2000; you know, when all the major studios were trying to act like they were indie too, this was Fox's indie wing, and they were trying to buy this nasty little book. If you've never read the book, it's as good as it gets—I nearly pissed myself, I was laughing so hard when I read it. The guy who became my agent, Josh Donen, who was trying to buy the book with me, had told me to read it. I was like, "I don't read books, and I'm in the middle of postproduction on *The Game*," but he said, "You have to read it tonight." So I did, and I called him back and said, "We gotta buy this." And he said, "You waited too long. Fox bought it. But go in and meet with Laura Ziskin." So I did and I told her, "I don't want to make the $3 million version of this; I want to crash planes, I want to blow up buildings and I want to do the thing that Hollywood really shouldn't do, material like this." She said, "Great!" and we agreed on this development process that I still hold true to to this day. You can't hold the hands of the people who are going to pay for this stuff and do anything marginally outrageous. You have to enter into a deal with them where you say, "We'll work with a writer that you bless, and we will go away. And when we're done and I'm ready to arm wrestle about the content of what that thing is, we'll bring it back and show it to you." She said, "Well, when will you be done?" And I said, "I don't know. It may take a year, it may take three, I don't know." So we hired Jim Uhls, who went off and wrote a draft of the screenplay that didn't have any voiceover in it. I read it and said, "This is sad and pathetic. It's just sorrow and people being horrible. Where's all the stuff where he talks about what he's thinking?" And he said, "Oh, that's kind of a crutch." And I said, "No, man, that's our only chance at being sarcastic and satirical." So he went back and put all that in. Then we came back to Laura, and we laid the script on the table, with a budget, schedule, and cast, and said, "$67 million, it's Brad Pitt and Edward Norton, and hopefully Helena Bonham Carter, and an eighty-nine-day shoot. You have seventy-two hours—let us know if you're in." And she went and scrambled Bill Mechanic and they came over, we walked them through the storyboards for the entire movie, showed them the whole thing, and they said, "Go do it." You can't make a movie like that, with that number, against the will of a studio. That's kind of what I tried to do on *Alien³*. But if you can get them to buy off on what it is, you can move an inch towards those things that will hopefully make them immortal.

MS: So you made it, and it came out, and it polarized people.

DF: Polarized—that's a very polite way of putting it. We opened at the Venice Film Festival, and I think to say that they hated it would be an understatement. Let's put it this way: the youngest person in the screening was Giorgio Armani. [audience laughs] They called for our hides, and we split town. We thought it was funny. Actually, Helena Bonham Carter's mother was three seats down from me and she was just laughing and laughing—she was the only one. [audience laughs] She's cool.

MS: Then it came out on DVD and everybody loved it. Did you feel vindicated that it's become a cult movie, although it's too big to be a cult movie now.

DF: No, it's a cult movie—it's just a big cult. [audience laughs] It's funny. There's a tricky thing: if you spend $15 million, it's not even a pimple on the ass of that kind of multinational media conglomerate. But if you spend $67 million, they gotta release your movie. That's a big number, they can't write it down. But by the same token, you get people who go, "So it's about fighting." And they went out and sold ads for this movie on World Wrestling Federation. [audience laughs] I said, "You know, the crowd who go to the WWF are going to be made a little uncomfortable. Certainly the opening weekend, they're going to be like, 'Dude, that was gay.'" [audience laughs] So we had this tremendous word of mouth that didn't work for us, and the movie just went into the toilet and no one ever saw it. It was sold to the wrong group. You can make movies for a select audience, but you have to market it to them. The spots that were running, were running on shows that the people who were gonna get this never watched.

MS: A boring, kind of geeky question. Sound is always amazing in your films. I think you've said that you have a psychotic attention to detail when it comes to sound.

DF: Well, I think it's half the experience. When you take twelve dollars or however much it costs to go to a movie here, and you're going to require their attention for two hours, and you're responsible for everything they're going to see and hear, it seems to me it's an opportunity to use those fifteen speakers to either do something intentional or do something accidental. I'd just rather do the intentional. I work with a guy called Ren Klyce, who's worked on all my movies since *Se7en*, and who I trust implicitly. He's just responsible for the sound. He helps choose the composer, helps spot the music and where it goes, and he works with all the source cues. On *Panic Room*, for instance, which is an interesting movie—maybe not from an audience's standpoint—but from a technical standpoint: you have an entire movie taking place in one space. To have that space evolve in some kind of way over the course of two hours, part of the thing he did was . . . he would record all the Foley, all the footsteps, all the doorknob turns, all the hard effects of everything, in the actual set that we were shooting in at the weekends. So we would shoot, and then he would come in on Saturday and Sunday and he would open the windows and shut them, jiggle the glass. He's insane about this, but it sounds so much better than the fake stuff. It's all just a lot of work. If you want to work really hard, stuff can sound good.

MS: So now we're going to throw it open to you in the audience.
Q1: Just a question on *Button*. Given that it's been kicking around for so long, and has been deemed unfilmable, where do you find the belief to say, "I'm going to make that movie, and I'm going to make it a success"?
DF: I didn't say the second part. I think Terry Gilliam looked at it earlier. There are just so many layers of complexity in terms of the period, the evolution of the background, that once you give up the idea of five or six people playing this one person, and you can kind of focus on one actor— that's what made it work for me. I know Brad will be able to describe this arc, he'll be able to figure this guy out, and I just have to create a world for him to do that in. The first time I read it, when I read Robin [Swicord]'s first draft of it in 1991/92, I think I was thinking of it then in terms of five or six actors, and it made my head hurt.

Q2: You always get an amazing performance from your actors—from Robert Downey Jr. to Morgan Freeman, Edward Norton. Do you just let them run with it?
DF: Can I just point out that you said, "You get such great performances from Robert Downey Jr., Morgan Freeman, Edward Norton." I think you answered the question. Cast really good people, find a way to get really good people in your movie and take credit for it. [audience laughs] For eternity.

Q3: This is your second film where you use a digital camera, after *Zodiac*. Do you plan to do the same for your next films, and why?
DF: It's not the camera. There are certain things that digital doesn't do well—but it's more about the workflow to me. It's about the way that I'm

able to make my movie. I like the idea that the first three takes, you're just rehearsing. I like the fact that actors never have to stop in the middle and watch somebody take a thousand dollars worth of film out the top of a camera and put another thousand dollars worth in. I like the fact that there's no guilt, you can just delete stuff. If something's not worth the time that it took for everyone to say it, you can just go beep and it's gone. So I like the plastic nature of how I'm able to work in digital. I like being able to work at really, really low light levels—we shot most of *Zodiac* and a lot of this movie, certainly the night exteriors, we shot it in 1.6 which, for anamorphic, you normally have to shoot at 2.8, 2.85, so it's one-third or one-quarter of the light that you would normally need to do that. You can work with more manageable units and it's a smaller crew. Also, you have a giant monitor that everybody, from the boom operator to the makeup artist to the actors to the dolly grip—everybody's looking at the same thing: this is the final, release print, it's not going to change. And everyone can see, that shit's out of focus, or her eyelash is coming off in the middle of that take, or she's got a spot on her teeth. You can see the background. One of the things I hate is when you can see extras in the background; for instance, two people at a table in a restaurant, and they're both talking at the same time. Unless they're married, that would never happen—one of them would have to listen. Things that you have in the back of your mind to keep a lookout for—so finally, everyone's talking about the same picture. And also, I hate voodoo. I hate the whole thing that you're going to see seven out of eight takes that are out of focus, and somebody's going to say, "But that last one's pretty good." And you can say, "When you're directing your movie, you can get one out of eight takes." No, as a way of working, I prefer having dailies in your lap, rather than waiting to see how much you hate everything you did.

MS: And in terms of takes, you are renowned for doing a few.
DF: This is bullshit. Look, you're spending $150 million, unbelievable amounts of money to ship period vehicles from Illinois down to Louisiana and get them working. There are teams of people making these cars work, all this stuff. So you get there and you're going to shoot three takes and then go home? Why? This is the whole reason we're here—we're here to do what's in front of the camera. And I find that actors—some people resent it and go, "My best stuff was when I had a lot of energy after my mochaccino and now my energy's gone," but a lot of actors work it out in their heads, they figure it out and have an idea of what they're going to do. I can see that and I like to move past that, to where they've

forgotten why they came, or who they are. And it is about choreography, where the eye of the audience finds that person and that person is revealed and they come forward and say their line. All those things in concert. So, you spend all that money to get there, so you might as well make sure you got it.

Q4: You've made films where improbable things look realistic. Did you ever consider making a superhero movie or fantasy, where things are bit more difficult to make believable?
DF: I was asked if I might be interested in the first *Spider-Man*, and I went in and told them what I might be interested in doing, and they hated it. No, I'm not interested in doing "A Superhero." The thing I liked about *Spider-Man* was I liked the idea of a teenager, the notion of this moment in time when you're so vulnerable yet completely invulnerable. But I wasn't interested in the genesis, I just couldn't shoot somebody being bitten by a radioactive spider—just couldn't sleep knowing I'd done that. [audience laughs]

Q5: I've always been impressed by your visual flair and atmosphere of your films. How do you conceive that look and feel in your mind and how do you convey that to your cinematographer?
DF: It's like finding a character. When I'm watching somebody act, it's a behavior editorial function—I look at someone act, and I might say, "I don't believe him when he says that." I don't know why I don't believe him, probably because the people that I've met, they don't act like that when they say stuff like that and mean it. I also have rules of thumb about dialogue. For example, I feel that most people, when they speak, are lying. So, I'm looking at the eyes, I'm more interested in the body and seeing how comfortable they are saying what it is they are saying than specifically what they're saying. I think the same thing is true of cinematography: you're presented with a room and a scene. You have a feeling about this, maybe it's Thanksgiving and it's the end of the day, so there's no direct sunlight coming in because the sun's going down behind trees. So you kind of talk about it in those terms. I never really start with a photograph or a painting—you always get in trouble with that because you look at it and you go, "Fuck, this looks so great and that looks so pale in comparison." So I tend not to do that any more. Where are the people, where do the people have to go, what do they have to do, what's my relationship to them? And what do I know about horrible

family get-togethers with these people and their weird guilt, and how everything's supposed to be so great on Thanksgiving and how it never is?

MS: What are you doing next? There's talk about *Ness*, or *Heavy Metal*?
Keanu Reeves's chef movie?
DF: I don't know. I'm going to sleep for about four months. We did *Zo-diac* and this movie back to back. We were shooting this movie when *Zo-diac* opened, so we were getting commercials sent to us over the Internet
at the same time that we were shooting days. I don't know what I want
to do. I just want to sleep.

Q6: I just want to ask about the technical element of your films—it's almost like a character in your films. In this film, it's time that is the main
character. How did you achieve that?
DF: We live in a silly time, and people go to the movies to see something
that they haven't seen before, and you have to promise to show them
that. In a horrible way, you have to promise them a special effect. And
we decided that the special effect in this movie was time and the effect
of time on the background, but more importantly, the one thing that
people had never done as ridiculously thoroughly as we intended to do
which was the effect of time on people's faces. We knew that we had to go
to Murmansk, we knew that we had to do battles at sea, we knew that we
had to go back to New Orleans in the sixties, and we knew we had to go
to New York in the forties, early fifties—we knew we had all these things
that were going to take place in the background but the thing was, how
do you see the same person un-etched or de-etched by time? I wanted
Benjamin as recognizable as Brad—this is a guy who can't walk fifty feet
in the civilized world without seeing a photograph of himself—so people are very used to seeing his face. So we wanted the audience to go,
"Wow, those are his ears, just bigger and droopier. That is his nose, just a
little bit bigger and droopier." And then when he comes back in the ballet studio, it's like him in *Thelma & Louise*. You look to spend the money
in the right place to take the things that are going to support the story. If
you're not doing that, that's not smart. So the special effect in this movie
was time, and we needed to do everything we could to support that idea,
and be as thorough as we could be. With Cate [Blanchett]'s face, it was
the other way: we had to take her head and put her on a ballerina when
she was seventeen. We did very subtle things because her skin's so good,
it's like porcelain. But we did different things to her eyes, and of course

we had to take her through to where she was the dying Daisy. I don't look at it and go, "This will be hard. It's going to be a really long movie and it's going to be hard. Let's do this." But you look at it and go, "If we're going to tell this story, where are we going to spend our money and where's the stuff where we can get in and do blindstitch?"

MS: Alas, we're out of time. David Fincher, thank you.

Social Network: Interview with Director David Fincher

Emanuel Levy / 2010

From EmanuelLevy.com, September 23, 2010. Reprinted with permission.

Emanuel Levy: This movie, at least on the surface, is a departure for you. Dealing with characters whose primary means of expression is verbal is not something you've had in your other movies—did you like that?
David Fincher: It was fine, but I think it's more like this—I don't know what directors are *supposed* to do except what the script wants. That's what the script was, and that's what it needed. Are you supposed to hoard your little corner of the Monopoly board? Are you supposed to say, *I'm Park Place and this is what I do.* That seems kind of dull.

The language is what's up front, but the thing that supports the language is the mouths out of which the language comes, the clothes on the bodies that carry the mouths from which the language comes, the houses and the rooms that the bodies inhabit. To me, the Chinese checkers of it is this: you get a couple of Aeron chairs and some computers, and the guys rattle off their dialogue in the way that they're supposed to.

But the three dimensional chess of it is to try and steep the viewer in the world of the movie, and to do so in a way that's effortless for him. I knew that I needed to make the surroundings of everything—where these people are, what they're wearing, all those details—feel right for Harvard, and right for these kids and their expertise. The fun of it is not *only* to find a handful of really bright, incredibly watchable kids to say these lines, but also to forge a world around them that makes them look like the kind of kids that would be saying this stuff.

EL: A world in which the events of the story are possible.
DF: Yes—but also a world in which they're *essential. Inevitable.* You want to build the drama—the inevitability of the fact that these kids can't be

159

friends or the fact that they're going to have to divide the spoils—by seeing this place that they all come from, with its bad prefab furniture and scratchy sheets and fire alarms in the middle of the wall and fireplaces that don't work. A lot of people think of Harvard as being like Camelot, or Hogwarts—but it's not. Of course Harvard is old and it's stately, but physically it's really this odd, colonial, kind of re-fabbed and refurbished place where every ten or fifteen years more conduit gets put on the walls and it falls apart a little bit more. Visually, these kids do sort of come from nothing. Whatever their family life was like—and I'm sure the Winklevosses lived well—you're trying to find this level playing field where they all meet. Everybody is peering into what each other's personal strengths or deficits are but you're not really privy to that. You're not seeing the Winklevosses in a Grey Poupon commercial. And that was great, I thought.

EL: When you read the script, did you know right away that this would be your approach? Did you immediately know how to do it?

DF: No. Again, it's not that you "know" how to do it—I don't have a map for how to get there, I don't necessarily know how to get through the woods—but I know where *there* is. You know what I mean? It's not like you look at the thing and say, *I've got to head east for a while and then I can cut back*—that's the reality of what you're presented with on a daily basis—but you can see Mt. Kilimanjaro in the distance and you can know where that is. I can look at that and feel like I know these kids—*part of me is this guy, part of me is that guy.* I know people like that, and I know what it's like to be that pissed off at somebody that you've known for so long, and I know what it's like to have that conversation where you go, *This is where it ends.* But any director that says they see the whole movie in their head is a liar.

EL: Unlike other movies that you've done, you came into this one with what was very close to a finished script—and yet it's very obviously a David Fincher film. How did you achieve that?

DF: I look at my job first and foremost as an interpreter. You're taking the written word and you're trying to have it make sense in terms of where people are in space, where they are in the frame, where they are in focus. I don't look at it as, *Oh my God, I have to find a script where the lead character is from Marin County and grew up in the 70s.* It would be just as boring for actors to do only what they know. I think you go into something like this and you say, *Here's a situation and here's a group of* *people—what do I know and what do I understand about this? What can I bring to this given situation?* I've been Mark Zuckerberg—there are times in my life where I've acted that way. There are times in my life where I've been Eduardo Saverin—where I've gone and made a scene and regretted it and where I've been emotional and felt silly and stupid. And there are times when I've felt self-righteous and I've acted out in this other way. You look at the whole of it and you make a patchwork quilt of what you relate to—what something looked like, what something felt like at a certain time—and that's what you draw on. And then you go in, and you get really good people to bring their trip to it and you sort it out. I don't think there's any way *not* to put your stamp on a movie because you're basically editing behavior. That's your job. You're basically responding to a behavior and saying, *I believe that or I don't believe that*—and so you're going to, in some pretty basic way, inform how the people behave.

EL: As a director, is that what makes every movie personal to you—or is it something unique to this one?

DF: Look, what Mark does is no different than directing a movie—it's what I do for a living every day. You grow something, and your job is to grow it well and to make sure it gets enhanced and to take care of it. That's the subject of the movie. And if you have to hurt people's feelings in order to protect that *thing*, that's what you have to do. It's a responsibility.

You want to love every character in the movie. You want to be able to understand them. You want to be able to see what's there. You want to be able to see their humanity. You want to be able to relate to them. But, as a director, the characters' behaviors are inevitably related to facets of moments in your own life. You look at the work and say, *Maybe I do know what that is.*

I've been the angry young man. I've been Elvis Costello. I know what that's like. The anger is certainly something I felt that I could relate to—the notion of being twenty-one and having a fairly clear notion of what it is you want to do or what it is you want to say and having all these people go, *Well, we'd love to, we'd love you to try. Show us what it is that you want to do.* It's that whole condescending thing of having to ask adults for permission because the perception is that you're too young to do it for yourself. And that's why I understood Mark's frustration. You have a vision of what this thing should be. And everyone wants to tell you, *Oh, well, you're young. You'll see soon enough.*

EL: And the movie, on some level, is a testament to Mark's work ethic—his relentless ability to execute that vision.

DF: Right. Mark does what no one else in the movie does and he's the guy who reaps the rewards—but he also pays a price. He was the one saying, *Advertising? I don't know—that's a way to go about it but I don't know if it's the only way.* And I totally concur with that.

EL: What is the movie saying about success? Is it something about the moment at which your fantasy of success collides with actual success?
DF: It's hard for me to even imagine the kind of success that the movie is talking about.

EL: But you had some significant degree of success when you were young.
DF: I do liken it, in a way, to the fraternity of the outsider that existed at a point in time with a commercial company that I started when I was twenty-five or whatever. And that was very much a bunch of people getting together because they couldn't find representation, because they couldn't make the jump from being music video directors to being commercial directors with this catch-22: *You can't do it until you've done it. But you can't have done it until you do it.* Nobody was going to give us our shot. It was a point in time when we were with Propaganda, during the whole movement of music videos becoming mainstream, and advertisers were looking for the MTV look. There was definitely a point where we were like, *Nobody at Pepsi is going to tell us that what we're doing is not going to sell records or sell soft drinks or sell sneakers. We're going to continue to do what we do until the world revolves and turns around and they beg us to come make television commercials for them.* Even though the impetus for us to be at MTV was that no one would hire us for television commercials. So I do understand what it is to stake your claim in the margins, to wait for the sun to illuminate your part of the world. And I think there's a little bit of that in Mark—he saw that if he could link all these things then people could have this sort of immediate connection in the same way as cellular phones. That's what it is—it's a cellular phone immediacy in the remaking of your image of yourself. *This is not who I am. This is who I want you to see that I am.* It's Narcissus.

EL: Is it your experience with Propaganda that made you want to do this?
DF: That certainly helped form my understanding of Mark and those

EMANUEL LEVY / 2010

guys—but it was before that. I graduated high school in 1980—and for three years, everybody just hung out on the weekends looking at Beta-Max and VHS tapes of movies. You have those little fraternities of people who are all movie makers or future movie makers or movie maker wannabes, all watching movies on technology that exists at the time and going, *He shouldn't have done that, he should've done this. This is where he went wrong and this is what's wrong with the narrative and here's why this lighting sucks and this is why this notion of being something could've been great but isn't.* You go and you do all that stuff as a young man. And then finally you get your opportunity. You get your "at bat." So I related to the notion of that, but I didn't go to college. I didn't have the dorm experience. I didn't have the fraternity experience. But I had my own dorm and my own fraternity.

In my life, I've been part of a lot of different little creative cliques—of young men who had ideas about technology or ideas about filmmaking or storytelling. I knew that world, and I felt like this tapped into it. It also seemed like it was talking a lot about where technology in the information age has taken us as far as innovation is concerned. You're talking about a world that no longer requires you to build a workforce and a factory to get a product out. Someone can disappear into his dorm room with a couple cases of Red Bull and, a few weeks later, come out with a beta of something that can be on six hundred desktops within nine days, and six hundred million within six years.

EL: Mark, for example, goes from being in the cracks to becoming completely mainstream.
DL: He owns the mainstream. He is the mainstream. He's the portal to the mainstream.

EL: Right. You can't get to the mainstream without him. Is that a good thing for him? What do you want us to feel about that?
DF: I don't *want* to feel anything about it. I don't think it's necessary to the story. I think it's ironic. I think it's ironic that creativity has to happen on the fringe. It has to. Creative change happens on the fringe of everything. It's always on the edge, it's in the margins, and then it's adopted by the herd. And I think it's ironic that a guy who seems to have issues with being able to communicate with other people has invented one of the greatest tools for communicating *with* people.

EL: Is it that failure to communicate that drives Mark? Mark says, *I* *built this thing and I'm going to hang onto it—and it's never going to be fin-ished.* What is underneath that?

DF: I think that there's an anger or this sense of not being appreciated—or rather there's anger *for* not being appreciated, at least for the right rea-sons or as completely or as much as Mark feels he should be. And I think that's human across the board. Everybody goes, *You know, I'm not so sure my parents appreciated me enough. I'm not so sure my siblings appreciated me enough. I'm not sure my friends appreciated me enough.* This story frames a slightly more exaggerated view of that feeling, but—as it relates to the notion of Mark never wanting to finish something—I think that's just the reality of invention in the information age. Nothing is ever going to roll off an assembly line and be somebody else's responsibility. It's going to reside on a desktop computer and provide a continuing relationship with that user and that user base, and I think Mark brilliantly understood that in a way that few people do. In the information age, Steve Jobs has a relationship with not only his product designers, but with the people who are buying his product for more money than competing versions of it. That's because of the relationship that he has to the design—the rela-tionship that he has to the message of it all, the relationship that he has to the empowerment of owning these things. Steve Jobs is an example of this in a way that Bill Gates isn't. And I believe that's what Zuckerberg wants to be, and I think that's what Zuckerberg has become.

EL: Is there a price that Mark pays for what he becomes?

DF: I think the price Mark pays is that, with every mounting hill he's able to climb—from five hundred early adopters to five hundred million later adopters—he's forced to realize the awesome responsibility of hav-ing your dreams come true. He learns that—if you want to be great at something—the next lap of the marathon you're supposed to shave a few seconds off, you're supposed to get a little leaner, you're supposed to get a little stronger. And Mark will do that—in the end, you see a guy who has a million users, but that means he has to stay late while every-one else can go celebrate. He's alone. He got what he wanted—but he's as alone as he is at the end of the first scene in the movie.

EL: What are the "seconds" that Mark shaves off—Eduardo and Sean and the Winklevosses?

DF: I think that Sean is as close to a kind of soul mate to what Mark is trying to accomplish as anyone else that he meets, but I don't think that any of those people you mention are willing to work as hard or as long, or think as deeply or completely or as uninterruptedly, as Mark is—and that's why *he* is Mark Zuckerberg.

EL: Because you have the vision, does that excuse the behavior?

DF: Only if you're right. One of the things that I always found very moving in this material is that it's about someone who's pursuing his own idea of excellence or his own idea of meaning. It's Galileo, but Mark is the only guy who sees that. Maybe it's because his social deficits make it so that he, in some way, has to believe that there's a future where you can connect in this other way—but I also think that there's this way in which life frequently tells you that the thing that you think is going to kill you is actually the thing that makes you what you are.

EL: That's what I'm asking—does brilliance come with a level of entitlement?

DF: Yes, in some ways—but it also comes with that awesome responsibility, which Mark discovers.

Mark takes very seriously his responsibility to his creation, but he also takes very seriously his responsibility to himself—some will say he didn't take seriously enough his responsibility to those around him. But we have as many articles that say, *It's ludicrous to think that Eduardo and I were best friends,* as we have to the contrary.

The movie is very clearly *not* saying that Mark thinks Eduardo is his best friend. The movie is saying that Eduardo *thinks* that's what Mark feels about him. It's never clear that this is reciprocal. If Eduardo were to forget what people say and just look at what they do, he would realize that it doesn't really matter what either of them is saying about their friendship. The fact of the matter is that they were young men trying to accomplish the same goal at the same time in the same room and, whatever their responsibilities were to each other, at some point there was a fork in the road. It's traumatic because one of them gets left in the dust.

EL: Who betrays whom in the movie? Does Mark betray Eduardo or does Eduardo betray Mark?

DF: I think that they both betray each other—I never saw it as cut and dried as Mark pulling the rug out from under Eduardo. I believe that Eduardo has a failure of imagination. He can't imagine that this thing could ever be worth anything or become profitable if he doesn't sell advertising, and I think that was the crux of their fork in the road. That's Eduardo's failure of imagination. And the Winklevosses, they never got out of the merge lane.

EL: There is an entire trope of American movies in which the Winklevosses would be the heroes and Mark would be the villain—and yet this is a movie in which Mark is the hero and the Winklevosses are the villains. **DF:** The only thing I can relate it to is this: in directing those scenes at the deposition, I would literally say to one side of the table, *This little weasel ripped you off and he's sitting in the chair that you should be sitting in, and without you, he's nothing.*

And then I would walk to the other side of the table and go, *Do you really think that there would be $15 billion worth of Facebook if you had made the Harvard Connection? Look at those douche bags. There's nothing—there are no spoils to divide—if not for the hard work and brilliance of Mark Zuckerberg. So look at them standing over there in their Brooks Brothers suits all smug trying to get a place at your table.*

EL: But you go to great lengths to say that Mark isn't in it for the money—so what's he in it for? **DF:** I believe that Mark is in it to fully realize his dream, which is to build an apparatus that allows him to connect to the world in a way that he's unable to do in his own life. People talk about Mark's borderline Asperger's, his horrific PR style, but I think that Facebook *required* someone with those kinds of limited social skills. If you're going to create an apparatus like Facebook, you have to start with somebody who's going to be able to understand how difficult it is to communicate. That's the progression.

EL: What do you feel about somebody who would say that it's not fair to make a movie about this guy who did all this stuff when he was nineteen and didn't know any better? **DF:** I don't know. Look, I don't think anybody involved ever thought we were sharpening our knives for Mark Zuckerberg. I think we thought of him as a compelling, interesting character for a movie—in the same way that Travis Bickle is. The same way that Rupert Pupkin is. The same way that the narrator in *Fight Club* is.

EL: You could also say Charles Foster Kane. **DF:** Yeah, exactly. And I would. I think the two are correlative. What we were able to glean from YouTube videos and *60 Minutes* interviews is that

Mark Zuckerberg is a young man, and a very young man at a time when this thing really caught fire. But there's no doubt that this is not a guy who goes to great lengths to ingratiate himself. So, I don't know how much of it is *him*. I don't know how much of it is youth and I don't know how much of it is lack of socialization.

EL: Is it the perfect storm, then? This cultural need for Facebook, the business need for it, and the vision of a nineteen-year-old kid who somehow found himself typifying the experience of an incipient Facebook user all colliding at the same time?

DF: I wasn't aware of Facebook as it was groundswelling, as it was a rumor, as it was furtive whispers. I was only aware of it as it became an inevitability. So I can't really speak to it as an early adopter. By the time I knew about it, it was K-Mart.

But you now have many portals into your life—you have doors and windows that allow you to walk out of your room and look out, and the facility of this technology has progressed to a point where you have a new window, you have a new door, and it doesn't allow you to just see your backyard, it allows you to see a backyard in Uzbekistan. It allows you to see the sunrise in Egypt, and it's amazing, the fact that you can so effortlessly and instantly take a picture with your phone, which is with you constantly, and, moments later, send it to somebody halfway around the world and say, *This is my experience right now*. Without that spark, you don't have the fire that is Facebook. But how that relates to people saying, *My God I almost forgot about you, we were neighbors in second grade,* I still don't know.

With all of this coming to in the maelstrom of those forces colliding, I do think Mark figured out something—and there's no doubt that it's in some way connected to American narcissism: the need to be on the cover of one's own *Rolling Stone*.

EL: Do you think there's a value to Facebook?
DF: Do I think it's worth $25 billion?

EL: No, do you think that Facebook is fundamentally a good or bad thing?
DF: I think that, like anything that is so flexible and so powerful, it's obviously both—it's alternating current, sixty times a second. It's like cell phones. Are cell phones a good or bad? No—thank God we have them but do we spend too much time on them? Do they create the impression

in minds that don't want to delve too deeply that we're somehow connected everywhere, when really all we are is riding around in a car filling our empty lives with, "Hey what happened?" "Nothing." "OK, call you later." You know, "What are you doing?" "Nothing, what are you doing?" "Nothing." I had a friend with one of the great quotes—I said, "So do you have an email address yet?" And he goes, "Nah, I'm not really into the Internet." And I said, "Why?" And he goes, "I don't like CB radio that you type." And I thought, that's kind of an interesting way of looking at it: CB radio you type.

EL: But isn't Mark using the computer in a way that goes beyond that? Is this hacking element something you could relate to?
DF: I didn't necessarily relate to it, to be honest—I don't really know any hackers—but I saw Mark as kind of like Banksy. I saw him as this outsider graffiti artist. Somebody who saw himself as a threat to society, in almost a fun way. I understand that there's this world of people who look at intrusion and dissemination and other ideas of this sort, but I didn't really relate to that as much as I related to the idea of a graffiti artist.

A lot of people have made movies about the Internet. There are a lot of bad movies about being sucked into a computer and having your life turned upside down—there's all kinds of nonsense like that. I think that the only way to talk about this notion of web-preneurship is to be able to speak cogently about the Molotov cocktail of the hacker. The first act of our story is this guy who hacks a Facebook at Harvard and decides, *Wait a minute, people are drawn to this*—it kicks off and sparks a whole different crop top that becomes something as ubiquitous as the Big Mac. Now, I think *hacking* is integral to the story, but I don't think it's essential—it's essential when you're discussing Mark Zuckerberg, I think it's essential when you're discussing Sean Parker. But I certainly don't think it has anything to do with what the Winklevosses were about.

EL: Or Eduardo?
DF: Right. I think Eduardo said, *Let's give the people what they want.* And I think that Mark is the other guy saying, *I'm interested in doing something like this,* and he stumbled onto something people would want, and he was able to see it as a next step. Meanwhile, the guy who was just thinking about giving the people what they want fundamentally couldn't.

EL: As an outgrowth of that, Mark reinvents himself in the same way that Sean Parker did—so what's the difference between Mark and Sean?

DF: I saw Sean Parker as a guy who's a veteran of the whole VC world—he's a veteran of having your ass handed to you by the people who would finance your dreams. He's the older brother who's been through it. I saw him way more as Wally than I did Eddie Haskell. I saw him as the guy who—when you're a kid—is the older brother of your friend, the one you look up to because he says, *Don't worry about that, worry about this. This is what's important.*

EL: Is part of Sean Parker a cautionary tale to Mark? In other words, all the things in Sean that lead him to continually attempt to destroy himself, we watch Mark *not* do.

DF: It's the birth of the CEO gene in Mark. But I saw Sean as a guy who—maybe it's not a chemical dependency—but certainly Sean's weakness is that he likes a good meal, he likes a good drink, he likes a good friend. I saw him as Jedediah Leland. I saw him as the guy you need to have around you who says, *No, be true to yourself.* And in his being true to himself, he becomes a bit of an albatross.

EL: One of the things in the movie that makes Mark sympathetic is that the world around him is moving so fast. He can't keep up with what he created. How did you achieve that visceral feeling of everything moving at such a relentless clip?

DF: I don't know that I ever consciously took what was happening in front of the camera *behaviorally* and superimposed it onto the accelerated world that we live in. I can't say that I knowingly used it as the graph paper against which to draw.

To me, it's how fast can you go and still have the audience understand what you're talking about. That's Frank Capra. The whole idea is, *Let's not be boring.* If you have to do this *Parent Trap* twins thing—which we did with the Winklevosses—part of what creates the impression that they're two different people is the degree to which they finish each other's sentences and cut each other off. It's not even so much the proximity of one to the other, but rather the way in which their speech dovetails into the next guy's idea because they're so familiar with each other's patois. They very quickly realize where that sentence is going and they can move on to the next thing, right over the top of their brother. To me, that was part of the speed—the effect of the text, and this hyper kind of righteous indignation, necessitated a pace and rhythm. The first scene in the movie is a girl saying, *I'm really having a hard time keeping up with what you're talking about.* Mark better be talking pretty quickly otherwise we're not going to have any respect for Erica, and we have a lot of respect for her—she's the one who comes back in and sets our stuff straight.

EL: How is directing kids of this age different from directing Cate Blanchett or Brad Pitt or Ed Norton?

DF: It's a lot of fun. Of course there's a lot to be said for having the right resources and skill sets from having made fifteen or twenty movies and having Hollywood revolve around you. There's a lot to be said for somebody who brings that to bear, but it's also a much different and more pressurized situation for that person, when you have someone in your movie who makes the movie *go*. It's a different thing for an actor like that, on a daily basis, than it is for somebody who has to be considered part of an ensemble. It's like *American Graffiti*—you look at that movie and say, *I don't think Richard Dreyfuss has ever been better,* but at that time and place, Susanne Somers had never been better. Ron Howard had never been better. It's great to be able to find people who are at this crossroads where they're no longer kids, and they're trying to find their way and define themselves. I will say another thing that I think is really interesting, which is that I went into this saying, *whatever happens, I'm not casting any of those Disney kids,* and they're *all* Disney kids, and they're all great! Thank God for the Disney kids, because they're awesome. Thank God for the Justin Timberlake and Brenda Songs of the world, and Joe Mazello, who grew up on movie sets. And Jesse! And Andrew. Andrew acted in his first movie when he was nine or something. I sort of said to myself, *I'm not going to go for movie brats, or television brats*—but now I have to say that they were *so* prepared. They were awesome. They knew how to work, and that was it. You want people who are going to come to this thing going, *I know what to do with this,* and then you want them to fall down a hill. You want to take them right to the edge and push them over so they find this other thing in it that's not the preconceived notion of who they are. And yet, the reason we cast Andrew, for example, aside from his incredible skill set, is because he is human. He is that guy who can be hurt, he is that guy who cares *that* much—so wherever and however we're going to lose our way, that is the guy who will feel it. And the same thing was true with Justin. My biggest problem with everybody that we looked at was, *I need somebody who understands the world like an agent does, or like a record producer does*—what it is to seat two people together and know that there's going to be annuity. You can tell an actor over and over and over what that is, but if he doesn't understand it, if he doesn't have that little twinkle in the eye of knowing *there's money to be made here,* that those two are getting along and there's the fruits of my labor—he's never going to get it.

I usually try not to get too bogged down with physical types, but we wanted to stay kind of true to the real people—but mostly to me it was the vibe. As far as directing twenty-five-year olds, God, it was a ball.

EL: It seems like everyone is playing, to some degree, at least some aspect of themselves.
DF: I wanted to find something human about everybody, and I never saw Mark as the villain. I don't see Sean as the villain. I don't see the Winklevosses as the villain. I don't see Eduardo's lack of imagination as villainy. I look at them all and go, *They're kids, they're going to make mistakes, they're going to fall into the right things for the right reasons, they're going to fall out of the right things for the wrong reasons.* It just happens, and so the thing was to find a bunch of people who wanted to do the work, have the fun, experiment, and not know what they were going to do. Once we'd blocked the thing that they were going to do—we knew they were going to have no choice but to go out on a limb so I could hand them a chainsaw.

EL: Was it like that with Trent? Can you talk about how that collaboration came about?
DF: Well, I knew Trent for a long time and we'd talked about the idea of working together. Now, I know how this sounds and I say this in jest, but all jokes have a little bit of truth to them—I really saw this movie as the *Citizen Kane* of John Hughes movies, and I heard the music in my head as being something from a John Hughes movie. I heard it as being this kind of cheeseball synthesizer stuff, and I thought that the synthesizer would be the perfect instrument for the world of the Internet—the hum of it, the drone of it, the pneumatics and the booting up, all this stuff with these weird sounds. And then I started thinking about the crush of that interfacing with something for that many hours a day—what your eyes feel like and what your skin feels like if you've been sitting in front of your computer. It's that kind of dead irradiating feeling that you have, and I thought that the only guy I knew who would get that and understand how to take synthesizers and make them operatic—and also understand the horniness of being the dweeb outsider—was Trent Reznor. And so I called him up, and he said no—but I kept calling him, and finally just said, *I don't have a reputation of being a pain in the ass for no reason.* I told

him, *You need to come and let me show you some of this movie so that you can understand what it is, because it's one thing to read the script and it's one thing to talk about it and it's another thing to see.* And so he came by and we showed him some scenes and at the end of it he said, *I'm in—I get what you're talking about.* I also think that he was a little exhausted at that moment in time and I think that he felt that he was going to have to drive the thing somehow—and I think when he saw the sequences he sort of thought, *Wow, I just need to interpret what the envelope is for this sonically. I need to help. I don't need to provide the cake—I can just provide the icing.*

EL: But on another level it's a completely unexpected score. It would be very easy to imagine this movie with a Phil Glass kind of modal pulse score and you didn't do that.

DF: Right. *Tangerine Dream.* We talked about that whole thing, but in the end I honestly don't know anybody more talented than Trent. People don't realize that he has an awesome sense of humor and that he's incredibly ironic, and I thought that he'd understand the irony of his involvement.

EL: Almost the biggest and most striking thing he does in the movie is his first cue. To take that journey from the breakup to Facemash and to make that a journey that's basically describing loneliness as opposed to energy is an enormously bold and brave choice.

DF: Yes—and it's both of those things. It has that sort of screeching sound underneath it where you know somebody is just welling up with hatred and vitriol and at the same time it comes from this other place. That cue wasn't written for that moment—he basically wrote fifteen or sixteen different eight- or nine-minute fugues and we took them and started moving them around and said, *Well, this sort of fits here and this sort of fits there.* He had seen the movie and he knew what the vibe of the movie was and he knew what we were talking about—and so he would just go and write. He just responded to it. It was gestural, it was empathetic. He and Atticus Ross would start sending us stuff and we would just try it over there, and try sticking it under here, and put this under there. And that piano piece that he sent—I remember when it came in an email—was just like *boom.* You played it and you just went, *Oh my God, what is this? This has to be up front and this has to be the Zuckerberg cue—this is him.* Of course we were trying to avoid putting it under the title sequence because I had this Elvis Costello piece that I wanted to put there, but it just became so apparent that the piece was exactly what the sequence needed. It had this incredible riptide kind of anger and revenge and darkness and then this intense childlike simple lonely piano over the top of it.

EL: I think that's the moment when you're watching and you say, *Oh, great movie—I wonder if they can go all the way with it.*
DF: And it's only nine minutes in. One scene with those two shots is nine minutes. It's the feeling you get with the driving cue at the beginning of *The Shining*, and the choice of using Ligeti there—it tells you immediately that there is more to it than a guy driving on a highway travelling to a hotel. There's something larger at work.

EL: The major question that remains is the one, which has sort of permeated the conversation about the film: Is the movie true?
DF: I think you can try to recreate every detail, you can make sure that people are wearing the exact same shoes that Lee Harvey Oswald wore, you can do all that stuff, but in the end, the thing that everyone will take umbrage with is, *But that's not the right point of view. You're looking at it from the wrong way. You have to be looking at it from the point of view of the person who was wrong. Or you have to be looking at it from the point of view of the person who won.* That's the whole magilla of doing anything that is based on the real world—the *Rashomon* of it is the thing that ultimately was interesting to me. We weren't here to sort out something. We're not making *JFK*. We're making a movie where the point is that these people don't get along—the point is that these kids were friends, to whatever extent, and they were there in the basement in the beginning for the foundation of this thing. Whatever happened by the time they got to the mezzanine *happened*. The movie is about how people set off to do the right thing by each other, and the right thing by an idea, and how they eventually decide they can't—that they won't complete this journey together. That's what is important.

Would this movie have been interesting had we made the exact same movie and called the thing "Mugbook?" And had the character be Mark Birkenstock? If we changed it all, would that have alleviated everyone's concerns? I think that would be fundamentally worthless because the job here is to basically say, *Here's an agreed-upon set of facts.* And our job is to take those facts and make a truth from it. Or three truths.

EL: Did you enjoy the multiple perspectives? Was that liberating for you?
DF: No, I thought it was essential to telling the story. I didn't think there

was any other way to do it. I wouldn't have done it had it been a lynch mob going after somebody. I'm not interested in taking the successful down a few pegs—I just thought he was an interesting, compelling force. I thought that considering all the stories—to have the *Rashomon* effect—was necessary to make a good movie. Otherwise I think people would be bored. There's also the idea, which Aaron and I have talked about, that one of the things we're trying to say in this movie is, *"No person is only one thing."* And the structure is a way of saying it. Otherwise it's just a biopic.

EL: There are big areas in the movie where you and Aaron are, in some ways, at opposite sides of the spectrum. Does it matter?
DF: No.

EL: Why?
DF: Because he has his view of youth and he has his view of invention. To Aaron, invention is somebody sitting alone in a room and literally hitting his head against a wall until he comes up with something, and then his fingers move and it appears on a screen and he hits send. That, for Aaron, is invention—and, for me, invention is swindling the right people, and saying things a certain way, and saying it near a window in the right way, and somebody takes a picture of that, and then you take that and put it with this other thing. So invention is a very different thing for me than it is for Aaron, and I would think invention is a very different thing for Mark Zuckerberg and the rest of the people in the movie. Everybody has his own take—you know you can spin anything in a lot of different ways, and thankfully that's what the movie is about.

EL: Is it the multi-fold perspective on these events that allows you and Aaron to not necessarily agree on what the movie is saying about the characters? Is that why the movie holds both your points of view?
DF: Yes, I think that is the case but I also think that it's a dramatist's job to essentially be reductive. Aaron is supposed to distill this whole breadth of events for us. And so even if Aaron is writing a story about this nerd—which may not necessarily be a subject I'm naturally drawn to—he described a character that I could totally relate to. We had these discussions about why the whole movie can't be about getting revenge against girls—it *can't* be that. It has to be about a moment in time and about an opportunity that presents itself that is so far beyond even the most delicious possible revenge. That was the scale of it—you're talking

about a kid who's doing something that will literally set the world on fire and make him a billionaire. So the two things encompass one another: one of them is driven by the groin and the other is driven by immortality, and there's room for both. I think both of our ideas for the movie can be intertwined while retaining the dramatic core that runs through the whole thing. One of the things that makes Aaron great is that he can say, *Here's something that's really dramatic and really simple. It's a guy who feels slighted—this is the reason that he does it. Otherwise, how do you explain his blog entries?* So rooted in this character is very primitive hurt, and Aaron uses that as a jumping off point.

The Vulture Transcript: An In-Depth Chat with David Fincher about *The Social Network*

Mark Harris / 2010

From *New York Magazine*, September 21, 2010. Reprinted by permission of Wright's Media.

David Fincher rarely gives interviews, but for the *New York* cover story on his new movie, *The Social Network* (which opens October 1), the director sat down with Mark Harris for a long, revealing chat. Only some of the conversation made it into the article, so we're presenting their entire, in-depth talk in full below. What better way to inaugurate our new recurring feature, the Vulture Transcript: extended, revealing, and virtually uncut interviews with fascinating cultural figures. Here, Fincher dishes on the enormous difficulty of speeding up Aaron Sorkin's motormouth text ("*Faster.* That was my only real direction."), his surprising "enormous amount of empathy" for Facebook founder Mark Zuckerberg, and much much more.

Mark Harris: I loved Aaron Sorkin's script, which was 162 pages, and when I went to see a screening of *The Social Network*, I asked how long the movie was and they said, 116 or 118 minutes, and I thought, *Oh, no, they've cut all the stuff I loved.* But it all seems to be there.
David Fincher: No, we just simply said, *faster.* That was my only real direction—take a minute out of that!

MH: I don't believe that.
DF: It's kinda true. The characters in the movie are people who need to get to the end of their thoughts before they can really focus on what it is they meant to say. And in describing it to them that way—I mean, Jesse

[Eisenberg, who plays Mark Zuckerberg] actually talks like that, he can do it—but a lot of people would come in and read and say, "Wait, what is he talking about at this point?" And I'd say, "There are people who need to work their way through the kelp beds of their own thought processes on their way to the exact idea they've been trying to fucking find, to get to *this word* and that's the word that's he's actually been looking for." And once they got that, they took to it like ducks.

MH: It was kind of shocking to hear Jesse Eisenberg doing Aaron Sorkin's dialogue, because you suddenly realize this is what he was born to do.
DF: We looked and looked and looked. We read every young actor in Hollywood. And it had been rumored on blogs and stuff that we were talking to Jesse Eisenberg. And you know, I hate to be told what to do by blogs, so I was like, "Yeah, we should probably see him but I don't know if this is his thing. . . ." And he put himself on tape reading the first scene, and I remember getting this thing on my computer and opening this little QuickTime, and here's this kid doing Sorkin: the first person that we'd heard who could do Sorkin better than Sorkin.

MH: But was that a language that everyone in the movie kind of had to learn?
DF: The studio initially said, "We don't know what you're gonna cut, but you're gonna have to get it down to a reasonable time limit, you can't shoot . . ." I think it was 166 pages. And Aaron and I went back to the office and I took out my little iPhone and set it down and put the little stopwatch on and said, "Start reading." And we went through it and he was done in an hour and fifty-nine to two hours. And I called the studio and said, "No, we can do this, it's gonna be about a two-hour movie." They said, "You're crazy." And I said, "No, I think it can be done that way. If we do it the way that Aaron just spoke it, it'll be two hours. It's up to me to have dialogue that pre-laps scenes, and to be able to establish places as quickly as possible." And when I opened this little QuickTime of Jesse Eisenberg, it was the first time I said, "We're gonna be under two hours!" He can just flat-out fly. And you can see in his eyes that he is searching for the best way to articulate something in the middle of articulating two other things; he's processing where he's going.

Oftentimes, you'll say to an actor that, you know, the notion of being present is not to be thinking of the next thing you're going to say but to actually be listening. You know, a lot of people are trained to give you the "thoughtful" thing, but at the same time, they're trying to process their next line. And Jesse can be half a page ahead, and in the now. I remember turning to Aaron and saying, "Okay, have we ever seen anything this good?" He just said, "That's the guy." We brought him out to LA and he came into my office and I said, "Hey, it's a pleasure to meet you." And he said, "Great, what do you want me to read? I've prepared three scenes." And I said, "No, no, no. You got the job. We're just having you here because we wanted to meet you and say hello, but you're in the movie." That's the fun part—to be able to tell them you enjoy what they do.

MH: The actors said the pace you set was really fast, but—and I know this isn't your favorite topic—you are known for doing a lot of takes. So how was a fast pace even possible?

DF: No, you know, I will normally trade helicopters and cranes and the incumbent extra technicians it takes to have toys like that for more hours, more time, more days. For $39 or $40 million, whatever it ended up costing, normally you're going to get about forty-five or fifty days of shooting. And we shot for seventy-two days, because we knew that was the kind of time it was going to take. You know, everybody had to know their lines, but we didn't necessarily know where exactly the scene was going to take place until we found the locations. There was a lot of negotiation going on with Harvard and different places in and around Cambridge that we wanted to use. And things would fall apart at the last minute, so something that was supposed to take place walking down the sidewalk would take place in a cab.

We rehearsed the notion of overlap—we rehearsed the idea of talking over one another very pointedly. The opening scene of the movie [an extended conversation in which Zuckerberg is dumped by his girlfriend], which is nine pages in under five minutes—we had two days to shoot that. And the studio said, "That's crazy." First they said, "It's one scene! You don't need two days for one scene!" Then they said, "It's nine pages! You can't do nine pages in two days!" We said, "Okay, make up your mind, which one is it?" We got through most of the scene in the first day, and then the second day was just going in to pick up certain things in close-ups. We shot ninety-nine takes.

MH: Of just that scene?

DF: Yeah. We put two cameras on it so that they could interrupt and talk right over each other. So it took an enormous amount of time to stage the background, probably close to the first half of the first day. And then we just started shooting. And then I would just go in and encourage them and say, "Here's what you're talking about here." Or: "Try to talk about this." Or: "Just get angry a little later." And the two of them are such facile creatures, they would just play. I look at it this way: You're gonna bring all this equipment, you're gonna bring all these people, you're gonna fly them all in and put them up in hotels, you're gonna run all this cable, do all this stuff, hang these lights . . . Then the actors have to have their time to fall face-first into it. Rather than say, "Okay, we'll do two, and let's move on," it seems like such a waste of talent to get somebody's second or third or even fifth or sixth thought at something. Especially with this kind of dialogue, it really needs to seem to fall out of their subconscious. Because a lot of what Sorkin does is think out loud. So it has to look like thought.

MH: One of the actors told me—
DF: [*Laughs.*] Which one?

MH: Two of them said interesting things about your process. Andrew Garfield [who plays Eduardo Saverin] said that you had them keep in mind that in any scene, anyone who's talking always thinks he's right. And Armie Hammer [who plays Cameron and Tyler Winklevoss] said that he thought the multiple takes were really helpful in ridding them of all of the things that they'd worked out in their heads that they thought were going to be their big moments the night before.
DF: So many Oscars are won in the tub! I'm not, like, trying to psychologically remake people, but look, it's an incredibly neurotic thing to want to do with one's life. It's incredibly hard to stand in front of a camera and be the focus of that attention and not be self-conscious. It makes you self-conscious, and to get beyond that self-consciousness, I absolutely want people to have their idea of what the scene is about, to have an idea of what their moment is. And then I want to take them through that process to a point where they've literally forgotten their own names. I want to take them past the point where they go, "But I had it all worked out." If it's still there but you're doing it a little bit later or doing it a little bit flustered. You know, it's an interesting thing: It happens very rarely, but invariably, when an actor's in the middle of a take and they go, "Uh, hang on a sec, sorry, my fault, can we start again?" always it's the best take. Always the best take before they cry uncle, before they go, "Wait a minute, I've lost my train of thought." And I can show them on the monitor: "Look at you here, that is you at your most present, when you're falling-down ill, like Dudley Moore in *Arthur*, ass-over-teakettle

trying to remember where you were in the thing, that's when you are stunning and real and amazing." Little things happen. There's this moment at the beginning of the movie where Rooney [Mara, who plays Zuckerberg's girlfriend] interrupts him and says "Mark!" And Jesse did this thing where he leaned forward in a very prodding way and said "Erica!" Oddly condescending. She gets really pissed off—and he'd never done it before. It was kind of great. I went up to him and he said, "Do you want me to do it again?" And I said, "No, but I bet you it's going in the movie." That's the kind of stuff you want to find.

MH: Let's go back to when you read the script. I feel like a lot of directors of your caliber, honestly, might have read it and said, "It's great, but there's not much for me to do here." I'm fascinated that you saw interesting directorial challenges in it.

DF: I think telling a good story is always an interesting directorial challenge. I read it and thought, "Oh my God, this is how I feel about the notion of the Internet and communication, and so much about the loneliness that characterizes much of modern interpersonal communication." I also loved the idea of old-world business ethics put to the test by new-world ability to beta-test and iterate. I thought it was an amazing idea. Harvard is this three-hundred-year-old institution built by people who understood business and innovation as: You find a place to cultivate a workforce and train them and create a factory or an assembly line, and you build a product and it comes out and everyone in this little village is rewarded by that. And that's innovation. Then there's this new world where somebody goes: If I've got DSL and enough Red Bull, I can prototype this thing! And then I can get it onto 650 desktops and then eight years later I can get in on 600 million desktops! That is a new paradigm.

MH: The movie seems to put two different kinds of ruthlessness in competition with each other.

DF: I don't know. You said ruthlessness? I don't know. I have an enormous amount of empathy for Zuckerberg. I felt like it was easy to do the *Revenge of the Nerds* version of this, but there was something more compelling about his wanting to do it his way. Because he was right. It shouldn't be done using an advertising model. The ultimate communication tool needed to be devised by someone who doesn't have the best communication skills. You see him with Lesley Stahl, you kind of go, "I'm not sure this guy should be speaking on his own behalf." But I thought it was amazing that this was the guy who figured out how hundreds of millions of people would want to connect with each other. I thought that was a great, ironic notion. It may indeed be dramatic license, but I thought Aaron did it beautifully.

MH: Do you mean dramatic license in terms of Sorkin's decision to shape him as that kind of guy?
DF: We know that Zuckerberg took out some of his vitriol on a woman in his blog, but I don't know that he continues to pine for her today. As a director, it doesn't seem to me that you should. There's a lot of directors out there who think, *Oh, this'll be great, I'm gonna get to go to Rome.* Or: *This'll be fun, I've never shot the London subways.* Or whatever. But I was just looking for a story and I thought, *Well, it's not* The Paper Chase *and it's not* Breaking Away *and it's not* Fight Club*, but it's a little bit of a lot of these things, and in an interesting way.*

MH: Aaron Sorkin told me that on the set, you were more insistent on the accuracy of small details than he was, that when there was push and pull between you, you wanted to hew closer to the record.
DF: Well, I don't know. I always think that if you have a bit of research, you can go, *I think it'd be cooler if the person wore this.* But if you have a photograph of him from that period of his life, you go, *Really, a T-shirt over a dress shirt with a tie?* That's such an odd thing, and yet there's something about that that speaks to who that person is. I feel like if you have something that in some way is real, it informs things in a different way. It's easy to make stuff look good or slick or cohesive, but I also think that if you're dealing with stuff that's real. . . . I mean, it broke my heart that we couldn't shoot at Harvard. And yet by the time we were done with all the bureaucracy, I was happy to go to Johns Hopkins. They were so helpful. They were so much easier to deal with that I didn't really care that it wasn't the real Kirkland because it was such a pain in the ass to deal with. And in those cases you just go, "Well, they shot a lot of interiors of *The Paper Chase* at USC, so screw it." But I do think reality informs things in a different way. Oftentimes it doesn't make things as clean in terms of storytelling, but it's almost always better in terms of character. Is [Sorkin] talking about the beer and stuff? [Indeed, there was a dispute over whether Zuckerberg should be drinking a beer or a screwdriver while he hacked into Harvard's databases.]

MH: He was. Small stuff like that.
DF: Yeah, originally, he'd written this thing about making a screwdriver,

and I was like, "That's great, except we have a blog. And in the blog it says, 'Here I am and I'm drinking Beck's.'" It felt like, well, he's a Beck's guy. I liked what it said: A nineteen-year-old guy with a case of Beck's in his dorm room. It doesn't say the same thing as Smirnoff and OJ.

MH: So were most of your disagreements on that scale rather than about, say, character?

DF: We almost never disagreed about intent. Remember, Aaron comes from a world where he generates a kind of page count on a daily basis that I can't even imagine, and he accomplishes an enormous amount. In his previous discipline, television, Aaron is used to thinking fast and making bold decisions. He works with a meat ax. The words are the important thing because it's what you're getting paid for. In television, you don't have the time to pick gnat shit out of pepper. But in the movies, my whole thing is, everything that we put on the screen is going to be debated and scrutinized in some way. So it's not even that there's an opportunity here to do more. It's that it's incumbent upon us, if we're going to put a prop next to somebody's hand and they're going to do three pages of dialogue with it, that prop is going to get a lot more important than it would in a two-page scene on television. It's going to be seen and scrutinized more, so we need to make sure it's not saying something we don't want it to say or undercutting anything about the environment or where they are in their head space.

MH: Do you feel comfortable with the idea that people will walk out at the end of this movie with differing opinions about whether Mark Zuckerberg is a good guy or a tragic hero or a bad guy? You've left a lot of room for people to disagree with the Rashida Jones character's assessment of Mark as someone who's not an asshole but is trying so hard to be. Some people will watch the movie and say, "No, actually, he's an asshole."

DF: Look, it's not my intention to crucify Mark Zuckerberg. Mark Zuckerberg is a guy who accomplished an enormous amount at a very, very young age. And I, not in the same way, not in the same world, but I know what it's like to be twenty-one years old and trying to direct a $60 million movie and sitting in a room full of grown-ups who think you're just so cute, but they're not about to give you control of anything. It's just, "Great—look how passionate he is!" I know the anger that comes when you just want to be allowed to do the things that you know you can do. In order to accomplish what he's accomplished, you have to have not only a great deal of drive, you have to have an unshakable, freakish confidence. A lot of people will look at that and wonder what kind of hubris does it take to know what it is that you want at twenty-one?

So I feel it would be irresponsible to say this is the story of a guy who betrayed his friends. I think Eduardo had a real failure of imagination, and I've been in those situations before. I've had companies where the partners were all in it for the right reasons at the beginning. And then four or five years down the line, when it's a commercial endeavor that's throwing off a lot of cash, you go, "I think you need to go in this direction." And other people say, "Everything's good just the way it is, let's just keep it here." You reach a point when you say, "We're working at cross-purposes, we're no longer aligned, you need to go do your thing and I need to go do my thing."

And I've been in situations where people say, "Look, it's best for everyone if this person is marginalized." Those things happen. So I have an enormous amount of empathy for everyone involved. I didn't want the Winklevosses to be the "Haves" who were surly and stupid. Cameron really has a strong sense of what it means to be a Harvardian. He's not joking. He was raised right.

MH: The idea of being gentlemen is very meaningful to them.
DF: Yeah! When we were shooting the phone call [to Cameron Winklevoss's father] I told him I wanted him to say, at the end of the call, "I love you, Dad." It's not in the script but that's the kind of kid this guy is. It should be surprising that this six-foot-five, 220-pound kid says that. And I don't know the Winklevi, but they'd somehow gotten a hold of the script because it was on the fucking Internet. . . .

MH: You don't sound like you're much more of a fan of the Internet than Aaron Sorkin is.
DF: I just resent the whole . . . I hate the idea of pre-auditioning clay pigeons for people. I really resent the idea of people reading screenplays that have yet to be produced. In any case, the Winklevosses got to us and said, "You know, that's not my dad's name." Aaron had changed the name originally. That was the one note we got. Little things like that were important to me. We were just trying to make the world as realistic as we could. There were times Aaron Sorkin and I would turn to each other and say, "What are we doing here?" And I said, "It's the *Citizen Kane* of John Hughes movies." Sean Parker is half of Jedediah Leland, and

Eduardo is the other half, the hurt half. It's not, "If I hadn't been so rich I might have been a truly great man." But: "If I'd known then what I know now, three years later. . . ."

Chasing the Dragon

Nev Pierce / 2011

From *Empire*, November 2011, 74–83. Reprinted by permission of Nev Pierce.

"This girl isn't a wound—she's scar tissue."

That was the direction David Fincher gave one well-known actress before her screen-test for *The Girl with the Dragon Tattoo*. "If you cry, it's over." She didn't get it. She wasn't alone. About seven or eight actresses—from Oscar-nominees to complete unknowns—shot samples with Fincher to play the title character in Sony's anticipated adaptation of Stieg Larsson's novel.

The part was almost impossible to cast, as the iconic researcher/hacker is a walking paradox. Lisbeth Salander is victim and avenger, vulnerable and violent, stunted and exceptional. Mercurial is too weak a word. And she's an icon already, both in the Swedish screen adaptation and in the imagination of millions: *The Girl with the Dragon Tattoo* has sold more copies than *The Godfather* and *The Very Hungry Caterpillar*.

Excerpt:
The Girl with the Dragon Tattoo
by Steven Zaillian
Based on the novel by Stieg Larsson

Lisbeth Salander walks in: A small, pale, anorexic-looking waif in her early twenties. Short, black-dyed hair—pierced eyelid—tattoo of a wasp on her neck; probably several more under her black leather jacket—black T-shirt, black jeans, black Caterpillar boots.

This isn't punk fashion. This is someone saying, "Stay the fuck away from me."

"There were discussions early on, where people were like, 'She's a super-hero!'" says Fincher. "And you go, 'No, she's not. Superheroes live in a world of good and evil, and she's far more complex than a superhero. She's been compromised. She's been subjugated. She's been marginalized. She's been swept into the gutter and she's had a part in it. She dresses like trash because she's somebody who has been betrayed and hurt so badly, by forces beyond her control, that she's just decided to be refuse."

So, Salander: a resourceful, intelligent investigator, within a pierced, pallid, dyed-to-death exterior. "She can sit anywhere she wants on the bus, because nobody wants to deal with her," says Fincher. "That's what her visage is about. It's not there to say, 'You fuck with the bull, you get the horns,' it's to say, 'You don't kick a garbage can—you ignore it.'"

The disguise may be part of her appeal. While not everyone can relate to beauty or brilliance, everyone has felt ugly or ignored. Everyone feels like damaged goods. For Rooney Mara, the girl who would eventually take the tattoo, it was someone else who first saw her as Salander. A friend of her mother's read the book and emailed, "Rooney has to play this part—she is this girl." So Mara looked into it.

"David didn't want to see me originally," she says. "It took a minute for him to wrap his head around it, because he only knew me as Erica Albright—and I only worked for four days on that film." That film is, of course, *The Social Network* where, says Fincher, he had "pictured her as this sort of Katharine Ross from *The Graduate*, the perfect one who got away [from Mark Zuckerberg]," fuelling the founding of Facebook. From the East Coast and well-educated, much like the actress herself, the character of Albright is about as far removed as you can imagine from the inked-up Swedish hacker. Mara's most significant screen achievement prior to that was getting through the remake of *A Nightmare on Elm Street* without looking mortally embarrassed. (Actually, no mean feat.) It took two-and-a-half months, three or four "real" screen-tests and about four or five on the side "that no-one knew about" to secure Salander.

She was called to Fincher's Hollywood Boulevard office for one final test, just about ready to blow. "I was like, 'You guys have to decide if I'm this girl or not, because I have to move on with my life at some point.' Of course, I didn't say any of that. I was like, 'Fine, whatever!'" She laughs. The process had been drawn out because, as Fincher has it, Sony was keen on someone else—a star who nailed the accent and attitude in auditions, but was ultimately beaten out by Mara's quicksilver quality.

"I just kept coming back to Rooney," says Fincher. "Just going, 'She's got something. . . .' Part of it was I kept coming back to the puppy that nobody wanted, you know? We kept putting her through more and more. I loved her work ethic."

The last test turned out to be an offer. "I was ready to kill someone. I went in there like, 'Whose ass do I have to ram a dildo up to get this part?'" says Mara, referring to one of the book's most notorious, violent passages. "And David gave some long speech. He said something like, 'Vivien Leigh was extraordinary in *A Streetcar Named Desire* but she will always be Scarlett O'Hara. And whoever plays this girl, if they do it right, they will be Ginger from *Gilligan's Island* for the rest of their life. You have to know that your life is going to change and I'm not even telling you that it's going to change for the better.'"

He then handed her his iPad, its screen shimmering with the press release saying she was hired, and gave her the choice. "I did not flinch. I was like, 'I've had two-and-a-half months to think about it. You can send it out.' And that was that."

Five days later, Mara was in Stockholm. Costume, hair, make-up, and piercings followed. Surprisingly, the transformation didn't trouble her. "I didn't freak out at all. Because at that point, I'd already been sort of in the part, like researching it, for two months, so to me the hair was weighing me down. I wanted to get rid of it. They were going to wait longer. I was like, 'You just need to do it!'"

"It was a tough process," says Daniel Craig, of Mara's marathon effort to land the role. "I went to read with her in LA, God knows, another lifetime ago, and I was incredibly impressed by how far she was into the character at that stage. Actually, I thought that's who Rooney was, but thankfully that's not who she is. But David had immense faith in her and I was convinced when I worked with her."

Craig plays *Tattoo*'s other hero, of sorts: Mikael Blomkvist, a journalist hired by retired industrialist Henrik Vanger (Christopher Plummer) to investigate the decades-old disappearance of his niece. After a rather unconventional meet-cute, Salander is also hired to help. The relationship between the two of them is pivotal to Larsson's three-book Millennium series (named after Blomkvist's magazine): he may teach her about trust, she may teach him about justice. Blomkvist is the story's Jake Gittes: a down-at-heel investigator not quite as clever as you think he thinks he is, but decent and dedicated. "He's a character with a moral compass," says Craig. "I mean, it may be skewed and it may have problems! He's weak and full of flaws. [Blomkvist and Salander] have a very odd relationship. They should never have even met each other in real life, but they're coming together—that's what makes it interesting. One of the reasons I like the book is because this relationship is so odd."

In London, on *Empire*'s first visit to the production in March, we witness this contrast in characters close up, as Salander takes him to a pub to meet other hackers who can help with their investigation. Craig has a sticking plaster on his forehead, which may be a sly tribute to Nicholson's gumshoe, but is probably just because he was wounded in a previous scene. Clustered around a dark wood table, the cyber-burglars, virtual strangers, sit in silence, ignoring the attempts of the journalist to engage. Fincher discusses the scene with Craig as they prepare to shoot: "You're just making conversation . . . with people that don't make conversation!" It's deliciously awkward.

Once wrapped, we head for a real drink—and you can see the truth of Mara's observation that "people sort of expect less of you when you look slightly different." There are a couple of sidelong glances at her, at the up-market Soho hotel the production is staying at, and she fades away from attention—preferring, as a person herself, to be "invisible." It's a position she may struggle to maintain as the marketing mounts up.

In June, in Stockholm, when we meet again, the poster has just been released—and engendered both outrage and adulation, for its image of her bare-chested in front of a brooding Craig, with the film's release date gauzing her pierced nipple.

People feel strongly about Salander—some say the poster is too sexual, that's she's presented as needing Craig's protection, that this is the "pornification" of a female icon. The range of reaction seems only appropriate to a film that certainly contains a good deal of sex and violence—and sexual violence.

"Which are very separate things, I would like to point out, because people are getting a little bit confused online," says Mara. "There is a distinction in the film and we are all very aware of that. Like, there's a lot of sex in the film that's consensual—these are very sexual characters. And there is also sexual violence—that's a huge theme of the film. But they're very separate. Just because you have one, doesn't necessarily mean you can't have the other. 'Cause I think some people have been sort of offended at our approach because she's been sexually abused, but I think just because someone has been sexually abused doesn't mean they can't be depicted as someone who is sexual."

Mara isn't meek. There's steel inside the waifish exterior, not simply in the twenty-six-year-old's surprisingly strong handshake. Comparisons with Noomi Rapace's much-praised performance in the Swedish films are inevitable, but Mara is making Salander her own. Her research has included speaking with people who are on the autism spectrum, or with Asperger's—the psychological syndrome Salander is said to suffer from, most easily characterized as making one socially maladroit—and also victims of rape.

Her strongest source was the books, naturally, which she read just prior to the casting process. "I'd seen the movie and was like, 'I can't be that girl—that scares me!' Noomi's incredible. But after I'd read the three books, I was like, 'Wait a minute, there's something here I can relate to, on a very extreme level, where I think I can be this girl.' Not only that, but I feel like I have to."

Violence against women—and the pervasiveness of it—was a large part of what motivated Larsson to write his trilogy. The author, who was, like his creation Blomkvist, an investigative journalist, died in 2004, before his novels were published to such worldwide success. Since then, a friend of his has claimed the writer witnessed a gang rape when he was aged fifteen, but didn't have the courage to intervene. So such violence, as well as moral cowardice, became themes in his work. When it was first published in Sweden, *The Girl with the Dragon Tattoo* had a rather more straightforward title: *Men Who Hate Women*.

Given the prevalence of violence against women, and how it is often marginalized or jokingly justified, it's a powerful subtext for a Hollywood blockbuster to possess. "Misogyny," says Fincher, "that's part of what's intriguing about [the material]: because it's so ugly and so widespread. And you don't have to be performing clitorectomies in order to be marginalizing women. It happens by varying degrees, by single digit percentage points, and it happens all the time."

But there are other elements in play here, even broader than misogyny, thinks Fincher. "People go, 'You don't want to be salacious about the fact that there's a lot of rape in this movie.' And yet, when everybody talks about the subject matter they go, 'Oh, that's the book with all the rapes in it!'" He pauses. "I mean, it is talking about rape—and that doesn't get a lot of people into the theatres—and yet there's something about her overcoming her . . ." His sentence becomes dislocated, uncharacteristically. He was quoted as saying Salander is an "avenging angel," but that's not it. "I was being facetious." No, this isn't a rape-revenge movie. Rather, it's about what he calls "the cultural legacy of denial," as well as, it seems, institutionalized abuse and all kinds of power and control. He continues: "I mean, everybody agrees rape is bad and rape visits a kind of psychosexual damage, but I think there are ideas in this that are bigger and more insidious."

Those ideas are more pronounced because of the Scandinavian setting. There was Internet chatter about transferring the story stateside, but never from within the product ion. Throughout, there was an insistence it remain in Sweden, right up to Sony chiefs Michael Lynton and Amy Pascal. "When Lynton was first telling me the story, I was like, 'I don't know.'" Fincher shakes his head. "'The Nazi thing . . . '" Lynton told the director, "No, you have to understand: this is a beautiful, socialist, free, women-are-equal society that is built on a particularly dark period of time where people sort of stepped back and said, 'It's not about us.'" This is when you remember: this calm country, land of ABBA and IKEA, was neutral during World War II.

"It's interesting. During the research, the photographs and stuff like that, seeing Nazi gatherings in central Stockholm," says Fincher. "I mean, they were obviously a fringe element and appropriately marginalized, but it's odd. It doesn't look like a Nazi rally in Decatur, Illinois, or whatever. Those people just look crazy!"

In contrast, the Swedish Nazis—and the most dangerous people in the film—look shockingly normal. "I think that's ultimately what's so scary about it, isn't it?" says Fincher. "It's the subterfuge, what's lying beneath the surface, the capability. And you can't say that's not what it is that makes Salander appealing for an audience, too. It's what she's capable of."

A sense of foreboding, a sense of fear, a sense of the unknown infects the material. Fincher remembers the day they filmed the drive up to the Vanger mansion, which was blanketed in unexpected snow. "I said, 'Call the ADs (assistant directors), make sure nobody walks in front of the house!' We shot the drive up for five or six hours, all different angles, and as we were shooting I was going, 'That's the fuckin' teaser. . . . ' I mean, it couldn't have been more beautiful or more menacing. There's a Swedish proverb, which we'll probably use for the final poster: 'What is hidden in snow comes forth in the thaw.' The one that's on there now, 'Evil shall with evil be expelled,' is a Swedish proverb as well. And when you start to look at Swedish proverbs and how uncompromising they are, you realize what Stieg Larsson was on about. When you're a little kid and one of the cultural touchstones is, 'Evil shall with evil be expelled,' if that's what's under the surface, you can see where this Goth version of Pippi Longstocking came from."

Kids' literature heroine Longstocking—first published in the forties and well-known worldwide—is another Swedish icon, while the proverbs were investigated at the suggestion of Stellan Skarsgård, the most prominent Swede in the cast (he plays Martin Vanger, nephew to Plummer's patriarch). The characters may all speak in lightly accented English (as does virtually everyone here in reality—even with regional accents, from Margate to Manchester), but the adaptation is aiming to feel Swedish, without being a retread of the first film. As Skarsgård himself has said: "I've seen the Swedish movie and I thought it was good, but I think Fincher and the writer Steven Zaillian can do even more with it."

Perhaps the most significant change to the story comes at the conclusion to the script from Oscar-winning *Schindler's List* scribe Zaillian—a change we won't reveal. Visually, though, there is a dynamism to this version that is unmistakably Fincher. It's being edited back in Los Angeles, as they shoot, so one evening Fincher shows *Empire* a substantial section of the picture. It's only on a laptop, but it's fair to say his comment, post-footage, is correct: "It's a very different movie from the one you've seen." Not that there aren't going to be some similarities. "There's going to be snow, there's going to be motorcycles, there's going to be tattoos. . . ."

But there's something about this film this year. *The Girl with the Dragon Tattoo* will be released into a world where a Scandinavian fascist has recently murdered seventy-seven people, where giant corporation News International is being laid low by hacking (albeit its own), and where the editor-in-chief of whistleblowing website WikiLeaks is currently fighting extradition to Sweden, with police waiting to question him about alleged sexual misconduct. From *Fight Club* to *The Social Network*, Fincher has a knack for picking the prescient. And this film picks the scabs of society to reveal what's festering beneath.

A day later, on a set in Stockholm—a painstakingly realized archive of Vanger Industries, all file boxes and fusty air—Fincher mutters to himself about a take: "aside from being completely unusable, it's fantastic!" They are close to wrapping the final Swedish stint of the production before flying back to LA, where they'll take the weekend off before the last week of shooting. "That gives me two days of uncontrollable weeping," says Fincher.

Today, they are using a motion-control camera to capture insert shots of Salander scouring maps for information. By the end of this long day, Mara could probably qualify for a second career as a Swedish cartographer. The process is effectively trying to photograph thought. As Fincher says of the challenge of externalizing the novel's deductive processes, "It's like, 'Oh, my God: how many Scooby-Doo moments?'"

Mara is aware that, as set visits go, this isn't the chariot race in *Ben-Hur*. She wanders over and asks Fincher why *Empire*'s been invited to the dullest week of the shoot. "Because we knew there'd be plenty of time to talk to you about your fuckin' bad attitude," he grins. There's a nice friendship here. Avuncular is not a term many would associate with the director of *Se7en*. Nor he with himself. But there's definitely a familial feel.

Between set-ups, Mara is reading a script on the iPad he gave her as a present after a particularly tough week of shooting. She brings up a picture and he tries to wrestle the tablet away to reveal more photos. It's hardly Roman Polanski and Faye Dunaway spitting hatred at each other on *Chinatown*'s set. Fincher may be sharp-tongued on occasion, but he's no tyrant.

"No, but I think he's sort of painted that way," says Mara, over lunch. "It's bullshit. I think the thing is that he doesn't care what people think about him. Fuck them. It doesn't matter. I think maybe where it comes from is that David is one of the rare people in this business who actually really, *really* cares and believes in what he's doing, and he's unwilling to compromise. . . . And generally he's always right." She pauses, before unconsciously echoing something Robert Downey Jr. said after working with Fincher on *Zodiac*. "He's *always* right. It's so frustrating! Every time I'm right I'm like, 'YESSSSS!'" She laughs.

"I think both Rooney and Daniel are my favorite kind of actors," says Fincher. "You know, Brad [Pitt] is that way too. They're very feline—they're always watching, they're always listening. They're always sort of taking in whatever people are up to. They're getting a vibe of all the elements that are in motion and then they're trying to find their way into it. And I like the fact they don't commit to something. It's, 'You want me to do that? How about if I try this?' 'Okay, great, let's see what happens.' I generally enjoy that process more. You come having prepared yourself, you have a notion of what your part is in the thing, your piece of the puzzle, but you're also reacting to what's around you. It can also work against you because somebody can be having a bad day and everybody starts to feel the pressure of, 'Uh-oh, the cats are upset.'"

Today, the cats are relieved. The near-year-long shoot is close to an end. If the first film is a success, there are the other two books to be filmed, probably back-to-back: *The Girl Who Played with Fire* and *The Girl Who Kicked the Hornet's Nest*. Craig and Mara are on board. Fincher will go as far as to say, "I hope to be asked." It will be interesting to see if he still feels there are ideas to be explored, exploiting his nose for the now.

The morning of our final day in Stockholm, we meet for breakfast at a hotel a few blocks from his rented flat. Caffeine, scones, and yoghurt dispatched, as we are about to head to the set another diner pauses at our table—a thirty-something Swede who resembles a geography teacher, like an inordinate amount of the men here. Appearances, though, as we know, can be deceiving. "Excuse me, Mr. Fincher?" he says, politely. "I just want to say: thank you for your work. You make the world more interesting."

Nev Pierce is a journalist and screenwriter. You can read more of his work at nevpierce.com.

Heart of Darkness

Brian Raftery / 2011

From *Wired*, November 22, 2011. Reprinted by permission of Brian Raftery, contributing editor, *Wired*.

A few months ago, David Fincher was having a problem with his new movie. This in itself wasn't especially surprising, as Fincher's productions seem to attract crises of the cosmic-joke variety, be they midshoot injuries (*Se7en*), last-minute casting switcheroos (*Panic Room*), or on-the-fly script rewrites (*Alien³*). Despite the director's meticulous planning—he can spend years preparing for a film—something usually goes awry. He's used to it. "All movies are a trial," he says matter-of-factly. "It's war."

But this latest battle was unique. In a roundabout way, it had to do with ABBA.

For much of the past year, Fincher has been filming *The Girl with the Dragon Tattoo*, his roughly $100 million adaptation of the macabre Swedish mystery that centers on a punk-hacker heroine with distinctive skin art. On one of the first nights of shooting, Fincher and his crew were in Sweden, filming a murder scene that takes place alongside a gloomy dock. But after a night's work, Fincher didn't have the shot he wanted, and the film's ultratight schedule meant he wouldn't be able to return for months.

When Fincher began planning the reshoot, he learned that the property had been sold to one of the guys in ABBA. Apparently, the new owner—either Benny or Björn, it's not really clear—wasn't thrilled at the prospect of having his evening stroll interrupted by a simulated drowning, and he refused to let the crew come back. Rather than find a new location or make do with the footage he had, Fincher decided to build his *own* Swedish dock.

Which is why, on a late-summer afternoon, we're standing on a Los Angeles soundstage, examining a replica of a rural-Scandinavia mise-en-scène: mossy rocks, foliage-fat trees, and—perched high above the docks, turtlenecking out of the woods—a squat, deceptively cozy faux cottage. Like most sets, it looks a bit weird naked. But once the lights hit and the smoke drifts in, we are suddenly in the land of stunted summers and moderately high suicide rates.

As usual, though, Fincher is not satisfied. He stands in the middle of the stage, arms folded, a coffee stirrer clenched in his teeth. He's forty-nine and trim, dressed in dark jeans, a gray polo, and sneakers, his mouth framed by a neat turf of mostly salty salt-and-pepper whiskers. He then starts pacing the set, calmly relaying what needs to be changed, tune-ups that range from the subtle to the barely perceptible: a branch that's sagging a few inches too low; a pair of lightbulbs with mismatched watt-ages; a patch of leaves that needs to be a little bit darker.

Most viewers won't notice the way the pebbles are scattered or how high the watermarks rise on the fake rocks. But Fincher will. Even in an industry full of control freaks, Fincher stands out as obsessive—a guy who will scrutinize and engineer every element in the frame until the images on the screen fit the ones in his head. Sometimes that means repainting a few leaves; sometimes it means doing fifty, sixty, even one hundred takes of a single scene.

Dragon Tattoo is Fincher's ninth film in two decades. And while the movies often focus on dark-hearted subjects—madness (*Se7en*), para-noia (*The Game*), nihilism (*Fight Club*), greed (*Panic Room*), obsession (*Zodiac*), and betrayal (*The Social Network*)—they're always beautiful to look at. Each is packed with so much careful detail—physical, aural, spa-tial—while also being so clean and composed that he's earned his own fanboy-bestowed sobriquet: *Fincheresque.*

Like *middle class* and *pornography*, the term is know-it-when-you-see-it elastic, but it's usually pinned on a scene that's darkly lit, darkly themed, and eerily beautiful. Think of the flashlights sabering through a shut-in's filthy apartment in *Se7en* or the skyscrapers exploding and folding like glass accordions at the end of *Fight Club.*

Moments like these have established Fincher as one of Hollywood's few accessible auteurs, a guy who can make commercially viable movies without 2s in their title and who never sacrifices his artful cynicism for phony uplift. "There aren't a whole lot of directors trying to find the bal-ance between commerce and—loath as I am to say it—art," *Se7en* writer Andrew Kevin Walker says. "Somehow, he manages to make something incredibly handcrafted and heartfelt on a big budget."

But Fincher's bleak yet captivating visions might also be why, despite all his success, he's never had an *Inception*-size box-office smash. Even a movie like *Se7en*, which pulled in $300 million worldwide, had the aura of a cult hit, if only because it felt weird to enthuse openly about a movie in which a pregnant woman's decapitated head is stuffed into a box. "My whole career has been pervy books, pervy scripts," Fincher says, only half kidding. "It wasn't so much about finding a niche. It just didn't seem to me like there was any need to be doing more of what everyone else was doing." It's not that Fincher's films aren't beloved—they are— it's just that sometimes it takes a while for audiences to come around to them. It's as if Fincher lives in the near future, releasing movies a year or two before the world is ready for them.

It wasn't until *The Curious Case of Benjamin Button* in 2008 and *The Social Network* in 2010 that Fincher made what could truly be called mass-market films. While neither was exactly upbeat—*Benjamin Button* is the story of a man aging in reverse, and *The Social Network*'s IPOs-before-bros maneuverings and legal takedowns were as brutal as anything in *Fight Club*—they were audience-pleasing efforts, and both earned Fincher Oscar nominations for best director.

Now, with *Dragon Tattoo*, Fincher is going further, plugging into a pre-sold, globally recognizable mega-property. Stieg Larsson's densely written (in every sense of the word) yet hard-to-put-down thriller follows a disgraced journalist (played by Daniel Craig) and an outcast hacker (*The Social Network*'s Rooney Mara) as they team up to investigate a forty-year-old missing-persons case. Before it's over, they'll have discovered a warped fiefdom of mass murder and hate-sex and you'll have discovered that your mom has been reading some really weird shit lately.

In many ways, *Dragon Tattoo* is the biggest movie of Fincher's career. It's the first time since his debut—*Alien³*—that he has committed himself to a fanatically awaited pop-culture property; Larsson's novels are easily the most feverishly devoured books since the *Twilight* series. If the movie works, Fincher could very well be looking at his first franchise, not to mention a third Oscar nomination. (Sony optioned Craig and Mara for the second and third installments, though Fincher hasn't been announced yet as their director.) Most important, the movie could finally nudge Fincher into the realm of Steven Spielberg and Martin Scorsese— bankable filmmakers who can define and mine the zeitgeist simultaneously and who get to do whatever they want. And for Fincher, getting to do whatever he wants is worth going to war for.

I meet Fincher at a very strange time in his life, in part because he's allowing me to meet him at all. Even as *Se7en* and *The Game* became hits in the mid- to late nineties—right around the time when directors like

Quentin Tarantino and Paul Thomas Anderson were becoming auteur superstars—Fincher kept a determinedly low profile. "I don't enjoy doing interviews, because I don't like being part of the noise," he tells me one afternoon as we drive between *Dragon Tattoo*'s LA sets. "I just don't want to be grist for the mill."

In person, Fincher is casually friendly. He says "dude" and "peace" more than you'd expect, and says "fuck" about as often as you'd expect, considering he's trying to get a massively expensive tent-pole movie into theaters by Christmas. And, like his films, Fincher is unexpectedly, almost disruptively funny; at one point, while scouting a new location in LA, he dryly jokes that private trailers will be needed for the actors, because of Craig's chronic masturbation habit. (Craig, for his part, calls the director "very witty. It's a valve that needs letting off, especially when you're doing scenes about anal rape.")

As a result of Fincher's low visibility—and perhaps this was partly intended—he has maintained a sort of scary-wunderkind mystique. The few known facts about the director make him seem such an unbelievable prodigy that even today they are like the stuff of fan fiction: that he lived down the street from George Lucas. Or that he skipped college and found a job at Industrial Light & Magic, working on movies like *Return of the Jedi*. Or that, by his early twenties, he was already overseeing video shoots with major-label budgets and giant crews.

But it all happened. And when you look at how Fincher grew up—in Marin County, California, in the early seventies—suddenly it's hard to imagine it *not* happening. By then, so many directors had set up shop in the San Francisco area—Lucas, Francis Ford Coppola, Philip Kaufman (*Invasion of the Body Snatchers*), Michael Ritchie (*The Candidate*)—that filmmaking seemed like a plausible, even admirable career path. "None of the kids in my neighborhood wanted to be doctors or lawyers," he says. "They all wanted to be moviemakers."

Fincher's father was an author and a bureau chief for *Life* magazine; his mother was a mental-health nurse who worked in a methadone clinic. At home, they'd discuss their work with Fincher. "My parents didn't keep much from me," he says. "They were like, 'Here's the world you're going out into.'"

They also encouraged their son to follow his singular, precociously realized goal: to make movies. In the third grade, Fincher was already taking an elementary-school film class; a few years later, he was directing super-8 movies with his friends. Figuring film school would be a waste of time, he worked his way into a job at ILM in 1982, when he was twenty.

"He knew what he wanted," remembers Terry Chostner, an ILM vet who was on staff with Fincher. "He kept telling people he was going to be a director. And this from a kid who wasn't even drinking age."

Fincher made his transition to directing by moving to LA to work in the nascent (and largely looked-down-upon) music-video industry. One of his earliest efforts was Rick Springfield's "Bop 'Til You Drop," a *Mad Max*–cribbing, dystopic-Jazzercise fantasy that involved slave labor, alien overlords, and laser beams. Though the clip's ominous story line was completely incongruous with the song's pro-bop message, the video established many of the hallmarks of Fincher's early director-for-hire career: light-bathed visuals, budget-straining production values, and a linear if only quasi-logical narrative.

Fincher didn't have much love for music videos, and he especially loathed doing commercials (and still does, though sometimes he will make one)—"they're awful," he says, "and they involve all sorts of bizarre, bureaucratic checks and balances"—but each assignment got him one step closer to making movies, and the money was spectacular.

After cofounding the famed production company Propaganda Films (which went on to produce works by directors from Michael Bay to Spike Jonze), Fincher directed dozens of clips throughout the eighties and early nineties, each increasingly daring and expensive: Madonna's "Express Yourself," a sweat-glistened, rain-soaked homage to Fritz Lang's *Metropolis*; Aerosmith's "Janie's Got a Gun," a disturbing child-abuse tale with a police-procedural story line; and Don Henley's "The End of the Innocence," a crisp black-and-white portrait of Reagan-era hardship, influenced by photographer Robert Frank's famed fifties travelogue, *The Americans*. "There's always been a deep humanism to David's work," says director Greg Gold, one of Propaganda's founders. "Even the characters in his music videos had depth."

Fincher's Propaganda duties often required him to deal with label brass and ad agencies, something he didn't enjoy, particularly when they got in the way of his ideas. An ad exec might show up at a Fincher shoot and find out he was banned from his own set. Nosy record-label employees were circumvented or simply ignored. "He was opinionated and difficult," says Sigurjón Sighvatsson, another of Propaganda's founders. "But he wasn't arrogant. He was confident." Kim Dempster, who helped produce several of Fincher's early projects, remembers the shoots as being "extremely stressful. You had to have it together for him. It was much harder than working for other directors, but it was a much better product."

When I mention an early nineties *Advertising Age* article about his supposed strong-headedness, Fincher dismisses the claim—though he doesn't exactly deny it, either. "You're supposed to have an idea of what it is you're trying to do, right?" he says. "Aren't you being overpaid to have that? My job is to know what the fuck I want."

Fincher's headquarters is a neatly outfitted modernist building in Los Angeles' Little Armenia district. Inside his office, there's a *Where the Wild Things Are* skateboard, a massive coffee table book dedicated to Stanley Kubrick's never-filmed Napoleon biopic, and a Segway. On his desk is a black-and-white printout of a scantily clad Mara, the actress playing the hacker in *Dragon Tattoo*, with a computer mouse covering her genitals. Fincher wonders if it might work to illustrate this story.

"What are your bosses like?" he asks. "Are they corporate suck-asses afraid of their own shadow?"

At first, it might seem odd that Fincher would still be raging at corporate suck-assery: His advertising clients have included such behemoths as AT&T and Levi's, and unlike many of his contemporaries—Steven Soderbergh, David O. Russell—he's never made a movie outside of the studio system. He has certainly been well compensated by the corporate fat cats he claims to loathe; at one point in the mid-eighties, he says, Propaganda was billing nearly $80 million a year. Undoubtedly, a reasonable portion of that ended up in his pocket.

Perhaps Fincher clings to his deep anti-authority streak because it has always served as a crucial motivator—almost a muse. It started back in grade school, when he bristled at the idea of being required to study nonfilm subjects, and it continued through his video and commercial career. "He was always a rebel," Propaganda's Sighvatsson says. "He was always fighting with somebody, whether it was the establishment or whatever. Always challenging the status quo."

But whatever animosity Fincher harbored toward corporate power was surely cemented by his experiences making *Alien³*. Released in 1992, Fincher's first movie tells the story of Sigourney Weaver's beloved Ripley character being stranded in an all-male outer space penal colony, where she shaves her head, learns she's pregnant with an alien, and eventually kills herself by falling, slow motion, into a giant vat of molten lava. *Alien³* was pounded by critics and largely ignored by audiences; the only way it could have done worse would have been if they'd actually called it *All-Male Outer Space Penal Colony*.

Fincher hates talking about *Alien³*, which started filming without a finished script and plunged him into daily battles with Twentieth

Century Fox over control (in the end, the studio recut Fincher's version). "At midnight, he'd have to get on the phone with Fox and justify shooting the next day's work," remembers Weaver. "I think it hurt his feelings and was exhausting."

Several years later, Fincher made nice with Fox and somehow persuaded the studio to bankroll *Fight Club*, his caustic, anticorporate buddy comedy about an unnamed, culturally emasculated claims adjuster (Edward Norton) and a charismatic anarchist named Tyler Durden (Brad Pitt) who form an underground brawling league/terrorist co-op. Adapted from a novel by Chuck Palahniuk, *Fight Club* was grotesquely violent, unnervingly kinetic, and darkly funny. The mere existence of *Fight Club* is kind of a joke—a treatise on the neutering effects of corporate America, underwritten by an international media conglomerate. "We were making a satire," Fincher says. "We were saying, 'This is as serious about blowing up buildings as *The Graduate* is about fucking your mom's friend.'"

Released in 1999, the movie caused a bipartisan freak-out: Conservatives condemned its violence, while Hollywood liberals complained that it focused unwanted attention on shoot-'em-up films and TV in the months following Columbine. For Fincher, this was all a point of pride. "There's a quote from a film critic that David had enlarged, framed, and hung in his conference room," says *Social Network* writer Aaron Sorkin. "It calls *Fight Club* 'amoral and Godless.' I think he'd rather have that quote than a Palme d'Or."

Though *Fight Club* was only a modest success in theaters, it has sold millions of DVDs. Watch the movie now and it's easy to see why: *Fight Club* has yet to age; indeed, its time may still not have truly arrived. The movie addressed build-your-life-around-our-brand consumerism well before the cult of the iPod was founded, and it provided an inadvertent blueprint for the sort of decentralized, shits-and-giggles anarchy that would later be adopted by web collectives like Anonymous. When people watch it fifty years from now, they'll probably assume it was made in 2011 or 2021 or whatever bleak period it will have turned out to presage.

Fight Club also exemplifies Fincher's curious relationship with the modern era: It's a movie about the perils of IKEA furniture and luxe gadgetry, directed by a Segway-riding gearhead. This is a paradox that runs through Fincher's life and work. He's a director raised on CG who's known for embracing new techniques and effects, from the reverse-aging wizardry in *Benjamin Button* to the subtle Winklevoss head-swaps in *The Social Network*. Yet Fincher has never been sucked too deeply into the whimsy-indulging, physics-bending cartoon rabbit hole of CGI that has engulfed directors like Tim Burton and George Lucas. And while his characters are frequently analytical brainiacs (hackers, coders, claims adjusters), they're often also prisoners of modernity.

Consider *Panic Room,* in which Jodie Foster's character takes refuge inside a Sharper Image–indebted, high-tech steel sarcophagus. Or *The Social Network*, which contrasted Mark Zuckerberg's frictionless online communication with his fractured real-life friendships. Even the solitary, decades-long hunt for a serial killer in *Zodiac* can be seen as a cautionary tale about informational fixation—an allegorical warning for the Internet age, when a time-suck can become a life-suck without your even noticing. In Fincher's world, the innovations that safeguard and enrich us are also the ones that do us in.

Back on the set of *The Girl with the Dragon Tattoo*, Mara's angry-hacker character, Lisbeth, is having her way with a treacherous Swede, courtesy of an imposingly huge chrome vibrator with a serrating buzz that sounds less like a joy machine than an irked Taser. This is Fincher's third attempt at the book's infamous rape-revenge scene, one of the key plot points in Larsson's story.

As it turns out, I'm not supposed to be here: Because the scene is so intense, this is a closed set—limited to essential cast and crew only. Before walking me in, Fincher makes me promise not to tell Mara I'm on set, then promptly finds me a seat right next to hers. I can't help but wonder if it's a semiplayful attempt to unnerve me. He denies this later, though I'm not sure I believe him. ("He is quite mischievous," Mara says a few weeks afterward, laughing. "But we were all pretty desensitized at that point.")

The relatively at-ease atmosphere on the *Dragon Tattoo* set is surprising, not only because of the subject matter but because stories of Fincher's endurance-test directing style are legendary: How he made Jake Gyllenhaal perform in *Zodiac* with a high fever; how he put Mara and Jesse Eisenberg through more than ninety takes of *The Social Network*'s opening breakup scene. "Challenging people," Mara says, "is one of his greatest joys in life."

Fincher's reasoning for putting his actors and crew through so many takes is simple: Making a movie requires flying people thousands of miles, putting them up in hotels, and spending days building sets. What's the point of all that preparation if you're just going to do your scene three times?

As grueling as it might seem to work under Fincher, he inspires loyalty among many of his actors and crew members. Rigidity, after all, also doubles as structure. "When you're working with somebody you trust, there's a really nice feeling of just submitting to their goals," says Eisenberg, who got an Oscar nomination for his role in *The Social Network*.

This confidence isn't limited to actors. "He really is the best technician I've ever worked with, ever," says Jodie Foster, who has directed four films. "He knows more about making movies than anybody I've ever met. He pretty much knows everybody else's job better than they do."

Still, at times Fincher has played God a bit too ferociously. At one point while filming *Panic Room*—a production so tense, according to Fincher's DVD commentary, that some people freaked out and needed to be escorted off the set (Fincher won't get into specifics)—Foster stood with him behind a monitor, watching him agonize over each take. "He looked at me, and he was like, 'I just don't know anymore,'" she says. "I'm like, 'You know what? I usually see what you're going for. This time, I don't see the difference between take two and take seven.' And he's like, 'Oh my God. I'm crazy, aren't I?' He recognizes it. He knows he has an issue. But he has to be 100 percent comfortable with the scene."

Fortunately perhaps for Fincher's current cast members, there hasn't been quite as much time for such micromanaging on *Dragon Tattoo*. It's his fourth film in five years, and it came together rather quickly—surprising, given its many ostensible obstacles. For starters, there's the fact that film versions of Larsson's three *Girl* books have already been produced in Sweden and are readily available on Netflix. And the movie came with an unwigglable holiday-season deadline.

There was also the material itself, a return to the gritty settings of Fincher's early career. "I try to choose things that aren't a rehash of places I've been," he says. "But I liked the idea of these two people navigating this odd world thousands of miles away. That was more interesting to me than the notion of 'Oh look, more depravity.'"

And hooooo boy, is the *Dragon Tattoo* book depraved (sample sentence: "The killer concluded his barbarities by shoving a parakeet up her vagina.") It's also unevenly written. For the first one hundred pages or so, it's almost impossible to believe Larsson's series has become a top choice for book-clubbers and frequent-fliers around the world.

But oddly enough, once you finish it you can't wait to see the movie. Maybe it's the animosity-flecked charge between the lead characters or the monstrous (yet recognizably human) villainy or the way it makes computer hacking seem like such a weirdly sexy calling. There's something undeniably dank and alluring about *Dragon Tattoo*, something almost . . . *Fincheresque*. With its sunless settings, multipronged cruelty, and emotionally bruised tech addicts, it's impossible to imagine any other director making it.

In fact, Larsson's gruesome work might never have found such a huge audience if Fincher hadn't long ago snipped off our eyelids and shown us the entrenched nastiness around us. Fifteen years earlier he would have had to fight to make a film as twisted as *Dragon Tattoo*; now it's set to be a holiday blockbuster. David Fincher's future, it seems, has finally arrived.

It's an early morning in Hollywood, and Fincher is listening to the words of a ghost:

"If a dove is the sinner's offering, the priest shall wring off its head, cleave its wings, and burn it upon the altar."

We're in a sound studio where dialog for *Dragon Tattoo* is being recorded. In the corner of the room, standing at a microphone, is Moa Garpendal, a fair-skinned, long-stemmed Swedish actress who plays Harriet, the teenager whose mysterious disappearance sets *Dragon Tattoo* in motion. As she reads the line—a short bit of voice-over that appears halfway through the story—Fincher paces the floor, making eye contact only when he has a suggestion.

"A little more finality at the end," he says. "Bring your voice down."

She gives it another reading. "Let's do one more," Fincher says. "Read it like a recipe. 'If you do *this*, then you have to do *this*, then *this*.'"

More tries, more notes.

"Give me a little more 'wring off and cleave,' just to make it more punitive."

"Try to make the inhale a little bit softer."

"Good. Do one more."

Sometimes, Fincher raises his glasses and pinches his eyes closed, shutting out everything but the sound. Whatever he's listening for this morning, whatever way the words fall together in his head, will not be arrived at quickly. At one point, he catches a noise deep in the background of the track and halts the session. "Are you hearing that?" Fincher asks the room. "It was like a truck passing."

They listen. There doesn't seem to be anything there.

"Maybe I'm having a stroke," Fincher says, shrugging. "Let's do one more."

They try again, the words rising into the air over and over again, finally landing somewhere only David Fincher can hear them.

You Better Be F—ing Serious: David Fincher on Directing

Fincher Fanatic / 2012

From FincherFanatic.com, 2012. Reprinted by permission.

"It was great. It's an adult movie, it's f—ing hard-R, and they were getting out of my way and let me do what I wanted to do," is what director David Fincher has to say of the experience of working on his new thriller, *The Girl with the Dragon Tattoo*. FincherFanatic caught up with him during the final days of editing.

First things first, David Fincher isn't one for vanity press. He didn't enter the movie business to become a celebrity. And that may be a reason why it is still rare and hard to get an interview with the man—particularly on camera—perhaps more so if you are writing a blog about him. "You know, I don't even like looking at my driver's license," Fincher says. "If I had wanted to be a celebrity, I wouldn't have picked this lonely job, that requires you to stay in a room in the dark, watching TV all the time." The very reason he started out directing music videos and commercials was *because* there was no screen credit, just a convenient opportunity to learn the craft and get paid for it. In Internet times, to see these works from the past rear their heads is not much to Fincher's liking. Which is why our conversation begins with his blunt question: Why would anyone in their right mind write a blog about him?

Fincher doesn't like to read about himself, nor does he like to be recognized. A two-fold discomfort: For one, Fincher doesn't want to be made aware of expectations towards his work. And understandably so: "There are so many things I wouldn't have done, if I had listened to that," he says. And as for being recognized, he adds: "You know, I used to live next door to George Lucas. When I was ten years old, he was the guy who had done *THX 1138*. By the time I was twelve, he was the guy who did *American Graffiti*. By the time I was fifteen, he had done *Star Wars*. By the time *Star Wars* came out, this guy couldn't go anywhere in town. He couldn't walk into some place and not be the focus of it. One of the things I like about being a director is, when your plane is late, you are doing homework. Because you are sitting there in the lounge, listening to people talk. That's your job. When you become the focus, when people feel like 'I can't act like myself, because that's the guy who did whatever,' all of a sudden you lose an advantage."

It's an intriguing motive for Fincher's publicity aversion. Yet each Oscar nomination and the anticipated roll-out of Sony's marketing campaign for *Dragon Tattoo* are not going to make that any easier—let alone Fincher's likely next, Disney's *20,000 Leagues Under the Sea*; a 100+ million dollar CG family adventure.

Fincher feels awkward at the thought, that he himself could have become an icon for a young generation of filmmakers. "Now, I understand Spielberg, Hitchcock, even to a certain extent George Lucas," he says—and thinks. But whether he likes it or not, 'Fincher' has long become a brand name. Still the director upholds his protest: "I don't want to be a Winchell's Donut. Even if my last name is 'Winchell.' I want to be able to make something like *Zodiac*. I mean, shouldn't your movies, if they are truly personal, change the way you change? Every seven years all of the cells in our bodies change, everything is in this process of evolution; so the notion that the director is a brand—?"

Well. Coincidentally, the theatrical trailer for *The Girl with the Dragon Tattoo* reads, "a David Fincher film," and "directed by David Fincher." Fincher's disapproval isn't very well hidden: "None of the trailers that I ever cut had my f—ing name on them. As I never tire of telling the marketing department, 'Remember, *Se7en* was from the director of *Se7en*, too, but it didn't say it on the poster.' So I work hard to fight against whatever my brand is. I would like my brand to stand for 'works really hard,' 'tries to make it as good as he possibly can.' If the brand is, 'it's gonna be dark and grainy,' I have no interest in that. It's just too reductive. It's just too stupid."

On the other hand, no matter how "reductive" and "stupid" these branding activities may arguably be, they are a good share, as Fincher admits, of why—despite debates over running time, final cut, and his infamously uncompromising nature—he keeps getting greenlights. "There is no doubt that that is part of why they put up with me. I am not easy to get along with. But I am saying to you, $100 million, that's the pain threshold in Hollywood. When you are talking about $100 million, you better be f—ing serious. When we're talking about $40 million, that is a low- to medium-budget movie."

Yes, 40 million. That was last year's Oscar favorite *The Social Network*. Now, *The Girl with the Dragon Tattoo* is looking at an estimated budget of exactly that $100 million Hollywood pain threshold. And you can rest assured: Fincher *is* 'f—ing serious.'

At the time of our meeting, Fincher and his Academy Award–winning editors, Angus Wall and Kirk Baxter, are working around the clock to get to that final cut—against a definitive deadline a mere two months away. "We gotta have a movie out in December! We're not making a movie, we're making a release date," Fincher says. And he's only half joking.

If you are familiar with Stieg Larsson's best-selling Millennium trilogy, it appears a perfect match of director and material. The first book, *Dragon Tattoo*, is a brutal thriller, centered around a murder mystery, riddled with themes of misogyny, rape, racism, serial killing—" . . . and ultimately it is a kind of love story," Fincher adds, "in some weird f—ed up way. It's not a serial killer movie. That is one of the elements of it, but it is really those two characters [Lisbeth Salander and Mikael Blomkvist]. What he and she have is really interesting. It cuts across generations, it's very nonconventional in Hollywood terms, of what gets them into the sack and, ultimately, what breaks them up."

The novels have sold in excess of sixty million copies, a graphic-novel adaptation is on the way, a Lisbeth Salander inspired H&M collection is due in December: The film is riding a wave of mainstream attention, which almost should guarantee a box-office hit. Yet it is looking at a running time of just more than two and a half hours, an R-rating, and promises to be the "feel bad movie of Christmas." And whether that is good or bad or completely irrelevant for Fincher's release, there's already a series of Swedish-language films based on the same trilogy of novels.

"I know," Fincher says, "we are playing into the European, and certainly the Swedish, predisposition that this is just a gigantic, monetary landgrab. You're coopting a phenomenon. Now, there is plenty of reason to believe that we can make it equally entertaining of a movie. But the resentment is already engendered, in a weird way. It's bizarre. But then there are British television shows, like *The Office*, that are being remade as American television shows. And we speak the same f—ing language." This is just as true for another of Fincher's slated projects: a reimagining of BBC's *House of Cards*.

But Hollywood is a different ballgame, as Fincher insists. In Sweden you have highly educated people, guys with master's degrees, pulling focus, working multiple positions. In Hollywood you have highly skilled but highly specialized people. "The American film industry is like the American auto industry: You got people who do one thing, and they do it great, and you don't have to tell them how to do that one thing. But you need a lot of people, because everybody does one thing. One guy does this, the other guy does this, the next guy does this. On my movies, dolly grip is important. I mean: We will wait for Michael Brennan. We want to start shooting at the beginning of January. Brennan is not available until February? So we'll start in February! He can save you three days of shooting over the course of the production, he's that good. When you are in sync with somebody like that, and they have your kind of aesthetic." Fincher spontaneously swings out of his chair and stages a scene. "I can say, 'I want the camera to start here and it's going to come around, and it's going to be over the shoulder.' And [Brennan] is watching, and he knows, that camera is thirty-three inches off the ground."

American films are more expensive, but they are (often) for a reason. "We shot seventy-eight days in Sweden, and I believe by the end of it the Swedish crew saw the difference between take six and take thirty. At the beginning they were definitely rolling their eyes. They were like, 'Hey, we made the first *Dragon Tattoo* for fifteen million bucks,' and I said, 'I realize that. But we're doing something different. It's going to be handled in a different way.' So at the beginning the Swedes were very much like, 'How could you possibly take this long to make a movie?' And by the middle of the shoot they were like, 'I get what the difference is. I get what it is to have these choices.'"

Nonetheless, the experience appears to inspire Fincher. He has talked about digital filmmaking on various occasions before; about the revolution in computer technology; about highly affordable postproduction software. "I think the Swedish film industry is probably more like the future. The directors of the future are going to come from YouTube. I'm telling you, Steven Spielberg tells me, 'check this out!'—and he's watching YouTube. People are sending him links to stuff. Here's some dude in Argentina, who's made some short, and he's watching it on Vimeo or whatever. It's totally decentralized."

Talking about his Netflix miniseries *House of Cards*, naturally Fincher had more to say than mentioning it as just another example of a Hollywood makeover. The original was a 1990 BBC produced series about political power, ambition, and corruption. "It was a brilliant TV show," Fincher says. "But today is a completely different universe. *House of Cards* was made during Thatcherism. It was a stiff-upper-lip look at parliamentary politics. Our thing is: Twitter, News Corp, hacking—and the notion of politics when you stand for nothing. Politics above all. And that was the thing that was transposable, nothing about the actual plot. But the notion of a guy, who can be in the middle of a conversation, turn to the audience and go, 'This is what pisses me off about people like this guy.'— 'Watch. This is how politics works.' That's what it's designed to do. It's the notion of, let me show you why politics is necessary: because that's how you validate people within a bureaucracy. The collective confusion is so much more important than singular clarity.'"

David Fincher taking on an up-to-date, sharp-witted political drama? Sounds like an exciting prospect. It also sounds like a new artistic stance for Fincher, whose movies so far seem to have made a point of avoiding being overtly (or in any way, really) political. And certainly Fincher tackling politics will be anything but shiny propaganda. "There is nothing optimistic about it, not in the least," Fincher confirms. "But it's fun. It's very fun. It's interesting in a good way. It's the kind of shit we should be talking about, which is: Why are we pretending that there are these choices?" Shooting for the series will kick off in March/April 2012, with an anticipated release some time next fall. "It's going to be on Netflix, so once we have five hours it's going to be on. So far the pilot is the only script we have, and it's great. It's by Beau Willimon, who wrote *The Ides of March*," Fincher says. (And this, listen, Fanatics:) "I don't know what my other responsibilities will be but I am going to do as many of them as I can."

In his recent *Vanity Fair* portrait of David Fincher, *The Social Network* screenwriter Aaron Sorkin had this to say: "The rumor about David is that he's gruff, harsh, and difficult to work with. The truth about David is that he's warm, honest, and an exceptionally generous collaborator. He's fine with the rumor." Going by every minute I was granted, I can only confirm Sorkin's positive observations. David Fincher is intriguingly easy to be around—for all I can truthfully say, this is true when you don't work with him—and aside from him being a personal idol and favorite director of mine, he's a bundle of trenchant anecdotes and sharp wit; dedicated to best-possible results and keenly enthusiastic about what he does. As much as Fincher hates branding and any kind of three-words-or-less approach, if I had to pick a label to describe my impression, I'd say 'Fincher loves movies.' Which can lead to curious conflicts.

"For the most part, people who are in the movie business don't go to movies," Fincher is ready to admit. "It's a pain in the ass. I have to be honest, I saw *Moneyball* for the first time last weekend. And I was like, 'How did this get to this point, where I am sitting in a theater, watching many friends of mine's movie, weeks after it opened?'—I just don't have time! I didn't get into the movie-business not to appreciate movies, and yet I find myself in the position, where I literally don't have the extra time to go see a movie. I saw the trailer for *Tinker, Tailor, Soldier, Spy* and I loved that trailer. I love David Dencik, love these actors, love the way it's photographed. But it's cut too fast. It's not appreciative enough of the hard work that's been put into it." It takes Fincher a second to realize that he got sidetracked. He wraps the thought up with a sigh: "So you find yourself in a situation where you haven't seen a movie in a year. It's weird."

But Fincher's love for cinema goes much deeper than consumption and enjoyment. In his own work, it's about making the most of every single frame. "I never fall in love with anything. I really don't, I am not joking. 'Do the best you can, try to live it down,' that's my motto. Just literally give it everything you got, and then know that it's never going to turn out the way you want it to, and let it go, and hope that it doesn't return. Because you want it to be better than it can ever turn out. Absolutely, 1000 percent, I believe this: Whenever a director friend of mine says, 'Man, the dailies look amazing!' . . . I actually believe that anybody, who thinks that their dailies look amazing doesn't understand the power of cinema; doesn't understand what cinema is capable of."

Fincher has been hailed (and snubbed) for his visual virtuosity, his films have been recognized and awarded for their writing, editing, and cinematography—and of course I make use of my opportunity to compliment the director on behalf of countless fans on the extraordinary ambition evident in his work. Yet surprisingly, Fincher feels tethered to it.

"Look, it's sweet," he says. "I am happy that people look at the way things go together or how they fit, because I look at that as my fundamental responsibility. I don't pride myself in technical virtuosity or finesse. I'm crippled by it. Brad Pitt said a funny thing. He said, he watches me watch the monitor, and 'I can actually see you flinch, when something . . .'—because I find myself, I'm watching and I'm in the moment, and I am watching her . . . and I am watching her eyes . . . and she looks over to him . . . and then all of a sudden this thing happens, and you go: 'Oh God! If I could just get rid of this distraction.'"

"I picked everything in that room, I picked the chairs, I picked the wall color, I put the lights where they are, I was here yesterday, making sure that everything balances. I have done all these things in my head, and then when you can actually do that and lose yourself in what's going on, and be concentrating on how one person is telling this story, and they are giving this moment, and the other person is picking it up at exactly the right place, and you are lost in it, and all of a sudden—doink!—this thing happens. You cut to camera and the shot should be three millimeters wider or something. And you go, 'God, if I could just carry the energy of that thing into the next shot.' So I appreciate that people don't have to go through that. They can see the final thing for what the intent is. They can be lost in it. But I'd be lying if I said it turned out exactly the way I imagined."

Which of course reminds me of an infamous Fincher quote, that has come to be one of my favorites over the years. As I come to find out, it holds just as much truth as it doesn't: "People will say, 'There are a million ways to shoot a scene,' but I don't think so. I think there're two, maybe. And the other one is wrong."

"Yeah, well the context for this was—and I was being funny—I kind of don't know how not to do it the way that I would do it," Fincher says. Within a second, he is up, staging another scene, making his point. "You watch what is happening here, then this person comes in, they do this, they say this, then she has to enter, and they have already talked about this. So we are seeing this from their point of view, so we need to be over them, certainly for a lot of it, and then we need to figure out a way to keep her at a distance." Fincher sits back down, retracing his argument. "So, yeah, I think that was in response to somebody saying, 'Don't you think there are a lot of different ways to do this?' And I was like, 'I don't know of them.' It's the horrible thing: You get into the interpersonal side of making movies, and the movie studio says, 'I don't know how to see your point of view.'" Fincher chuckles. "I get paid to see my point of view, I get paid to see it one way. And I get paid to be able to elucidate what that perspective is. I am fundamentally against this notion of auteurism. I think it worked for those guys. I think the Yippiekayee guys from the 1960s got a lot of mileage out of it. But your point of view is all you've got. Your take on things. And so I was saying that, no, you cannot do anything other than what you do. Martin Scorsese once said an interesting thing to me, 'The things you do badly are as much part of your style as the things you do well.' And I can look at stuff that's been done by other filmmakers, and I go, "Why are they doing it this way? Why is it so simplistic?' And that may be the thing that this filmmaker looks at and goes, 'I have to, at this moment, be so blunt and so simple in the presentation, so this is what I am going to do.' And that may be the thing that rubs me raw: That I may look at it and go, 'Ugh, why do you have to be so close? Why wouldn't this shot include another person? Why wouldn't there be a move to it?' But they may go, 'Look, I can do all this stuff around it, and in the end what I really want is to not have anything embroidered or filigreed around this moment.' So that's a choice that they make. That's their thing. I may look at that and go, well, that's that storyteller's shortcomings, is they don't chose to make this moment, or juice this moment, or pull this moment—but that's what it is."

"Anyway, I think it was something I said about an idea of perspective. And I was basically trying to say, 'I don't think you cannot have a perspective.' You answer three thousand questions a day, all about, what do you want? What do you want to see? Where do you want to see it from? Where should we put the money? Should we paint this with nine layers of fucking lacquer, or should we . . . ?—And that's what you get paid to do. You get paid to say, 'This is where we are going to spend the money, and this is where we are not.' Because we don't get to build the whole f— ing world, we only get to build the pieces of it that we see. So, no I don't think there's a thousand ways to skin a cat—I think there is a couple. And most of the time you shoot for two or three different ways, and you go, 'Duh! Here's the one. This is how it shakes out.'"

We already know that for David Fincher directing is more than drawing neat little pictures and showing them to the camera man. Directing means painting a picture with a walkie-talkie and a crew of eighty people holding the brush. Directing means total control over everything the audience sees and hears for two hours; forging their experience of the story. And this requires the filmmaker's attention to the whole and to detail in every department and along every step of the process.

"There are a lot of people, who don't understand what staging is. It's the most important thing directors do, and not a lot of people realize that. Not a lot of people know why they like Steven Spielberg. They don't know the difference between having their eye directed, and having coverage edited for them. But the truth is," Fincher continues, "film is too expensive to teach. You can't teach how to make Hollywood movies. What you can do is make people look at the language of cinema. Why do we need a close-up? I got a master, I got an over, I got close-up—what's the best, what's the most effective way to move people who are watching it, who don't know what this person is or don't know what the circumstances are; how do I engage them? And you can do that anywhere. You don't have to go to London, you don't have to go to Pinewood, you don't have to go to SC. Creativity happens on the fringe. It does. It's too bad. But you can get there. Start in the fringe, meet those people, write your scripts. I always wanted to give a lecture at film schools. You go in and you see all these fresh faces, and you say: 'You! Stand up, tell me your story. Tell me what your film is going to be about.' And they start, and you go: 'Shut up and sit the fuck down!' And if they do, you go: 'You're not ready.' Because the film business is filled with shut-up and sit-the-fuck-down. You got to be able to tell your story in spite of sit-down and shut-the-fuck-up. If you are going to let something like that derail you, what hope do you have against a transportation department? What hope do you have against development executives?"

To me, that is the essential Fincher: Trust yourself, trust your perspective on your story. Fincher has no qualms to admit there are commercials he has done for the paycheck. Nowadays, however, he signs on only if there is a high enough concept, something in it he wants to do—and he's ready to walk away if there's not.

"I am nothing if I am not honest to people," Fincher says. "We are meeting with commercial clients here and I will say, 'Here's what I am going to do, and I am not joking, and I am not teasing, I am not just backing you off to be incendiary. This is what I know how to do, this is what I want to do with this. And if you don't want to do it, don't hire me."

It's true for his commercial work, yet you can easily see this is true for his films as well. *Zodiac* was a passion project. *Fight Club*, as Fincher says, was "the giant movie studio version of a movie that should never be made by a movie studio." And as for *Se7en*, producer Arnold Kopelson thought Fincher took "a perfectly good genre movie and turned it into a foreign film."

"I know that I am true to the things I am interested in," Fincher says. "I like stories to unfold in certain kinds of ways, and I don't like short-hand, and I don't like to be told who's evil. I don't want to know who the villain is, I don't want to know who the hero is. If it happens over time that's great. You know the thing is, with Robert McKee and these people, who go, let's distill it down. The thing is: Let's not distill story-telling down. That's what makes it so interesting. I'm telling you, I'm reading *Se7en*, and about thirty pages in I'm going, 'What the fuck? The old cop, the young cop. . . .' I throw it across the room and call my agent, I go, 'Why would you send me this shit?' He goes, 'No, no, no, no! Read through to the end.' So I read it . . . and all of a sudden John Doe gives himself up. And I know there's f—ing twenty pages left. But I'm going: 'How do you . . . ? You can't do this here! This can't be done.' That was fun! To be in that place, to be sitting in the theater and going: 'He's covered in blood, he walks into the police station? That's crazy! This movie could be starting, it could certainly start over, but it could be going for another two hours. Where are we in this?' That was Andy's [*Se7en* scribe Andrew Kevin Walker's] creation. It's not the seven deadly sins; that's easy. It was that! And all of a sudden, once you realize there's the head in the box, you go, 'Oh my God, this is not going to be one of those movies. It's a totally different thing.' It's like, now this guy has to deal with evil. He's no longer dealing with plot devices—he's dealing with pure evil."

Key Resources

Asterisked interviews are reproduced in this book.

Interviews/Profiles

Abele, Robert. "Playing with a New Deck." *Directors Guild of America Quarterly*, January 2013, 34–39.

Albinson, Ian, and Will Perkins. "David Fincher: A Film Title Retrospective." ArtoftheTitle.com, August 27, 2012.

Berger, Warren. "When Hollywood Come a Knockin'." *Advertising Age*, June 1, 1998, 28.

Billington, Alex. "David Fincher Discusses Having Final Cut, Themes, and More." FirstShowing.net, December 23, 2011.

*Blair, Iain. "David Fincher Interview." *Film and Video* 13 (October 1997): 15–18.

*Bowles, Scott. "A Curious Case of Friendship." *USA Today*, November 28, 2008.

Braund, Simon. "Hall of Fame: David Fincher, Fighter." *Empire* 155 (May 2002): 110–17.

Brooks, Xan. "Directing Is Masochism." *The Guardian*, April 24, 2002.

Brunner, Rob. "The Girl with the Dragon Tattoo." *Entertainment Weekly* 1181 (November 18, 2011): 40–44.

BT. "David Fincher on *Zodiac*." *The Times of India*, July 21, 2007.

Burman, Mark. "A Real Horror Show: The Filming of *Alien³* Was a Nightmare for Its Director David Fincher." *The Independent*, August 21, 1992.

Calhoun, Dave. "The Greatest Asset to an Actor Is Their Ego." *Time Out*, December 8, 2011.

Calhoun, John. "Power Plays." *American Cinematographer* 94 (February 2013): 18–22.

Carr, David. "Giving Viewers What They Want." *New York Times*, February 25, 2013.

Cashin, Declan. "Inside the World of *Dragon Tattoo* Director David Fincher." *Irish Independent*, December 16, 2011.

Cheney, Alexandra, and Amol Sharma. "Netflix Wins More Respect with Showing at Emmys." *Wall Street Journal*, September 23, 2013.

Cohen, David. "The Game." *Total Film*, November 1997, 48–49.

*Cooney, Jenny. "The Head Master." *Empire* 101 (November 1997): 128–134.

Coyle, Jake. "In *Dragon Tattoo*, Fincher Taps Another Network." *Metro News*, December 29, 2011.

Davies, Dave. "Spacey and Fincher Make a '*House of Cards.*'" Fresh Air (npr .org), January 31, 2013.

Desowitz, Bill. "Fincher Talks *Benjamin Button* and VFX." *VFX World*, January 9, 2009.

Dombal, Ryan. "Trent Reznor and David Fincher." Pitchfork.com, September 27, 2010.

Doogan, Todd. "Todd Doogan Interviews Director David Fincher." TheDig italBits.com, May 11, 2000.

Douglas, Edward. "The CS Interview with David Fincher." ComingSoon.net, December 19, 2011.

Eimer, David. "Game Boy." *Time Out*, October 8, 1997.

*Epstein, Daniel Robert. "Inside *Panic Room*: David Fincher, the Roundtable Interview." DavidFincher.net, 2002.

Faraci, Devin. "Exclusive Interview: David Fincher." Chud.com, January 8, 2008.

Farber, Stephen. "A Meeting of Tough Minds in Hollywood." *New York Times*, August 31, 1997.

*Fincher Fanatic, "You Better Be F—ing Serious: David Fincher on Directing." FincherFanatic.com, 2012.

Fincher, David. "Jake Gyllenhaal." *Interview*, October 2007, 138–43, 190.

Fincher, David. "Rooney Mara and David Fincher." *Interview* 41 (December 2011): 50–52, 140.

Foley, Jack. "*Zodiac*—David Fincher Interview." IndieLondon.com, 2007.

Fuller, Graham. "Fighting Talk." *Interview*, 24 (November 1999), 1071–77.

Galloway, Stephen. "David Fincher: Punk, Prophet, Genius." *Hollywood Reporter* 417 (February 9, 2011), 55–59.

*Gilbey, Ryan. "Four Walls and a Funeral." *The Independent*, April 19, 2002.

*Gilbey, Ryan. "Precocious Prankster Who Gets a Thrill from Tripping People Up." *The Independent*, October 10, 1997.

Goldman, Michael. "With Friends Like These . . ." *American Cinematographer* 91 (October 2010): 28–42.

Goldrich, Robert. "The Collaborative Network Behind *The Social Network*." *Shoot* 52 (January 21, 2011).

Goodykoontz, Bill. "Man Behind the *Dragon Tattoo*." *Arizona Republic*, December 17, 2011.

Grossman, Lev. "Face-Off: Why David Fincher and Aaron Sorkin Made a Facebook Movie." *Time* 176 (October 4, 2010): 71–73.

Guyot, Paul. "David Fincher: *Seven* and *Fight Club*." DVDTalk.com, 2002.

Halbfinger, David M. "Lights, Boogeyman, Action." *New York Times*, February 18, 2007.

Hanas, Jim. "The Rise and Fall of Propaganda." *Advertising Age*, December 1, 2001, 26.

Harris, Mark. "Enter the Dragon." *Entertainment Weekly*, January 6, 2012, 26–35.

Harris, Mark. "Inventing Facebook." *New York Magazine*, September 27, 2010.

*Harris, Mark. "The Vulture Transcript: An In-Depth Chat with David Fincher about *The Social Network*." *New York Magazine*, September 21, 2010.

Heath, Chris. "The Unbearable Bradness of Being." *Rolling Stone*, October 28, 1999, 66–74, 116.

Henkel, Guido. "David Fincher: Fighting the Odds." DVDReview.com, May 23, 2000.

Henry, Michael. "Entretien avec David Fincher: Le pandémonium de l'existence." *Positif* 576 (February 2009): 9–12.

Heuring, David. "Power, Politics and Pixels." *Digital Video* 21 (March 2013): 20–23.

Hooper, Barrett. "Not One to Get Boxed In: *Panic Room* Director David Fincher Took His Own Sweet Time to Get It All Right." *National Post*, March 27, 2002.

Horowitz, Josh. "David Fincher Didn't Want to Make 'Another Serial-Killer Movie . . . Until *Zodiac* Came Along." MTV.com, January 3, 2008.

Horowitz, Josh. "David Fincher Discusses Reunion with Brad Pitt, Possible *Fight Club* Musical." MTV.com, January 7, 2008.

Hosoki, Nobuhiro. "David Fincher on *Zodiac* Director's Cut." Hosokinema.com, 2007.

Huddleston, Tom. "Close-Up: David Fincher." *Time Out*, January 29, 2009.

Huddleston, Tom. "Warning Signs." *Time Out*, September 18, 2008.

James, Nick. "Face to Face." *Sight and Sound* 19 (March 2009): 28.

Japan, Warner. "Une breve rencontre avec David Fincher." *Cahiers du Cinema* 642 (January 2009).

Jeffrey, Morgan. "David Fincher; *House of Cards* Q&A: Kevin Spacey Is Just Naughty." DigitalSpy.com, January 26, 2013.

Jenkins, David. "Pay Attention, or You're Going to Miss a Lot: David Fincher on *The Social Network*." *Time Out*, October 14, 2010.

Jolin, Dan. "The Total Film Interview: David Fincher." *Total Film*, May 2002.

*Kaminsky, James. "Mr. Fincher's Neighborhood." *Advertising Age*, November 1, 1993, 17.

Katsikas, Loukas. "Pretty Hate Machine." *Cinema* (Greece), March 2000, 68–70.

Kilday, Gregg. "The Making of *The Girl with the Dragon Tattoo*." *Hollywood Reporter*, January 14, 2012.

King, Dennis. "Director Met Challenge of Film's Complex Casting." *Oklahoman*, December 21, 2011.

Lawson, Terry. "David Fincher Talks *Zodiac*." *Detroit Free Press*, March 2, 2007.

Lee, Stephan. "*Gone Girl*." *Entertainment Weekly*, January 17, 2014, 18–21.

*Levy, Emanuel. "*Social Network*: Interview with Director David Fincher." EmanuelLevy.com, 2010.

*Levy, Shawn. "David Fincher of *Zodiac*." *Oregonian*, March 2, 2007.

Lewis, Keith. "Director of *Gone Girl* Talks about Life behind Camera." *Southeast Missourian*, October 13, 2013.

Liberatore, Paul. "Director Fincher Got Taste for Film Growing Up in Marin." *Marin Independent Journal*, December 12, 2008.

Lim, Denis. "Directing What She Knows." *Los Angeles Times*, October 26, 2008.

Luscombe, Belinda. "10 Questions for David Fincher." *Time* 178 (December 19, 2011).

Maher, Kevin. "When I Saw It My First Thought Was: This Is Too Good to Be True." *Times of London*, January 30, 2013.

Martin, Kevin. "David Fincher." *International Cinematographers Guild Magazine* 79 (December 2011): 24–26.

McGrath, Charles. "Obsession, Reignited." *New York Times*, December 7, 2011.

McWeeny, Drew. "Interview: David Fincher Discusses *The Social Network*, *Fight Club*, and the Digital Age." Hitflix.com, January 3, 2011.

Miller, Prairie. "David Fincher Interview: *The Girl with the Dragon Tattoo*." *Long Island Press*, December 31, 2011.

Mockenhaupt, Brian. "The Curious Case of David Fincher." *Esquire* 147 (March 2007): 158–63, 210–12.

O'Regan, Nadine. "David Fincher *Benjamin Button* Interview." *Sunday Business Post*, January 27, 2009.

Osborne, Bert. "Panic Attack." *Creative Loafing*, April 3, 2002.

*Pierce, Nev. "Chasing the Dragon." *Empire*, November 2011, 74–83.

Pierce, Nev. "David Fincher Exclusive: The Making of *House of Cards*." Empire.com, March 2013.

*Pierce, Nev. "Forget the First Two Rules of *Fight Club*." *Total Film*, April 2006, 120–127.

Pierce, Nev. "Geek Tragedy." *Empire* 256 (October 2010): 114–19.

Pierce, Nev. "History in the Making." *Total Film*, October 29, 2008, 82–87.

*Pierce, Nev. "In Conversation with David Fincher." *Empire* 235 (January 2009): 163–68.

Pierce, Nev. "Political Animal." *Empire* 285 (March 2013): 112–17.

Pierce, Nev. "*The Curious Case of Benjamin Button*: Romance, Death, and Director David Fincher." *Empire* 233 (November 2008): 20–23.

*Pierce, Nev. "The Devil Is in the Detail." *Total Film*, March 26, 2007, 62–67.

Probst, Christopher. "Anarchy in the USA." *American Cinematographer* 80 (November 1999): 42–53.

Probst, Christopher. "Playing for Keeps on *The Game.*" *American Cinematographer* 78 (September 1997): 38–40, 42, 44, 46, 48, 50–52.

Pulumbarit, Oliver. "David Fincher: Cinematic Style and Substance." Multiply.com, December 1, 2007.

*Pulver, Andrew. "Fight the Good Fight." *Guardian*, October 29, 1999.

Quint, "David Fincher and Quint Talk About Everything from *Alien³* to *Zodiac!!!*" *Ain't It Cool News* (AintItCool.com), January 1, 2008.

Quint, "David Fincher Chats with Quint about Harvard Tilt Shift (and Lack Thereof), *The Social Network* DVD, and Gives an Update on *The Goon* Movie!" *Ain't It Cool News* (AintItCool.com), January 12, 2011.

*Raftery, Brian. "Heart of Darkness." Wired.com, December 2011.

Rich, Katey. "*Dragon Tattoo*'s Mara, Craig, and Fincher Talk Motorcycles and Suffering Take After Take." CinemaBlend.com, December 20, 2011.

*Richardson, John H. "Mother from Another Planet." *Premiere* 5 (May 1992): 62–70.

Rocchi, James. "David Fincher of *The Girl with the Dragon Tattoo.*" MSN.com, December 21, 2011.

Rose, Charlie. "Conversation about *The Curious Case of Benjamin Button.*" *The Charlie Rose Show*, December 25, 2008.

Rose, Charlie. "Interview with the Cast of *The Girl with the Dragon Tattoo.*" *The Charlie Rose Show*, December 15, 2011.

Rose, Lacey. "Netflix's Ted Sarandos Reveals His 'Phase 2' for Hollywood." *Hollywood Reporter*, May 31, 2013.

Roug, Louise. "*The Girl with the Dragon Tattoo*: An Interview with Rooney Mara, Daniel Craig, and David Fincher." TheDailyBeast.com, December 18, 2011.

Rouyer, Phillippe. "Seven." *Positif* 420 (February 1996).

Ryan, Mike. "David Fincher on *The Girl with the Dragon Tattoo* and Working on *Return of the Jedi.*" Moviefone.com, December 19, 2011.

Ryzik, Melena. "David Fincher's Embargo Solution." *New York Times*, December 7, 2011.

*Salisbury, Mark. "David Fincher." *Guardian*, January 18, 2009.

*Salisbury, Mark. "Seventh Hell." *Empire* 80 (February 1996): 78–85, 87.

Schaefer, Stephen. "Brad Pitt & Edward Norton: Two of Hollywood's Hottest Thirtysomethings Embrace Mayhem and Millennial Meltdown in *Fight Club.*" MrShowbiz.com, October 1999.

Schneller, Johanna. "Two Heavy Hitters Put Their Muscle Behind the Controversial *Fight Club.*" *Premiere*, August 1999, 68–73, 100.

Schruers, Fred. "David Fincher's Bizarro Game." *Rolling Stone* 757 (April 3, 1997): 52–53.

Sciretta, Peter. "Eleven Things I Learned From LACMA's Conversation with David Fincher about *House of Cards*." Slashfilm.com, March 8, 2013.

Secher, Benjamin. "David Fincher Interview on *The Girl with the Dragon Tattoo*." *Daily Telegraph*, December 20, 2011.

Sepinwall, Alan. "*House of Cards* Director David Fincher on Making 13 Hours for Netflix." Hitflix.com, January 29, 2013.

Smith, Christopher Allan, and Michael Tunison, "David Fincher Interview." *Cinescape*, May 2002.

*Smith, Gavin. "Inside Out." *Film Comment* 35 (September/October 1999): 58–62, 65, 67–68.

Sragow, Michael. "Testosterama: The Men Behind the Ballsy *Fight Club* Talk about Anti-Consumerism, Annoying Boomerisms, and How to Make Soap out of Human Fat." Salon.com, October 14, 1999.

Stasukevich, Iain. "Retro Style." *American Cinematographer* 94 (May 2013): 14–18.

Stone, Sasha. "David Fincher: Through a Glass Darkly." *Awards Daily*, February 16, 2011.

Svetkey, Benjamin. "Blood, Sweat, and Fears." *Entertainment Weekly* 507 (October 15, 1999): 24–29.

Taubin, Amy. "Amy Taubin Talks with David Fincher."*Sight and Sound* 6 (January 1996): 24.

Taubin, Amy. "David Fincher Interview." Filmcomment.com, January/February, 2009.

Taubin, Amy. "Nerds on a Wire." *Sight and Sound* 17 (May 2007): 24–27.

*Taubin, Amy. "Twenty-First-Century Boys." *Village Voice*, October 19, 1999.

Uncredited, "David Fincher Talks Violence, Unpleasant Revenge, and the Odd, Perverse Relationship that Drew Him to *The Girl with the Dragon Tattoo*." IndieWire.com, 2011.

Uncredited. "Dark, Edgy *Dragon Tattoo* a Love Story, Fincher Says." *Toronto Star*, December 17, 2011.

Uncredited. "*Fight Club* Director David Fincher." Scotsman.com, September 18, 2008.

Uncredited. "The Minds Behind the Butt-Kicking *Fight Club* Special Edition DVD Tell the Tale of the Disc." B&N.com, July 11, 2000.

Uncredited, "A Walk on the Dark Side." *Sunday Business Post*, January 25, 2009.

Vachaud, Laurent, and Christian Viviani. "Entretien David Fincher: Le film d'action est sur le déclin." *Positif* 443 (January 1998): 82–84.

Van Meter, Jonathan. "Playing with Fire." *Vogue* 201 (November 2011): 248–57.

Verdiani, Gilles. "Fighter Fincher." *Premiere* 272 (November 1999): 116–121.

Virtue, Graeme. "Room with a Crew." *Sunday Herald*, April 28, 2002.

Walker, Andrew Kevin. "David Fincher Making Audiences Wish They Could Buy Anti-Anxiety Insurance with Their Popcorn." *Interview*, March 2002, 78.

Weintraub, Steve. "David Fincher Exclusive Interview!" Collider.com, December 2010.

Wise, Damon. "David Fincher Interview." *Neon*, November 1997.

Wise, Damon. "Menace II Society." *Empire* 126 (December 1999): 100–106.

Zeichner, Naomi. "The Way Out Is Through: An Interview with David Fincher." *Fader*, October/November, 2013.

Books

Astrom, Berit, Katarina Gregersdotter, and Tanya Horeck, editors. *Rape in Stieg Larsson's Millennium Trilogy and Beyond*. London: Palgrave, 2013.

Browning, Mark. *David Fincher: Films That Scar*. Santa Barbara: Praeger, 2010.

Dyer, Richard. *Seven*. London: British Film Institute, 1999.

Fincher, David, Eric Roth, and Robin Swicord. *The Curious Case of Benjamin Button: The Making of the Motion Picture*. New York: Rizzoli, 2008.

Hanson, Peter. *The Cinema of Generation X: A Critical Study of Films and Directors*. Jefferson: McFarland, 2002.

Kagan, Jeremy, editor. *Directors Close Up 2: Interviews with Directors Nominated for Best Film by the Directors Guild of America: 2006–2012*. Lanham: Scarecrow Press, 2013.

Kolker, Robert. *A Cinema of Loneliness*, 4th edition. Oxford: Oxford University Press, 2011.

Lacey, Nick. *Se7en: The Ultimate Film Guide*. London: York Press, 2001.

Littger, Stephan. *The Director's Cut: Picturing Hollywood in the 21ˢᵗ Century*. New York: Continuum, 2006.

Marks, Craig, and Rob Tannenbaum. *I Want My MTV: The Uncensored History of the Music Video Revolution*. New York: Plume, 2012.

Mayshark, Jesse Fox. *Post-Pop Cinema: The Search for Meaning in New American Film*. Westport: Praeger, 2007.

Schuchardt, Read Mercer, editor. *You Do Not Talk About Fight Club: I Am Jack's Completely Unauthorized Essay Collection*. Dallas: Benbella, 2008.

Swallow, James. *Dark Eye: The Films of David Fincher*. London: Reynolds & Hearn, 2006.

Thomson, David. *The Alien Quartet: A Bloomsbury Movie Guide*. New York: Bloomsbury, 1999.

Wartenberg, Thomas E., editor. *Fight Club*. London: Routledge, 2012.

Waxman, Sharon. *Rebels on the Backlot: Six Maverick Directors and How They Conquered the Hollywood Studio System.* New York: HarperCollins, 2005.

Documentaries

Murder by Numbers (Mike Hodges and Paul Carlin, 2004)
Side by Side (Christopher Kenneally, 2012)

Index

ABBA, 190, 194
Abrams, J. J., xi
Abyss, The, 11
Academy Awards, 128, 142, 196, 205
Adams, Ansel, 13
Adidas, 143
Aerosmith, xiii, 25, 43, 68, 198
Affleck, Ben, 63
After Hours, 53–54
Albee, Edward, 109
Albright, Erica, 186
Ali, Muhammad, 12
Alien, xiii, 6, 8, 11, 24–25, 30–31
Aliens, 11
Alien³, xii–xiv, 3–17, 19, 24–25, 29–31,
    33, 38–39, 41–44, 49–50, 62, 65, 67,
    71, 94–99, 126, 130, 132–33, 139,
    149, 151–52, 194, 196, 199–200; as
    Fincher's Waterloo and baptism
    by fire, 19, 149; Fincher as being at
    the helm of the *Titanic*, 4; Fincher
    loss of and need for control, xii–
    xiii, 95–97, 133, 139, 149, 199–200;
    mismanagement, 25, 29–30; pre-
    production, 6–12; post-production,
    15–16; production, 3–5, 11–15;
    Special Edition DVD, 149
Allen, Arthur Leigh, 117, 121
Allen, Woody, 13, 39
All That Jazz, 144
All the President's Men, 120
American Cancer Society, 8, 20, 22,

91–92; "Smoking Fetus" PSA, xiii, 8,
    20, 22, 91–92
American Express, xvi
American Graffiti, 56, 147, 170, 205
Americans, The (book), 198
Anderson, Paul Thomas, xiii, 197
Anonymous, 200
Another 48 Hours, 7
Antonioni, Michelangelo, xvii
Apocalypse Now, 9
Apple, xvi, xix
Armani, Giorgio, 153
Armstrong, Bill, 123
Arquette, Rosanna, 61
Arthur, 179
*Assassination of Jesse James by the Cow-
    ard Robert Ford, The*, 128
AT&T, 18–19, 199
Avery, Paul, xvii, 117, 120
Ayer/New York, 18

Babbit, Jamie, 35
Baby Boomers, xv, 109–10
Bacon, Francis, 107
Banksy, xii, 168
"Barkley on Broadway" Nike ad, 20
Basic Instinct, 45
Bauchau, Patrick, 80
Baxter, Kirk, 206
Bay, Michael, 198
Beadle, Jeremy, 40
Beastie Boys, 83

Lightning Source UK Ltd.
Milton Keynes UK
UKOW04f1048031117

312116UK00001B/345/P